In the Shadow of the Wind

In the Shadow of the Wind

Copyright © 2014 Ann Christine Fell

Printed in the United States of America

All rights reserved.

No part of this book may be reproduced or transmitted in any form or by any means electronic or mechanical, including photo copying, recording or by any information storage and retrieval system without written permission from the copyright owner.

* * * * *

Author Edited

Cover by Ryan Fell

Formatting by Debora Lewis arenapublishing.org

* * * * *

ISBN-13: 978-1502478375

ISBN-10: 1502478374

In the Shadow of the Wind

A story of Love, Loss,
and Finding Life Again

To Evelyn
May you forever soar on
the winds of the Spirit.
Z

Ann Christine Fell

All the best - Ann Fell

To Phoebe Dawn
With Love

Author's Note

The following story is based on actual events. I have relied heavily on journals and letters from early in my life, as well as the occasional topic researched online. While discrepancies with factual data may arise in the following pages, they are purely unintentional. Most names have been changed to protect the privacy of friends.

In the Shadow of the Wind

"We are the fruits of the wind—and have been seeded, irrigated, and cultivated by its craft."
Lyall Watson

Lord, make me an instrument of Thy peace.
Where there is hatred, let me sow love.
Where there is injury, pardon.
Where there is doubt, faith.
Where there is despair, hope.
Where there is darkness, light.
Where there is sadness, joy.

O divine Master,
Grant that I may not so much seek to be consoled
as to console;
To be understood, as to understand;
To be loved, as to love.

For it is in giving that we receive.
It is in pardoning that we are pardoned.
And it is in dying that we are born again
into eternal life.

St. Francis of Assissi

Lord, make me an instrument.
If it be Your will, use me as Your pen.
Make my mind like a blank piece of paper
And write upon it Your truths and Your wisdom.
Lord, make me Your instrument.

Ann Christine Fell 1985

PROLOGUE

"It's okay, Daisy Pup," I said. The small spaniel whined. I drew her to my chest and we cuddled together. Thunder exploded in the air above our little tent. The after-rumbles faded. Seconds later rain pelted the nylon roof of my fair-weather shelter. Daisy shivered in my arms. "It'll be okay." I tried to convince myself.

I felt foolish. How could I have thought this was a good idea? How could I have dreamed that I would be able to withstand forty days in the wilderness? The rain turned my plan into a futile effort that bordered on the edge of insanity.

A drop of water stabbed my forehead. In the gray afternoon light, I saw hundreds of droplets hang heavily from the inside of the tent roof. The threat of a cold shower hovered inches away.

"Good Lord, Daisy—it's going to rain inside the tent."

There was no escape from the chill in the air. No escape from the fingers of cold that crept up from below. No escape from—"Oh, my God, the sleeping bag is wet."

I shifted sideways in the orange tent and discovered we huddled in a growing pool of water, now about an inch deep. "Oh, God, this is crazy."

My canine companion stood and shook.

"You need to go out?"

She wagged her stubby tail and shook again. I unzipped the door and she jumped into the deluge. I grabbed my boots and began to pull one over a damp sock. On second thought, I tied the laces together, removed my socks, and backed out of the low-slung tent. I pulled my backpack into the soggy afternoon, zipped the tent door shut, and stood barefoot in black ooze.

Daisy splashed through standing water. She located a slight rise, squatted, and relieved herself. I glanced at the sodden landscape. Water stood everywhere, and I was already soaked to the skin in the downpour. What were we to do? I turned in a circle and searched for shelter. An old railroad boxcar, the only farm structure that remained on the abandoned farm, stood behind the tent.

I stooped to look under the boxcar. We could wiggle under it. I quickly discarded that idea. The prospect of lying in muck was no better than sitting in a wet tent. Though padlocks secured the sliding doors of the boxcar, the aged wooden sides looked weathered. One ragged gap at the leading edge of the north door panel appeared almost large enough for me to wiggle inside.

I slogged to the side of the boxcar and grasped the lower edge of one wooden slat. Frantically, I tugged on the worn end. I put my entire weight behind my efforts and ripped panels, inches at a time, until the opening had grown twice as large.

"Come here, Daisy. Let's check this out." She was instantly at my mud-covered heels. I patted the dark floor of the boxcar, which stood forty inches off the ground. Daisy leaped. With an assist from me, she scrambled into the dark interior. I stuffed my backpack behind her, slogged to the tent and pulled my boots and the bedding into the storm. I struggled to maintain balance as I slipped back to the hole in the door and crammed the bundle of blankets inside. Then I leaned into the darkness of the abandoned car and jumped. On my stomach, legs dangling out the opening, I snaked forward a few inches. With flailing arms, I reached into the darkness in search of something to grab.

There. Something metallic. Perhaps an old piece of farm equipment. I didn't know. I could see very little. But it didn't budge, so I was able to pull myself into the relatively dry interior of the old boxcar. Across the car, Daisy explored the darkness through her nose. She snuffled and sneezed a couple times. I stood and felt my way around the area. After locating a pile of old shingles along the south wall, I propped the backpack on the floor beside them. I shook the bedding. All of it felt damp. My clothing was soaked through, so I wrapped the blankets and sleeping bag around my shoulders. I sat on the shingles and leaned against the wall of the boxcar.

Daisy jumped lightly onto my lap. We shared each other's warmth as the deluge continued outside. Moments after we both settled down, I heard scratching noises inside the boxcar. Light-footed creatures scampered about the interior now that we sat still. I hugged Daisy a little tighter. I could see pinpoints of light here and there, small eyes that reflected the afternoon light filtering in through holes in the wall. *Oh, my God.*

Rats. Lots of them. I screamed.

"I am such a fool, Daisy. Why do you put up with me?"

She licked my chin.

I spoke to my husband Craig. "What am I going to do? I can't do this. I can't live without you."

He didn't answer. I was on my own.

Time is a funny thing. To a child, a year seems a long time. Ten years, an eternity. To a grandmother, those same ten years are but a blink of an eye. For Craig and me, a young couple in love, ten years before us was hard to visualize. But the decade passed too fast, too soon. If we had known that all our joys and memories, our plans and dreams, would have to be packed into one decade would we have spent our days differently? Would our choices have been laced with more love and wisdom, or with desperate lunacy? Based on the law of averages, we had every reason to expect several decades together.

Yet there was barely one.

"It's not fair! It's not fair!" I railed against the universe.

Daisy whined softly and licked my chin again as if she understood. The storm mirrored the anguish in my heart. The entire universe wept with me. "What are we going to do, girl? I don't know where we're heading. I only know where we've been."

Part I
Tie it up with a Ribbon

1

A Tree Fell in the Forest

A decade earlier

My hand trembled as I knocked on the front door at 410 West 8th Street. Was this a mistake? I couldn't imagine what I was getting into this evening. Reeling from the impact of a recently broken engagement, I had answered a notice in *The Daily News* about a writer's meeting. Here. Tonight. "Ann," I told myself, "you have to get out of the house." I made myself go.

Through the small square window in the front door I watched a slight figure move slowly, unsteadily. My pulse quickened. All I could see was a man's broad forehead, covered sparingly with thin gray hair. Why was he moving so slowly? Maybe I had the wrong house. No, the number was clearly 410. I fought the urge to run and I waited.

I took a deep breath. Then another. I willed my breathing to slow. My heart rate dropped to a less frantic pace.

The door inched open. A thin man stood on legs fused at the knees and barely movable. His fingers draped uselessly across his palms. He opened the door with a lever rather than a doorknob. His head angled downward, frozen in that position so that he had difficulty seeing anything at eye level or higher. However, his eyes turned up in their sockets. He looked at me and smiled. My trepidation vanished.

"Hello," he said. "Are you here for the writer's meeting?"

"Yes," I answered in a mouse-like voice.

"Come in. I'm Marvin Swanson. Glad you're here."

"Ann Harris."

I entered the living room of Marvin's house and I stepped into my future.

I found a seat on a worn couch while he perched on a wheelchair nearby. We chatted as we waited for others to arrive. "What do you write, Ann?" he asked.

"Poetry, mostly."

"Are you a student at Fort Hays State?"

"Yes."

"English major?"

"Well, no. I'm a geology major."

"Geology!"

I nodded. "The study of the earth. I figured that would cover just about everything I'm interested in."

"I see. I know a lot of biology majors who live here or have lived here. They rent rooms from me."

"Not English majors?"

Marvin chuckled. "No. Though I do teach a correspondence course in creative writing for the University of Kansas. Perhaps no other writers are coming tonight. Bad timing. There's a game at the Coliseum. Did you bring any of your poems?"

I nodded.

"I'd like to hear one if you'd like to read it."

I opened my notebook. "Here's one I wrote after a field course to Yellowstone between semesters this year.

We saw lots of wildlife, including more than a dozen moose. This is for Moose Number Seven.

We chased a moose too far on a snowy highway,
Chased him involuntarily,
And watched his long beating legs
Cloud the snow at his feet.
Reluctant to leave the smooth road
For the shoulder-high drifts,
He raced until lather from his heaving ribs
Splattered the ice behind him.

Moose Number Seven, let us learn together
That the easiest roads of life
May be its most dangerous roads.
And the longer we wait to leave them
For the places we belong
The harder our detours will be.

"Very interesting," Marvin said pensively. "Do you think you've been following a wrong path? An easy path?"

"Yes. More or less. I just broke an engagement. We'd been going up and down for months, and the longer we waited, the harder our inevitable break-up seemed to be."

"Have you ever thought about the difference between love and infatuation? I've seen quite a few relationships come and go with my roomers."

"What do you think the difference is?"

"I think that infatuation seems stronger and more short-lived," Marvin explained. "Love abides. But sometimes it goes into hibernation. Then the sound of a voice, a memory, an object, a passage from a book—something—wakens it and you know it has been there all the time.

"Sometimes," he went on, "a crisis awakens it. Sometimes standing on a peak of suffering before a cliff, it not only awakens but floods your being. The last kind, though, transcends the love of a person for a person and embraces all."

The evening progressed. We shared many tidbits of philosophy, poetry, and the beauty of life's tragedies. We talked of writers' moral responsibilities to readers and the uncomplicated love of children. I learned that he suffered from rheumatoid arthritis, which began afflicting all his joints decades earlier, before he reached the age of twenty.

Shortly after nine-thirty, the back door of Marvin's house opened as his roomers returned from the basketball game. One young man entered the living room before heading upstairs. Marvin introduced us. "Craig Darr. Ann Harris. Craig is one of Dr. Blankenship's Mexican boys."

I looked at Craig's flashing blue eyes and blonde hair and said, "You don't look very Mexican to me."

He laughed. "I'm not. We were in Chiapas doing ornithological research. I'm a good old Kansas farm boy at heart, even though I grew up in Wichita."

"How did someone who grew up in Wichita end up at Fort Hays State?"

"A neighbor up the street from where I lived came here. He told me I ought to check it out."

"Craig selected biology as his major," Marvin chimed in. "And met Jim Brown."

"The rest is history," Craig said.

"Craig had a rather unique experience in Mexico," Marvin said. "He saw a tree fall."

"Really." I gazed intently at Craig.

"Why don't you tell us about it?" Marvin prompted.

Craig sat down across the room. "Around the first of June last summer," he said, "I grabbed my bag and water thermos and headed out to Net Ten, below Berriozabal. Ella, the camp's pet spider monkey, followed me for a ways. Then I shooed her back to camp."

Craig explained how he wound his way through the rain forest to the bird net, noted the identification and health conditions of four trapped birds, and checked them for bands. Two already wore the tiny numbered anklets. The other two he banded before releasing all four to the forest.

He repacked his gear and turned back down the trail. Not in any particular hurry to return to the station, he cleared a space on a rock part way back and sat down. He closed his eyes and let his mind wander.

A ray of sun split the canopy and found his rock. There was not a breath of air stirring, though, and he soon squirmed in the tropical heat of early summer. A clicking noise broke into his thoughts. He opened his eyes and glanced in the direction of the unidentified noise. He saw nothing out of the ordinary. He closed his eyes again. Moist heat rose from the green plants around him. To relieve the rainforest sauna, he shifted sideways slightly, wishing he could doze.

Again. Clicking noises. Maybe more like cracking now. Somebody cracking nuts? Big nuts. The noise lasted longer this time, but he still could not identify the source.

The crackling faded once again to silence. But soon it returned, louder and more insistent than before. He gave up on any kind of nap. The crackling intensified and began to sound like rapid gunfire. "Is someone hunting?"

At that moment, a tree twenty feet up the trail began to shudder. He watched, transfixed. The cracking increased in volume while the tree swayed and drooped. Then in one long crash, it thundered to the ground at the edge of the clearing. Leaves and twigs dispersed in all directions.

"I jumped from my rock and ran a few yards up the trail," Craig concluded.

"It just fell over? Nobody cut it or pushed on it or anything?" I asked.

"Nope. It just fell down, right across the path between our camp and Net Ten. We had to walk around it the rest of the time."

"It made a noise."

"No question about that. They heard the tree fall in camp half a mile away. Hey, do you want to get some ice cream?"

He stood up. "Do you want some, Marvin?"

"Make mine vanilla," Marvin beamed.

"We'll be right back then," he said. "My car is the Volkswagen out back."

"Better a Volkswagen than a limousine," I said with a grin and followed him out the back door.

The ice cream run was my official initiation into Marvelous Marvinsky's commune, as the roomers fondly called his boarding house. Each student rented a private bedroom, and shared the main kitchen facilities and living space. Though neither an official roomer, nor even a biology student, I was soon included in weekly dinner gatherings. Later in the spring, the dinners moved into the backyard where we enjoyed many picnics. Craig and I became the best of friends. Binoculars in hand, we explored area parks together and watched for returning spring birds.

Toward the end of the semester we gathered for a Friday picnic in Marvin's backyard. Jim Brown sat opposite Craig and me at the table. "Have you gotten any strange letters yet?" he asked me.

"What?"

"Like, maybe on a mouse skin?"

"Say what?"

"Yeah, your friend here is noted for pullin' stunts like that."

I looked at Craig. He just grinned.

"I kid you not," Jim continued. "I stuck my head into his room a couple years ago and he was writing a note to Jennifer on a mouse skin that he'd stretched and dried like a hunter's trophy."

"No, it was a note to my grandpa."

"I figured that you really sent it to Jennifer and that's why we never saw her again." Jim teased.

"Who's Jennifer?" I asked, eyebrows raised.

"She's history now." Craig wrapped his arm around my shoulder.

"He keeps stuffed bull snakes under his bed to keep the cleaning lady out too," Jim said.

"I don't like her snooping around my things."

"Then your room doesn't get clean, either."

Craig turned to me and flashed a grin, his smooth cheeks dissolving into deeply grooved dimples at the corners of his mouth. "Just the way I like it."

"You trying to scare me off?" I asked Jim. "Not happenin'."

He shrugged. "Just sayin'. You ought to know this stuff."

I looked at Craig. We all laughed.

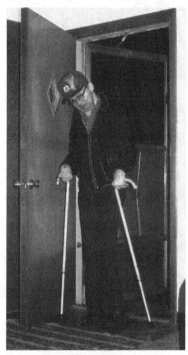

Marvin

Ann and Craig

2
FRIENDS FOR LIFE

"Did you see that? Did you *see that!*" Craig shouted. He stomped on the brakes of his blue Volkswagen Beetle. We careened to the side of the gravel road.

After the semester had ended in May, Craig accepted a job offer with the federal government, a range conservationist with the Soil Conservation Service. He moved from Hays to Alma in the Flint Hills of eastern Kansas. That August, I transferred to Kansas State University in Manhattan as a graduate student in geology. We were thirty miles apart and spent many weekends together, exploring the Flint Hills.

"I saw it. What was it?" To me it resembled a bird transporting another bird. I thought of a mother cat who picked up and moved her kittens from place to place.

"I'm pretty sure that was a loggerheaded shrike," Craig said.

"A shrike?"

"Sometimes they're called butcher birds. They catch live prey and store it on thorns or a barbed-wire fence. I think it headed for that locust tree."

"A predator that stores its prey?"

"Yeah. They impale what they catch on something sharp and return for it when they're hungry. Or use it to mark their territory. Let's go see."

We trotted to the locust tree. Sure enough, a dead cotton rat swung from a locust thorn. "I've seen them do that to grasshoppers and other insects, but this rodent catch—that's a first for me," Craig said.

"That was a bird carrying a mouse almost as big as itself?"

"Apparently."

One Friday afternoon in September, I parked in the alley behind Craig's home in Alma. He met me at his back door, eyes flashing and a big grin on his face.

"Hey, c'mere," he said. "I want to show you something."

We walked to the south doorway which opened onto a screened-in porch. Rocks littered a corner under the porch table. A large tray of water sat next to the rocks. Small tree branches hung around the porch, wired into place at the corners. Three doll-sized baby bottles sat on the table. One held a milky liquid. I heard a high-pitched chirring. "What's that?"

Craig nodded in the direction of a large hollow stump in the corner opposite the doorway. A tiny black head peeked out of a hole in the stump. "That's Blackie."

He picked up the filled bottle and sat on the porch chair. A small black squirrel scampered up his leg. Craig opened his left hand. Blackie made himself comfortable on Craig's palm and suckled eagerly at the tiny bottle.

"He's so cute," I cooed. "What's the story?"

"I was out mowing on Tuesday and this little fellow started following me. Back and forth. Back and forth. I stopped the mower and he came right up to me, chittering away. He even let me pick him up."

"You're kidding. Is he a wild squirrel?"

He nodded. "Born and bred in that elm tree in front of the house."

"Why would he let you pick him up?"

"I couldn't figure that out either. Then I saw his mother. She'd been killed by a car and was just a lump of black fur on the street. The little guy was getting hungry."

"That's sad. I've never seen a black squirrel."

"Me either. Alma has a few though."

"You've sure gone out of your way to make him feel at home."

"You like my habitat room, do you?"

I nodded.

Craig nurtured Blackie through the fall and winter months that year. The squirrel grew bolder and feistier every time I saw him. By spring, he'd gnawed on the porch furniture and woodwork. He'd graduated from the doll bottles to a diet of mixed nuts and grain. Craig hid the nuts and let Blackie search them out.

Blackie

"I want to let him go," he said.

"Before he gnaws through the wall of the house? I guess you're teaching him how to find his food."

"Trying, anyway."

In April, he announced, "I think it's about time to find a new home for Blackie."

"Are you just going to open the porch door or what?"

"No. I want him to be out in nature, away from streets and cars."

"He won't meet his mother's fate, hopefully."

"He also won't keep depending on me. He'll be on his own, back in the wild."

"Where are you going to let him go?"

"Out at Beth's place. I already asked her."

"Your office secretary?"

"Yeah. Want to come along?"

One Saturday in April, we took Blackie to a large oak tree in a remote corner of the pasture at Beth's ranch. He chattered with excitement. Craig placed him on the ground. He immediately scampered up the tree, without even a parting chirr. Our last view of him was high in the greening limbs of the oak tree. We bade him farewell and sent a wish on the breeze for his long and happy life.

On the first day of May that year, I drove to Alma with a basket of flowers, cookies, and strawberries. I placed the basket just outside Craig's front door and rang the doorbell before I retreated to a corner of the house. He came to the door and looked around. He didn't see the basket so he went back inside the house.

I returned to the door and rang the bell a second time. Again I retreated to the corner of his house. He came to the door and yelled, "All right. Who's there? What's the deal?"

I peeked back around the corner.

"What are you doing?" he asked, a hint of annoyance in his voice.

"Well, it's May Day."

"So...?"

"You mean to say, you've never had anyone bring you a May basket before?" I pointed to the basket of goodies at his doorstep.

A grin crept onto his face. "No. What's a May basket?"

I shook my head and rolled my eyes. "When people bring you a May Day basket, they ring the doorbell and run away. Then you find the basket and you have to chase them. If you catch them, you kiss them. Kind of takes the oomph out of it if I have to stop and explain it all."

"Oh," he said. He lunged toward me. I ran. But not far. In three strides, he caught my waist and whirled me around. Then there was a delicious kiss.

"I like May Day baskets," he said.

"So do I."

"Let's go for a drive. It's early and the day is gorgeous."

We packed a lunch and left to observe a great blue heron rookery two miles south of Matfield Green. A nearby farmer informed us nobody would mind if we observed the birds where they nested in a tall sycamore tree. From the road, we saw nests and birds silhouetted against the sky. They flew when we stopped to park. Quietly we made our way into the copse of trees. From a blind of low shrubs, we watched the herons return to their nests. Our cameras clicked away as we observed the activity at the rookery.

Heron rookery

We drove toward Wichita to visit his folks. In Butler County, we skirted a couple of small lakes which would soon be swallowed by a new reservoir. A hint of a breeze perfected the sunny spring day. Exhilarated after the rookery, the words of "Who Will Buy" from *Oliver!* came to my mind. I burst into song as we trundled along. "Who will buy this wonderful feeling? I'm so high I swear I could fly." Craig looked sideways at me from the driver's seat and laughed.

After supper, we headed back to Alma, arriving about ten thirty. I didn't want to leave. I lingered in his living room. He slipped his arm around my shoulders and drew me close. We shared our hundredth kiss for the day and he whispered, "Do you think you want to marry me?"

"Oh, of course, Craigie, of course," I answered without a moment's hesitation. Then there was the hundred-and-first kiss for the day. When I returned to my home at two a.m., the full moon glowed in a ring of mystical light, the perfect ending for a magical day.

As my head hit my pillow, I thought, "Thank you, God, for giving me a friend like Craig to be with for the rest of my life."

3
WEDDING AT TWO ELMS

In June, Craig and I stood under the Two Elms at the old home site on my family's farm. He spread his arms and let his palms brush the tops of ripening wheat. The field came right up to the trees.

"What do you think?" I asked. "After harvest we could clear a large area for chairs and keep it clear until August."

"There's lots of shade here." He nodded. "A good possibility."

"I really want an outdoor wedding."

"Me too," Craig said. "But you know August can be hot."

"What if we planned a morning ceremony?"

"Fine with me."

"With a picnic lunch for everybody afterwards," I added.

"And home-made ice cream."

We grinned at each other.

The invitations went out the first week of July. We made them ourselves, printed on very thin Kodak photographic paper and folded into a four-by-five-inch card. A photo of ourselves, silhouetted against a setting sun, adorned the front.

Inside, "We would be honored by your presence at our wedding celebration, Saturday, August 6, 1977,

10:00 a.m. at the Harris Family Farm seven miles northwest of Americus, Kansas. A picnic lunch will follow." A map to the Harris Farm was included.

People began to arrive for the event on Friday. Late in the afternoon, Craig and I headed to the Farm. After setting up borrowed chairs and tables, we cut wild flowers and tall grasses and arranged them into decorative bouquets. A lattice arbor centered between the Two Elms framed the location where we would recite our vows.

The next morning, I headed to the Farm in my handmade white A-line dress. To add a splash of joy, an embroidered yellow rose adorned the bodice of the white cotton fabric. Craig's new summer suit included a white shirt with a small yellow rosebud embroidered on the lapel.

Guitar chords struck the introduction to an old hymn, "Let Us Ever Walk With Jesus," and our ceremony began. At my father's side, I entered our natural sanctuary.

"This is the day which the Lord hath made. Let us rejoice and be glad in it." The reverend welcomed us.

We stumbled through our vows prompted by the minister. Craig's sister-in-law sang a solo with guitar accompaniment. "I walk alone... I'll walk with you..."

The minister concluded, "May the peace and grace of God, the blessings of His Son, and the grace of the Holy Spirit go with you always in your lives together. Amen."

The guitarist strummed a joyous, "Now Thank We All Our God." Together Craig and I greeted our guests. Then we adjourned to the tables of food at the edge of the Neosho River for a feast to start our future. Warmed by the August sun, the elation I felt as we started our life together made me feel like I floated. All I needed to do was fill my lungs with air and I could drift from guest to guest. Craig must have felt much the same. His smile, a permanent fixture on his face that day, gave me confidence that we could face anything as long as we had each other.

That was the way we dreamed it would be. In reality, due to the oppressive August heat, we moved everything indoors. Our native bouquets provided a link to nature, and everyone remained comfortable in the air-conditioned country church. We celebrated with an indoor picnic, complete with homemade ice cream for all.

After a short honeymoon camping near the headwaters of Tuttle Creek reservoir, we headed home to Meade, where Craig had begun work as the range conservationist with the Meade County Soil Conservation District. We rented a two-bedroom farm house from some Mennonite folks. Five miles out of town, it nestled in isolation at the end of a gravel road. North of the house an apple orchard covered about three acres. A windmill turned on a knoll in a field to the east. Farm buildings sat to the south and west and included a long-empty chicken house. At our first opportunity, we headed to a hatchery in Dodge City to order two dozen California white pullet chicks.

The man behind the counter at the hatchery raised his eyebrows slightly. "You want to order chicks now? They won't be ready until September. You'll be nursing chicks through the winter."

"Can you hatch them now?" Craig asked.

"I can hatch them any time."

"Then yes, we want to order them now. Will you call us when they're ready?"

"Sure." The man nodded and wrote our phone number on his order book.

Three weeks later, he called. We drove to Dodge City to fetch our chicks. I held the box all the way home, playing with the little beaks that emerged now and then through holes in the box. The fuzzy chicks flitted from side to side. Their tiny feet scratched the cardboard. We listened, delighted. Having spent our lives in homes on paved streets of various towns, the discovery of country life provided continuous enjoyment for us.

Our nearest neighbors, a Mennonite family living half a mile west of our home, provided tips about raising the chicks. A clean chicken house, heat lamp, water, and chick feed awaited our brood.

By mid-September the apple trees behind our home drooped, heavy with fruit. Craig stood under one tree, a long-handled hoe in his hand and two bushel baskets at his knees.

"I'll give each branch a little shake. We can pick up what falls." He reached the tip of a low branch on the corner tree and shook it. Half a dozen apples dropped to the ground. I gathered them into a basket.

"Over here, Annsy." Craig selected another fruit-laden tree. He shook several branches, reaching higher ones with the hoe. Apples rained onto his shoulders. Our two bushel baskets were soon full.

"Do you suppose that's enough?" I asked.

"For now. It's a good start."

During the next few days I peeled, cored, and cooked apples into sauce and apple butter. I pored over cookbooks and instruction manuals to learn how to safely can the fruit for winter use.

Craig stepped into the cinnamon scented kitchen each day after work. "Smells like home." He wrapped his arms around me while I stirred the pot of apples on the stove. Selecting a paring knife, he began peeling more apples for a second pot of sauce.

One Saturday morning Craig called "Hurry every chance you get."

"I'm coming. I'm coming." I swung a backpack onto my shoulders and dashed out the kitchen door. He stood in the front yard, stretching his leg muscles in preparation for our excursion. A fitness buff, he'd decided to jog the county road around the section, a distance of four miles. The stretching done, he tied a bandana around his forehead and headed out the driveway. I rode along on my bicycle and soaked up the morning sun.

Halfway around the section we came to a corner and stopped briefly to examine the stand of native grass in the roadside ditch.

"Here's one we don't have yet," Craig said. "I think it's little barley. You got a bag?"

I dropped the backpack to the ground and unzipped the main compartment. Inside were several plastic bags. I handed one to him.

He removed a couple of seed heads from the little barley and slipped them into the bag. "We'll check the ID when we get back."

The plan for the little barley included pressing the collected seed heads in a botanical plant press. We would mount them on cardboard, add a label, and include them in a collection of native grasses that eventually grew to include forty different species.

The baby chicks grew fast. By the end of October they were feathered and half grown. Still awaiting the first frost of the season, grasshoppers had become so abundant they were a nuisance.

One day in late fall, I snatched a grasshopper from a knee-high milkweed plant that grew along our driveway. Caught by one hind leg, it wriggled furiously. I closed my fingers around the insect, winced slightly as its legs pummeled my palm, and opened the jar lid a crack.

"In you go," I said and stuffed the two-inch grasshopper inside my jar.

"How many you got?" Craig called from across the yard.

I looked at the jar. "Oh, about fifty."

"That's enough for now. Let's see what happens."

We slipped into the chicken house with our grasshopper catch and went out into the fenced yard. I set my jar on the ground about six feet away from Craig's jar. Together we removed the lids.

Grasshoppers began shooting from the tops of the open jars. The chicks took a fraction of a second to react. In a flurry of flapping wings, they scrambled for the freed insects. The yard exploded with a cacophony of peeps that were becoming clucks, excited chickens and frantic grasshoppers. Once a chick caught a grasshopper, it banged the insect against the ground, tore legs and heads from bodies, and gorged on the insect parts.

"They must really like bugs," I said. Laughing, we dodged the birds. We retreated to a safe vantage point outside the chicken yard.

"They're going crazy," Craig said. "It's a regular grasshopper rodeo."

"Mayhem—absolute mayhem," I shrieked between giggles.

The following spring, my sister Kay and her husband Gary brought our six-month old niece Becca for a visit during their spring break. Born just three days before our wedding, the first child of a new generation in my family captured the hearts of all her aunts and uncles, not to mention grandparents.

"Put on a Ronnie Milsap album," Craig said.

Ronnie Milsap's golden baritone voice filled our little house. Craig grabbed me. The dancing started. We danced almost every week, shoving our little kitchen table to the window and transforming our humble farm home into a dance hall for two. This week, Kay and Gary joined the festivities. Becca sat in her high chair. She clapped her little hands as she watched.

When the next song started Craig picked up the giggling girl. We sandwiched her between us and danced and danced. "Someday," he said quietly in my ear, "we'll dance with our own little baby."

During a visit to Manhattan, we found a piano. The beautiful Victorian era Kimball immediately caught Craig's fancy. Delicate leaf carvings adorned the golden quarter-sawn oak panels of the music desk. He liked the oak more than anything. We both fell in love with the piano and moved it across the state to our country orchard home in Meade County. To Craig's delight, I played every day.

At the end of the summer, he was transferred to Morton County as the District Conservationist, his training complete. We moved everything—including Fluffy the farm cat, two dozen laying hens, the new workbench he'd built, a box of sentimental rags that I hoped to construct into a quilt, and the piano. We moved from one farm house to another a hundred miles further west.

One Saturday afternoon, the two of us were piddling on the old Kimball, improvising harmonies to favorite songs. "I'm beginning to think buying a piano for its looks was the wrong idea," I said.

"What do you mean?" Craig asked.

"It sounds really bad. I wonder how we go about finding someone who tunes pianos."

"Why don't we just tune it ourselves?"

"Right." I was skeptical.

"No, I'm serious. How hard could the job be? I tune my guitar. A piano just has a few more strings."

"A few?"

"I've got wrenches, even a crescent wrench. Maybe some pliers or vice grips would help. You know what it should sound like."

"More or less."

"I'll get the tools."

While Craig assembled his tuning kit, I cleared the piano and folded the top lid back on its hinges. I could barely peek over the front music desk panel, but inside were the tuning pins.

"Wow," I said on his return. "There sure are a lot of pegs."

"How many do you think? A hundred or two?"

"Looks more like a thousand."

"Nah—can't be." He peered inside, played a key and watched the hammer strike its strings. "Well, looks like nearly every key has three strings."

"What did I tell you?"

"It still isn't a thousand." He rolled his eyes. "Where do you want to start?"

"Maybe Middle C?" I played the note.

"How does it sound?"

"Low, I think."

He reached in with a little wrench. "Play it again." Craig found the C unison and turned the tuning pin.

"Whoa—wrong way!" I said.

"Okay. I'll go the other way. Is that any better?"

The tones ringing into the room raucously disagreed with each other. "I can't tell."

"Here, I'll pinch off the other two wires." Craig reached inside and squeezed the outside strings with his fingers to damp the extra tones.

"Yeah. I think that's about right," I said.

He manipulated the remaining tuning pins for middle C. "Next."

I moved up to C sharp. We repeated the procedure. "I think that's about right." Again my ears guessed.

"Hold on. I need a ladder," Craig said. I raised my eyebrows. "It's getting hard to reach over the top of this board."

I nodded. "Yeah. I could barely see over it myself."

Craig brought the ladder and we continued up the scale, a half step at a time, until we reached the next C.

"Let's do all the C's," I suggested.

I began to play matching notes, first one, then another. I listened and offered judgement as Craig manipulated the pegs.

"Higher. No. No. Now a bit lower."

When we got to the lower octaves, overtones seemed to create additional listening challenges.

"Why don't you get down lower," Craig suggested.

"Like—under the keys?"

"Yeah. We can take off this front board below, so you can hear better." He squeezed the retaining spring and the board tipped out.

"You on the ladder and me on the floor."

Craig nudged me playfully. "That's the way it should be, right? Me, always on top."

I rolled my eyes and smiled as I dropped to the floor and reached up to the keys. "I can't tell which key I'm playing," I said.

"I'll play them. You listen."

The following afternoon as we completed the arduous process, I shook my head. "There has to be a better way to tune a piano. I'm not altogether sure it sounds better than it did earlier."

"Why don't you learn how to tune pianos then?" he suggested.

4
A CRACK IN THE ICE

I heard it again that November night. Something—
something big—was moving around in the walls of the
house. Definitely bigger than a mouse. Very likely bigger
than a rat. It squirmed and brushed along in the walls of
our bedroom at night's beginning and end.

"Should we call the landlord?" I asked Craig.

He nodded. "Wait. There's the hired hand. I'll tell
him."

Before he left for work, he and the rancher's hired
hand surveyed the exterior. Set on a slab with no
basement or crawl space, the old farm house was a cozy
place two miles from Elkhart on the sandy ground of the
Cimarron River basin.

The two of them located a hole under the west wall,
hidden by bushes and shaded by an elm tree. "Looks big
enough for a 'possum to get under the floor," Craig said.

"Maybe a raccoon. Or a skunk," the hired man said.
"I'll set a trap. See if we can get whatever it is."

Next morning the trap had been sprung and dragged
underneath the house into the six-inch tunnel. "What is
it?" Craig asked.

"I can't tell. It's too dark in there. I've got a twenty-
two in my truck, though. We'll get whatever it is."

Before the plan had been thoroughly discussed, the
ranch hand produced his weapon and fired blindly into

the hole. The chain attached to the trap went slack. When he pulled the trap back out, he dragged a skunk with it.

Phew! What a stench. Inside an hour the whole house was rank with skunk musk, strong enough to make a person sick. The odor infiltrated every room, every closet, every cupboard, every inch in the house. We opened windows and turned on fans.

We drove to town, desperate to locate some kind of fragrance that would subdue the stench. I bought incense. Craig bought cigars. We burned incense all day, and both of us—though non-smokers—puffed on cigars until we couldn't any longer. At day's end, defeated by the skunk, we checked into a local motel. We spent two nights away from home, but weeks passed before the odor faded enough to be unrecognizable.

Given the skunk situation, Craig began to dream about reviving his hunting skills.

"I've always wanted a bird dog," he announced one morning. He'd read a classified ad for a litter of registered Brittany spaniel puppies. They lived around the corner and two blocks east of the house we were building in Elkhart. When we went for a visit, three little fuzz balls scampered in the pen, clamoring for attention. "Only one is not yet claimed," the breeder informed us. "She is this little one here, the runt of the litter." He lifted a squirming pup. Craig cradled her in his hands and scratched her belly. She crawled up his chest and licked his chin. He beamed at me with twinkling blue eyes. I knew we had a dog.

Though a registered Brittany spaniel, with liver brown spots on creamy white fur, little Daisy Fleabane never grew to typical spaniel size. She stayed small and delicate. Her sunny temperament captured our hearts and she became our first beloved child. Her stubby tail wagged ferociously most of her waking moments.

Under Craig's direction, we set about training the pup. She eagerly mastered "Sit," "Stay," and "Come," both on voice command and with a whistle.

Pup on the prairie

Craig hooked a quail wing on a fishing line. "Watch this," he said as he cast the wing into a far corner of the living room. "Go get it, Daisy. Find the bird." She danced happily along the edge of the room, sniffing every hidden nook until she detected the "quail." She froze into an instinctive puppy point while Craig manipulated the wing. "Get the bird, Daisy." She pounced to collect her prize and trotted proudly to Craig. The hunting games delighted all three of us.

Early on, it was clear Daisy was a jumping dog. Craig found that with a bit of encouragement, he could get her to jump into the back of our pickup—over the side rails. Later, after we moved east two hundred miles to a Barber County ranch, she started climbing trees. She surprised more than one cat when they sprinted away from her. With a smirk of feline satisfaction at having escaped the dog, the cats turned to find this particular dog quivering behind them on the tree branch.

Daisy was also a water dog. She loved to join one or the other of us in the bathtub. When hiking in the Cimarron National Grasslands, she headed for the pools and puddles and splashed happily through them. Always ready for a trek, she eagerly ran to the car with us, dancing with excitement. Craig designed a carpeted doggy platform which fit neatly between the bucket seats of our Volkswagen. On our outings, she perched on her seat and watched the road over our shoulders.

Daisy chasing a cat up a tree and Daisy in the tree.

One spring morning when Daisy was four months old, our alarm rudely filled the stillness of the wee hours of the April night.

I groaned. It was four-thirty a.m.

"Rise and shine," Craig said cheerfully.

"You shine. I will try to rise," I mumbled.

"C'mon. We have to get there before first light, or the birds won't come out."

Minutes later we bundled into flannel shirts and hoodies. We grabbed our cameras and binoculars, scratched Daisy good-bye and headed to the waiting car. This was an activity which our little dog would have to miss. Craig handed me a flashlight and scrap of paper. "You navigate," he said.

We disembarked for the National Grasslands. He'd learned the location of an active booming ground for Lesser Prairie Chickens. Directions were noted on the scrap of paper in my hand.

With the flashlight, I read the directions as we carefully wound through sandy land, brush, and the short grass prairie native to western Kansas. By five-thirty we had arrived in a spot that looked very much like the middle of nowhere. A few hummocks dotted the ground around us. They cast low shadows in our car's headlights. Craig scrutinized the area. Gesturing for the flashlight, he opened his window and shone its beam out the side.

"This is it," he said. We'd arrived at the lesser prairie chicken lek. He killed the car engine and doused the lights. "Get your camera ready. Stay in the car—and no unnecessary noise."

"Okay. I don't want to scare them off."

A good forty-five minutes passed. Gradually the sky brightened. The chill of the pre-dawn air penetrated my jacket. I began to rub my hands along my thighs to warm them.

"Sh-sh-sh. No noise," Craig whispered.

A short chirp sounded outside my open window.

"See anything?"

I strained my eyes. Nothing. The light was far too dim.

Another chirp resounded from another direction. Then another. "They're coming out," Craig mouthed silently.

Soon we were surrounded by the unique vocalizations of the male prairie chicken, a sort of a bark combined with a cough. As dawn progressed more of the birds strutted through the little mounds. Prior to each chirp, a male planted both feet, reared back his head and filled a balloon in his neck with air nearly to the bursting point. Then, in an explosive expulsion of the air from his gullet, the chirp resounded across the grass. He had just boomed.

Prairie chickens booming

Activity grew as the day dawned. We were captivated by the behavior. We turned from side to side and pointed with frantic but silent arm gestures. More birds appeared while we watched the show of a lifetime.

Finally the day was bright enough to attempt some photos. Resting long lenses on the open window frames, we both clicked away. The booming began to dissipate when the sun peeked over the horizon. The birds disappeared, uncannily blending back into their prairie surroundings. When the last one was gone, we quietly stowed our cameras. Craig started the car and we wound back to the sandy road in the grasslands area. The elation of witnessing this unique event carried me through several days. What had started with reluctance to leave a comfortable bed turned into an unforgettable experience, completed before seven in the morning. Craig went to work at eight, as usual.

After only one year in Morton County, Craig resigned from his government job. He jumped at the chance to work as a ranch hand in the red hills of Barber County, previously only a dream for this city man with a country heart. I began to think we should not even unpack our moving boxes from one move to the next.

Life on the ranch proved to be full of adventures. One December evening, the full moon illuminated snow-covered hills to make the night hours nearly as bright as day. But it felt unquestionably cold when we met Randy and Marla at a watershed pond on their ranch. As the moon rose in the east, we sat down to lace ice skates onto our feet. Randy lit a campfire on the shore of a cove. Its flames flickered tentatively against the piercing cold, then found the cedar logs and blazed to warmth and brightness.

"You're sure the ice is thick enough?" I asked.

Randy affirmed that it was. "It's been below zero for the last five days. Dad took a core this morning. It's nearly four inches thick in the center. We'll be fine." He glided away from the firelight to join his wife.

Shaped somewhat like a kidney bean, the fifteen-acre pond curved around a small hill. Once my skates were tied securely, I warmed my gloved fingers at the fire for a moment before pushing myself onto the nubbly surface.

"Just watch for twigs," Rhonda called from the pond's center. "You don't want to catch your runners on sticks."

I looked for Craig. He slid along like a ghost on the other side of the pond. I felt a moment's aggravation. Sporting activity came much easier to him than to me. He sailed along like he'd just come off Olympic training. I made a good two passes around the pond with tense uncertain strokes before I found my ice legs. Though not totally new to the ice, skating was not something I experienced regularly in the fluctuating temperatures of Kansas winters. Never before had I skittered across a pond this large. And never before in moonlight.

Every few minutes the fire welcomed us to its circle of light. I hovered over the friendly blaze, soaking up the warmth that radiated into the sub-zero air. Marla steeped a pot of hot chocolate over the fire. With feet freshly toasted, I pushed off again into the cold embrace of the winter night. Icicles of water vapor seared my throat and chest as the air I breathed warmed in my throat.

Away from the fire, on the far side of the pond, the stillness was complete. Beyond the scratching of the skate blades not a sound met my ears. Craig swooshed to my side and squeezed my shoulders. We set off together, hands crossed in front of us, skating in perfect synchronization. Right. Swoosh. Left. Swoosh. Right. Left. Swoosh. Swoosh. The enchantment was perfect.

We ventured further onto the ice, closer to the center and then toward the fire and back around the edge again. Some sections were smooth. Others felt rough. Between the sides of an inlet about twenty-five feet across, the ice even sloped downward away from the shore so that we could skate downhill and gain speed.

Alone at the far side of the pond, we came to a rest momentarily to warm up with a hug. The silence around us was ominous. I could hear nothing besides our breathing and my own blood rushing through my veins.

Suddenly a wrenching boom shattered the stillness. The ice thundered beneath our feet. A long crack passed across the pond, all the way below our feet to the nearby shore. It echoed for a few seconds in the night air. Then all was still again.

When we next met up with Randy and Marla, the moon had arced two hours across the night sky since our arrival. The hot chocolate had disappeared and the fire had ebbed to a few glowing coals. Our moonlight skate on the farm pond drew to a close.

"Did you hear the ice crack?" Craig asked the others.

"What? No," Randy said.

"All the way across the pond—or that's what it sounded like."

"Did you think you would fall through the ice?"

"Well, yes."

"Sometimes the pond does that," Randy explained. "The ice will shift and then you have little ridges to skate over. But it's not like you're going to fall in."

The brilliance of a December night followed us home. We brought out a comforter, pulled Daisy onto our laps, and curled up in front of our little cedar Christmas tree.

5
DAWNING OF A NEW DAY

I couldn't keep a straight face. Craig pushed open the door of our little mobile home. His head peeked around its edge and his eyes sought mine. Try as I might I couldn't stop myself. I beamed back at him.

"Well?" he asked.

One little nod from me and he burst into the room. "Yes?"

"Yes," I said. "We're expecting."

"A baby." He grabbed me and whirled me around in the middle of the room. "We're Craignant. We're Craignant," he chanted as we danced a little jig. "Have you called your folks? I want to tell Mom and Dad."

"No. I kind of wanted to tell you first."

"Let's call the Ma's and Pa's—they'll soon be Grandma's and Grandpa's."

Craig's days as a ranch hand had come to an abrupt end more than a year before. A major disagreement with the rancher spurred our hasty flight from the Barber County ranch. Though we had not fallen through the pond ice that December night, the resounding thunder beneath our feet seemed to portend a shift that left us floundering in the uncertain tides of life. We floated homeless and jobless for a few months and finally settled in Butler County when Craig found employment at Boeing aircraft manufacturing in Wichita. I found a job in the printer room of Boeing Computer Services. Both of us worked the second shift. We bought a twenty-acre lot half an hour east of Wichita and moved a small mobile home there until the day we could build our own country home.

Our dance of joy slowed to a tender embrace and we swayed back and forth. "I just can't quite believe it," he whispered.

"Me neither."

"This time next year we'll have a teeming little monster in the house."

When I mentioned our expectant situation at work, my supervisor became concerned.

"You know the toner in our printers is a known carcinogen and mutant."

"What's a carcinogen, TNF?"

"Yes. The tri-nitro-fluoronone. We got a memo about it several months ago. I'll see if I can find it."

A few minutes later he brought me the memo. There, in black and white, was an advisory statement that the TNF was a chemical known to increase the risk of cancer and genetic mutations.

Later that evening, I shared this tidbit of information with Craig in the cafeteria. "TNF is a major component of the toner in the printers I work with," I said. "I think I should quit."

"Will they let you take leave so you could return later?" Craig asked.

"Maybe. I'll ask. But even if they say no, I don't want to take any chances with the baby."

Boeing allowed me leave to await the birth of our child. I returned to our small mobile home and busied myself with preparations for the little one. One day I bought a pattern for newborns, cut out a baby kimono, and stitched it together. Craig arrived home from second-shift about eleven-thirty.

"Look," I said, holding up the tiny outfit.

He gave me a squeeze. "I can't believe any person could be small enough to fit in that nightgown. We need to celebrate. What do you say about a campout this weekend?"

"Sounds fun," I said. "Where do you want to go?"

"It might be fun to go to your folks' farm. You know, the Farm, where we planned to be married. Have you ever camped by the river?"

"That sounds like a great idea. Next year at this time, maybe we can take the baby there again."

Friday afternoon, we loaded our tent, sleeping bags, camping gear and ice chest into the car. Daisy leapt into the car and we piled in after her. Two hours later, we unloaded our gear and set up camp at a location which was once the yard for stock outside a long-ago barn. Trees now towered over the flattened space at the edge of a soybean field. After pitching the tent, I crawled inside to unroll our bags and zip them together. Craig gathered fallen wood for a campfire. After he had one roaring he cut a couple of willow twigs and we roasted hotdogs and marshmallows for supper.

Evening faded into a moonless night. We sat by the fire and gazed at the sky. Stars dotted our canopy.

"Aren't they brilliant?" I asked.

"They really pop."

"We're far enough away from Emporia that you can't see city lights."

He looked over his shoulder into the trees. "It's going to be really dark tonight."

"This is a good place to see the constellations." I waved abstractly toward the west. "Right over there is where I set up a camera a few years back to take pictures of the stars. Look—there's the Big Dipper." I pointed upward. "And Cygnus, the swan."

"You sure can see the Milky Way, can't you? I've never seen it so clearly." Craig tilted his head backwards.

Eventually we retired into the tent and crawled into bed.

The next morning, I was up early. I let Daisy out of the tent and headed to the ice chest to rustle up some breakfast pancakes on our camp stove. When the first pancake was ready, I called Craig to breakfast.

He didn't respond. I let him sleep and ate the first two pancakes myself. When I unzipped the tent door and crawled in to wake him, he shivered in the sleeping bag, eyes closed.

"Hey, want some pancakes?"

He moaned.

"Craig?"

"Headache," he muttered.

I crawled to his head, knelt beside him and cradled his temples between my hands. He moaned again.

"That bad?"

"A killer."

I mentally ran through an inventory of supplies we had packed the previous day. "Rats. I don't think we brought anything for a headache."

Craig tightened his eyelids and breathed heavily.

"Shall we go to my folks' cabin? They probably have aspirin or something."

He nodded once. Eyes still squeezed shut, he said, "You drive."

I set the bowl holding the rest of the pancake batter inside the ice chest, turned off the camp stove and headed to the car. Craig staggered out of the tent. Before he reached the car door, he bent forward and retched. I opened the door for him and he sank onto the passenger seat, eyes still closed. I let Daisy in through the driver's door and we were off.

Mother dug in her medicine cabinet and produced a bottle of Tylenol when we reached their cabin. Craig downed a dose and we tucked him into bed. He soon slept.

"I guess I should go back and clean up the camp," I said.

"Want some help?" Dad offered.

I didn't object. We returned to the camp site and rolled up the bags, pads, and tent. I put everything back in the car.

By noon, Craig had pretty much recovered. But our fun weekend of camping was over. I settled into the driver's seat for the drive home. "Man, that was some headache, wasn't it?" I said during the journey.

He agreed. "Must have been a migraine. I've never had one of those before. I sure don't want another." A few minutes later, he slept again.

Autumn arrived in flaming colors. I settled into a daily routine, centered around our child. One day, I sat at the piano, music spread across the Victorian carvings of its face.

"Good morning, Baby," I said softly to my belly. "Can you hear me? How about a little Beethoven?"

I now had the time to sit and play until my aching fingers could play no more. Or until I had to dash to the bathroom and heave with morning sickness. This pregnancy thing was far from what I had imagined. First came the excitement and anticipation. Then the sickness took over. I became miserable. My joints ached so that I could hardly walk across the room. I felt fat. I had never weighed so much in my life. And we had months to go yet. But, like all mothers-to-be, I knew I would make it. I just had to take one day at a time.

"Hey, Little One. How about a hymn now?" I opened the hymnal and found a couple of favorite hymns. "I thank God for you, Baby. I'm looking forward to the days when I can jog and ride my bike. I'm also looking forward to the time when you can jog and ride bikes with me. I sure hope you can hear through your walls of flesh. I wonder if you like music. I hope so, Baby. I dream of the day you and I can play duets together. How about a little Chopin?"

I pulled out a prelude by the master composer.

"Baby, I hope you know how much we love you already. I wonder what you'll be like. Will you be good? Or cranky? What kind of person will you become? How much will you change our lives? Most important, can I still be me or will I be lost within your countless needs?"

By mid-November, Craig was able to transfer to first shift. As Thanksgiving approached, we felt thankful for many things. Heading to Wichita for a turkey dinner with his folks, a stiff breeze buffeted our car.

"Look out for that bird!" I yelled. "Why do they do that?"

"Do what?" Craig asked from the driver's seat.

"Fly at the car. You know, when we're driving along, it seems like most of the birds sitting on the roadside wait until we're almost there and then jump into our path. Haven't you noticed? That last one was a close call."

"You've heard of bird brains, haven't you?" he teased.

"Very funny. Well then, why don't half of them fly the other way? It's crazy. No wonder so many birds get hit by cars."

"There's another reason."

"What's that?"

"The wind. It depends what direction the wind is blowing. Watch. There are a couple of meadowlarks up on the crest of the next hill. They will jump into the wind—right at us—to get airborne."

Rarely was there a day when the air didn't stir in Kansas. The state was even named for a group of Native Americans whose name, Kanza, meant "People of the South Wind." The northerly breeze of the last two days had shifted direction and came from the south today.

I studied the three birds as we approached. Sure enough, just before we achieved the crest, they each leapt directly into the path of our car. They swerved sharply and fluttered to the north, over a dormant winter pasture.

"But why? Why not just fly away from the car to begin with?"

"They get lift a lot faster if they jump into the wind," he said.

"Really? You mean they couldn't fly if they didn't meet the wind head-on?"

"Pretty much. It probably depends on wind velocity. I think if the wind isn't too strong, they could take off with a breeze, but it would take more effort to get airborne going with the wind. You see how they turn and go with the wind once they get in the air?"

We watched another pair of meadowlarks follow the same pattern.

"Instinctively they know they can get up faster heading into the wind."

"So if the wind is strong—"

"They may not be able to get lift unless they face into it," Craig finished my thought.

"And if they can't get airborne soon enough, they fly right into a car."

We watched in silence for a couple of miles before I said, "If a little bird found shelter from the wind on the wind shadow side of a rock, in order to fly it would have to meet the wind?"

"Wind shadow?"

"You know—that area on the leeward side of a solid object where you get some relief from constant wind."

"Oh. Wind shadow. Yes. Okay, then, in order to fly, the bird would have to get out of the wind shadow and leap into the wind."

Half an hour later, we pulled onto the driveway of his parents' Wichita home. We'd spent the remainder of the trip counting near-misses with birds flying at the car. "At least a dozen," I said.

"Fourteen to be exact."

Craig delivered a blessing for Thanksgiving dinner. "Thank you, God, for our little home in the country, and for allowing me to experience country life. For my favorite things—the smell of fresh cut alfalfa; cattle in the corral and the crisp north wind; feeding silage; quiet Kansas sunsets; frozen morning air; dusty wind; rain;

the time following a storm when the sun comes out; quiet stillness on a frosty morn; greasy hands; muddy boots; bacon and eggs in the morning; fresh milk in a bucket; fried chicken; wild marigolds along a chalky road; a cold glass of water on a hundred-and-ten-degree day after baling alfalfa; picking up bales and stacking them in a barn; the breeze through the trees on a spring afternoon; the smell of love—the country.

"I thank you God for the country life, and for our little baby. I look forward to helping our child discover the wonders of the world. Amen."

Three weeks later, I spoke to my child. "Hey, Little One, today marks six months. We're two-thirds of the way to the day we hold you in our arms. This is your daddy's and my last Christmas alone. I wonder what next Christmas will bring? We brought home your crib today and set it up in your tiny room. I'm so excited." I paused in my reverie to give a little hug to my bulging belly.

"Your daddy heard your heart-beat today. The rate says you're supposed to be a girl. Won't we be surprised if you aren't?If you're a girl you are probably Phoebe. If you're a boy, we're starting to like the name 'Gabe.' Hey, Phoebe-Gabe," I patted my belly. "It's so exciting to hear your heart-beat. And to feel you move. I go around glowing and smiling a secret smile of silent pleasure and quiet thrill."

As a new year began, we grew restless in the confines of our small home. Craig tossed the magazine he had been reading to the end table. He stood and walked down the hall. Two seconds later, he walked back. He came to the kitchen, pulled a dish towel from the drawer and began to dry the dishes I'd washed.

"You seem kind of tense," I said. "Is something wrong?"

"I don't know. I've been pretty edgy today and I'm not sure why."

"Looking forward to tomorrow? You'll be changing decades at ten-ten in the morning."

"Well, yes and no. Here it is the eve of my thirtieth birthday and I'm lost. I ought to have my life together and be on the road to a career, but I don't feel like I'm there at all."

"Maybe it would help to look at what we do have," I said and pointed to my belly.

"I know. I feel grateful for the baby every day."

"And we have our own place."

"Yes. But there's more to my unease than that. I really can't explain it."

"Maybe a hug would help?" I dried my hands and turned to embrace him.

He stood for a moment, not responding. Then he squeezed me and spoke softly into my hair. "I'll have to look to God to pull me through—to pull us through whatever I'm experiencing right now. I pray on the eve of my birthday for Him to give us a new sense of direction in our lives."

He looked in my eyes and forced a smile.

"What would you like for dinner tomorrow?" I asked. "Home cooking or eat out?"

He shrugged. "Doesn't matter. What I want this year is for God to be with you and the baby, and for God to pull you through the birth in good health. That would be the best present I could have."

"I'm sure everything will be fine."

"Well I hope so. But I can't help thinking that something is just not quite right."

Craig building a chicken house

The little mobile home

Part II
Angel's Blood and Tears

6
EMPTY ARMS

Four days later, I stretched out on the exam table for a prenatal checkup. The doctor smeared gel across my belly. I winced. It seemed extra cold this winter morning. He worked the monitor's sensor in small circles across the prepared area, searching for the baby's heartbeat.

"Ah, there we go." He smiled.

I listened to the tiny echoes and smiled as well.

"Pitty pat... pat... pat."

The doctor's smile disappeared. He repositioned the sensor. "Pat... pat." His brow furrowed.

"Is something wrong?" I asked, my voice barely louder than a whisper.

"I'm not sure. The heartbeat seems irregular. Let me try again." He moved the sensor to a new location.

"Patter... pat..."

"It's not any better there. The fetus may be under stress for some reason. I think I'd better admit you to the hospital so we can monitor Baby."

"Today?"

"Yes. Right now. As soon as you can get there. Go home and pack your bag. What time does your husband gets off work?"

"Two o'clock."

"Have him bring you right down. I'll see you later this afternoon."

I swallowed hard and left the clinic in a daze. At home, I packed a small bag and tucked the little baby kimono on top. I patted my belly gently and paced the length of our mobile home, singing softly to my little one while my heart pounded as if it would jump out of my chest.

"Hurry, Craig. Please come home." I walked back and forth, up and down, to and fro. Daisy watched. After a few minutes, I sat beside her on our sofa and we watched the door, as if staring would bring him a little faster.

Finally his pickup came into view. When he opened the door I met him, dressed to go. He looked into my worried eyes and his smile disappeared.

"What's wrong?"

I described my visit to the doctor.

He gathered me into his arms. "Okay then. Let's go."

An hour later, I lay in a hospital bed, trussed up to a fetal monitor. The second-shift nurse searched for our baby's heartbeat. She ran the sensor back and forth across my belly, until I felt bruised. Finally, she shook her head. "I'm just not having much luck right now."

She caught the agonized glance between Craig and me.

"I'm not too worried yet," she said. "Sometimes the little

fellows get turned so you just can't get a good signal. Tell you what. We'll give it a rest and try again a bit later."

She backed out of the room and shut the door.

"What do you think?" I asked Craig.

"I don't know what to think. I hope she knows what she's talking about and we'll hear the heartbeat later."

"How long can you stay?"

"As long as you need me."

"I really don't think much is going to happen."

"Maybe I'll go home and do chores. I'll call you later for news." He leaned over to kiss me.

About ten o'clock, the nurse came in again to check for the baby's heartbeat. "Now that's more like it." She smiled as the sensor detected a steady beat. Pat-pat. Pat-pat. Pat-pat. "That's what I thought. He was just turned funny before. You get some sleep."

I woke refreshed the next morning. "They found the heartbeat at ten last night," I told Craig when he called. "It sounded good and strong. I think everything is fine."

"I hope so, Sweetie," Craig said. "I'll be there right after work."

The day nurse did not have the same good luck as the night nurse. "I'm not too worried," she said. "The placenta pulse is strong. We'll try again a little later." But each time she tried, there was no echo to be found.

"I'm not going to lie," she said about noon. "I am worried. We should be able to find something. I'll check with your doctor. See what he wants to do."

Early in the afternoon, a technician wheeled a machine into the room. "Doctor ordered a sonogram. Let's get some pictures of your baby."

The process filled the better part of an hour. I tried to lie still and cooperate, but I so wanted to see a reassuring little wiggle. I craned my neck to see the monitor screen, but it was aimed away from me. The technician said very little. But finally, "Okay. Guess we can get you covered and warmed up again." Then he disconnected the machine and left. Too frightened to say anything, I shrank into the covers.

Later, when the second-shift nurse entered, I asked her about the results.

"Doctor wants to talk to you himself. He'll wait until your husband arrives. Sorry. I can't say more than that." She left. I tried to rest and doze, but it was impossible to quiet the panic that grew inside me.

Craig finally arrived from work. I told him about the day. He held my hands and squeezed them each time my voice caught. He smoothed the hair from my eyes and raised my chin. He kissed me tenderly. Then we waited, holding hands as daylight waned into an early winter evening.

The doctor arrived at the very end of his rounds. He breezed into the room, shut the door, and sat on the foot of my bed. "Okay," he said in a voice full of sadness and compassion. "Your baby is dead."

Hours later, I squirmed in the hospital bed. Uncomfortable, agitated and totally alone in the dark hospital room, I couldn't sleep. I raised my eyelids to squint at the dimly lit clock on the opposite wall. "Three-o-seven? Oh, God."

With reluctance, Craig had gone home to tend to chores after the hospital staff connected me to an intravenous system. The drug used to induce labor slowly dripped into my veins. I could feel gentle contractions on a regular, mechanical interval. A monitor in the corner registered the contractions on its moving graph. The line labeled for the baby's heartbeat stretched in one long flat line across the screen.

The sonogram had revealed two things. One, the baby was deceased. Two, she was a girl. *My poor child. My poor sweet girl.* I wept silently at each contraction. I gazed out the window near my bed and studied the stars. Up there somewhere in that infinite dotted blackness, our baby slipped away from me. I felt small and far away.

For the first time in years, I thought of my maternal grandmother who had lived with us for a time during my childhood. Her death introduced me to the imperfect world of loss and grief. Now she smiled at me from the stars. She lifted her arms in welcome and an infant floated to her. She cradled the child, cooing in the distance. My arms ached with emptiness. Grandmother looked at me again. She cocked her head slightly to one side and smiled a tiny smile. Then she nodded once, as if to reassure me that all was well. And they were gone.

At three in the afternoon the following day, I was still alone. Beyond the closed door of my hospital room, the daytime bustle of the maternity floor filtered to me in muffled noises. Nurses kept the door closed to make it easier for me, they said. Was it easier? Maybe it was.

The pitocin dripped into my veins. Contractions squeezed my belly gently every quarter hour.

I heard a baby's distant cry through the door. Tears flowed down my cheeks as I listened. My baby would never cry. *My sweet, precious child.*

Another night passed, and the sun shone brightly the following morning. "No—don't close the shades. I like to see out the window," I told the day nurse.

"I'll leave them open for you then. I just didn't want the sun to bother you."

I looked into the bright January morning outside my window. Another contraction started. I closed my eyes and breathed deeply. "How long does it usually take to induce labor?"

"It can take a while. Let's see. You're past thirty-six hours now. Do the contractions feel stronger?"

"No. About the same. I'm getting really tired."

"Hard to sleep, isn't it?"

I nodded.

"Well it won't be too much longer. Tell me, have you thought what you'll do after the delivery?"

"I don't know. I haven't thought."

"Most parents of stillborn babies need the closure of a few minutes with the baby. You get to decide if you want to see her or not."

"Oh. Okay. I hadn't thought."

"I'm just saying what I've heard. The parents... if they don't see their child after delivery they later wish they had."

I looked down. The nurse placed her hand over mine and gave a gentle squeeze. "Did you have a name picked out for this baby yet?"

I nodded.

"Are you planning to name her then? I think you should. Go ahead and name your child."

I looked at the nurse and mustered a small smile. "Thanks." She bustled about for a few more seconds and slipped out of the room. I turned to gaze out the window, blinking rapidly to stop the tears from spilling out of my eyes.

When Craig arrived after work, I reported my conversation with the nurse. "She said we should go ahead and name her."

"What name are you thinking?" he said.

"I like the angel idea. Let's find an angelic name."

"Like Gabriel?"

"Maybe."

"Or... Gabrielle for a girl."

I thought for a few seconds. "Gabrielle. I like that."

"So do I." He nodded. "Our little angel. I made arrangements at the funeral home this afternoon. They told me we could bury her on our own land, but they didn't recommend it since we might move someday."

"What did you decide?"

"There's a section for babies at the cemetery in Winfield. They're going to arrange a plot there. We can have a small service at the burial."

"Will it be private?"

"That's what I figured. Just you and me and our folks. I think we should have our folks there, don't you?"

"Yes. I'd like that."

"I'll let the minister know."

At ten that evening, I noticed a change in the contractions. "I think it may be tonight," I said to Craig.

"Really?"

"The contractions seem to be stronger."

"I guess that's a good sign. Are you ready?"

"In a way yes. I'm so ready for this to be over."

"Me too. It's been more than forty-eight hours now."

I nodded. "I'm exhausted. Oooh—there's another one." I grimaced in preparation for the discomfort.

"Breathe, Annsy," Craig coached me. "You're supposed to breathe."

I willed myself to breathe slowly and deeply. I struggled to relax as the contraction strengthened. When it abated I said, "Yes. I'm ready for this to be over. But I'm sad too. This is the last night we'll ever spend with our little girl."

Craig squeezed my hand. The room was silent except for the mechanical beeps of the monitor.

It was three twenty-four on the morning of January 17. "Okay. One more push," the doctor instructed. "I can see the head."

"Come on, Sweetie, you can do it," Craig said.

I took a deep breath and willed my exhausted body to bear down one more time. And it was over. The baby slid from her dark enclosure, slipped through the hesitant hands of the delivery team and landed on the floor with a wet slap, like a fish tossed onto a boat deck. The physical intensity within my body dissipated instantly. I wilted.

The delivery room was silent—no laughter, no exclamations, no baby crying, no weighing or measuring, and no holding the baby for me to see. Nobody knew what to say. There were no smiles of congratulations. No bustling about to tend to a newborn's needs. No baby crying.

"You did it, Annsy," Craig whispered in my ear. "It's all over now."

After a few moments of deafening silence, the doctor asked, "Do you want to see the baby?"

"Yes," I said weakly, remembering the nurse's counsel. "But later. Can it be later? All I want to do right now is sleep."

"Okay," he answered. "We'll arrange a viewing later. You get some rest. What's it been, a couple of days?"

Craig answered, "Fifty-four hours since the labor began. She hasn't slept for almost three days." His voice dimmed as my consciousness waned. Soon I slept, a heavy, dreamless sleep.

Fourteen hours later, at the end of his daily rounds, the doctor arrived in my room with a wheel chair. He settled me into it and wheeled me to the elevator. Craig walked at my side, holding my hand. When the elevator door opened, we entered the hospital's basement. The doctor pushed me to the morgue where our child waited on a table. She lay covered with a towel, a tiny mound on a large table.

Craig helped me stand and together we stepped to the table, clinging to each other for strength. The doctor removed the towel. We gazed at little Gabrielle. She was a beautiful child and looked a little like both of us, I think. Her hands lay at her sides, like tiny pale starfish marooned away from the sea. Her eyes were closed and we forgot to see what color they were. I think they must have been blue. Short fuzzy wisps of hair stood out from her head. I squeezed Craig's hand and I didn't cry.

"She's so tiny," I whispered.

"She looks like she's asleep. So peaceful," Craig murmured.

"Do you want to touch the baby?" the doctor asked.

I reached to caress her cheek. It was soft and smooth. And cold.

"Could we get a picture of her?" Craig asked.

"I'll ask the staff to take a photo for you," the doctor said.

"And a lock of hair. I'd like a lock of her hair," I said.

"Okay. Shall we go back now?"

Later that evening the doctor slipped into my room. He carried a sealed envelope and handed it to Craig. "Here's your baby's hair," he said. After he had gone, we broke the seal and peeked inside to see the tiny clip of light brown hair. I closed the envelope and folded it in thirds. Standing, I clutched the precious envelope tightly in my left hand and reached up to wrap my right arm around my husband.

"Guess you go home tomorrow," Craig said. "Are you ready?"

I nodded. "More than ready."

The following day I reminded Craig, "Today is seven months. Two more before Gabrielle's due date."

He parked our car at Highland Cemetery and helped me out. We were the last to arrive at the graveside services. I squeezed his hand and we joined our parents, the minister, and the minister's wife to stand around a lovely satin-covered box under a huge mound of rosebuds.

We held hands through the short ceremony. Under my other arm I clutched my purse. The envelope with Gabrielle's lock of hair rested safely in a zippered pocket. I didn't hear much of what the pastor said. Both our mothers dabbed at their eyes with tissues. Though a slight breeze played in my hair, the bright January sunshine warmed us as we stood on the hill. As the brief service concluded, we parted company with our folks.

"Are you ready to go home?" Craig said.

"No. I dread it. It will be so sad to go home to an empty house with an empty nursery and empty arms."

"There's no hurry, I guess. Let's take our time and do what we do best."

"What's that?"

"Wander the countryside. I brought our cameras. We could look for things that visually express what we're feeling right now."

"That makes sense. We bonded over Nature. We can start healing there too."

We drove north toward home. Craig chose a circuitous route traversing the hills between the cemetery and our house. We stopped several times along the way to snap photos of scenes that expressed the anguish and sadness in our hearts, the loss of our dream.

We found an icy shoreline at the city park, a broken and separated cream can enveloped in prairie grass, a stone bridge over a dry stream, an abandoned house at the end of an overgrown path across the prairie, and the flaming sky of sunset which silhouetted twisted and pleading tree limbs at day's end. Cold. Lonely. Abandoned dreams.

"Here we are," Craig announced as we rolled up the driveway. After I climbed the three steps to our front door I hugged Daisy. She danced with excitement to see me. "What do you think?" Craig asked as we hooked our coats on the hall tree.

"It's so quiet here. My arms are so heavy—they ache," I said. "They're empty—there should be a baby in them, but they're empty."

Reflections in Memory of Baby Gabrielle

7
DREAMS AND SIGNS

"Hi, Little One," I whispered as I stood reverently at Gabrielle's grave. The heat of an August afternoon enveloped me like a sauna. Shading my eyes from the afternoon sun, I lowered myself to my knees and sat on the hardy buffalo grass near the small marker bearing Gabrielle's name and birth date.

"Hey, guess what. I just heard the news—you'll have a little brother or sister next spring. It's true. I just confirmed that at the doctor's office. This little baby is due next March, the same month you were due. Only it will be later, the end of March.

"Guess what else. I didn't go back to work at Boeing. I just couldn't, considering how things ended for you and the possibility that the TNF contributed to your problems. No. I'm going back to school. I start later this month at Wichita State University to work for a teacher's certificate. Whoever would have thought? Me, a teacher. A science teacher at that."

I studied the turf over Gabrielle's resting place. There was hardly a clue that the ground had been disturbed within the last year. A little wild rose bush from home clung precariously to life in summer's heat. Around the isolated grave marker, unbroken sod stretched twenty feet in all directions. Suddenly I shivered. An image of a second satin-covered box near this grave flashed into my mind. I shook my head to remove the image. No. I wouldn't think about that. This baby would be fine. He or she had to be fine. I forced the thought out of my mind.

The fall semester started, keeping me busy with my studies. I met fellow education students for lunch daily. We shared life stories, and favorite recipes. One young woman from Iran showed me letters she received from home with holes cut in the pages.

"What's this?"

"Censored." She nodded. "Somebody didn't like that particular word."

"You mean somebody opens and reads all the mail?"

"Yes. For letters heading to the U.S. You're so lucky here. You have your privacy. And good education,... medical care. How are you feeling anyway?"

"Doing well, thanks."

"In my country, married women, especially if they're expecting, wouldn't be allowed to attend classes anywhere."

"I think I'd go stir-crazy if I couldn't get out."

Mother called often. "I feel much better than last time," I told her one autumn day. "I'm more active. I haven't had the nausea nor the swelling."

"That's a good sign," she said.

"I certainly hope so. We'll take it as a good sign anyway."

"Is Craig staying busy?"

"Very much. He's gone by six every morning. Then he's also taking a Tuesday evening class at WSU to learn computer programming. That involves lots of study on the other days."

"Computer programming. That was a difficult class for your dad fifteen years ago."

"I remember. I think Craig is trying to stay busy enough he won't start worrying about the baby. I wish I could convince him it's different this time."

With Craig gone a lot, I spent long hours in the company of only Daisy and the baby. I often read aloud.

"'Fish gotta swim and bird gotta fly,'" I read one morning a few days before Thanksgiving. "'Insects, it seems, gotta do one horrible thing after another. I never ask why of a vulture or shark, but I ask why of almost every insect I see.'"

The morning sunlight filtered through the roof slats of our covered wooden patio. I rocked in a deck chair as I read aloud to Baby. This morning, we continued with Annie Dillard's *Pilgrim at Tinker Creek*. My days were tightly scheduled with classes and activities leaning toward Baby's healthy development. Each day included exercises for me, walks along the county road, music at the piano, quiet reading time, and naps. The plan seemed to be working. This baby responded with frequent, energetic kicks. In fact, I now was doubtful that Gabrielle had ever kicked, after experiencing this child's energy.

I set the book aside. Resting my hands lightly across my abdomen, I smiled as the baby stirred. "Okay, Little One. That's enough Annie Dillard for today. Let's go for a walk."

I lay on an exam table at the Winfield hospital. Craig stood at my side, holding my hand.

"Now, watch," the technician said. "Here's the head, a little shoulder." She moved the sensor over my belly and static vague images appeared on the monitor screen.

Craig said, "I guess you really need a lot of training to see it well."

"Yes. Practice helps." She continued to move the sensor over my belly. "Here's a little knee—oh look. Baby kicked. Did you see that?"

We had. Craig squeezed my hand. We looked at each other and both of us beamed. Then we looked quickly back to the screen, not wanting to miss a thing.

"This is all very normal. Very good, as far as I can tell," the technician said. "Our in-house physician will review the images later today and your doctor will give you a call. But it looks normal so far. Baby even kicked for us. Go ahead and get dressed now."

When she had gone, I looked at Craig and we both smiled.

"Is this a sign?" I asked.

"This is definitely a good sign."

"Now, maybe we can go ahead and get excited."

"Whatever you say, Mommy."

"Return to your seats and fasten your belts." The captain's voice over the airplane's speaker crackled with tension. I reached across my distended belly to assure that my belt was indeed fastened. The airplane careened wildly and dove. My head spun.

The moment of impact pitched everything into chaos. We must have hit water. The forward areas began seeping after just a few seconds. The nose filled, and our aircraft tilted forward. The submersion accelerated.

Icy water reached my toes and the cold shot like lightning through my entire body. The water bubbled up to my thighs. I frantically clawed at the seat belt clasp to release it, but couldn't. Water encircled my waist, and rose over my belly. I flailed my arms. We were going down. There was nothing I could do.

I woke with a start, my chest heaving. In the darkness, Craig's breathing confirmed that he rested in a deep sleep.

"It was a dream... a nightmare." I forced myself to inhale slowly and deeply. Gradually, my heart rate slowed. But the sense of dread hung heavily over me. I hugged Baby gently, lovingly. "You're okay, aren't you, Little One?"

Why else would I dream of an airplane crash? Was something amiss? What if this baby died too? What would we do then?

The sense of dread hung over me until dawn. I lay in bed, weeping quietly for what seemed like hours. When Craig

rolled over and opened his eyes, he saw my stricken face. "Is something wrong?"

"No. I just had a bad dream."

"Another nightmare?"

I nodded. "I don't know why the nights are so hard. Everything is fine in the daytime."

"Baby still moving?"

I nodded again. "A lot."

He squirmed closer and kissed my forehead. Then he kissed my swollen eyelids. I forced a tight-lipped smile and nodded.

On Christmas Eve I grabbed Craig's right hand with both of mine and tugged him gently toward the couch in our crowded living room. "I have something for you," I said. "Please sit down."

Craig lowered himself to the sofa. He watched me go to the tiny Christmas tree adorning a table in front of the window. I pulled an envelope from a branch of the tree and presented it to him. With great ceremony, and a twinkle in his eye, he broke the wax seal on the envelope. He extracted papers from within and read. After a few seconds, he reached for my hand and pulled me to him. I leaned my head against his shoulder as he continued to read silently.

To Craig

The world is a merry-go-round which spins faster and faster, surrounding me with so many details I overlook the essence of life. I am so wrapped up in petty things I rarely see what's important, like the specialness of my loved ones. Even more rarely do I express the underlying depth of my feeling.

Perhaps you don't even know...

...How weak I would be and powerless to handle the world without your quiet strength behind me.

...How sometimes when I really look at you and see every detail of your beloved face, time stands still and I feel a frozen moment of eternal peace.

...How content I feel wrapped in your arms. It must be what Daisy feels when she is curled against you and gives one of those lingering sighs.

...How I swell with uncontainable love when I see a sign of the beauty of your soul, like the way you love country smells, the crispness of a winter morning, the peace of nature, farms, and wildflowers.

...How proud I feel when I stop to think of all the things you do and do well.

...How confident I am that you can do anything you want to do.

...How ashamed and undeserving I feel when I see an expression of your love toward me and I've been caught up in the merry-go-round again.

...How happy I feel when our baby moves inside me and how grateful I am that she or he will have a daddy like you.

...How I want to do for you what you do for me but I fear I lack the strength.

Perhaps marriage really is a circle like our wedding rings—never ending, never beginning, always turning back on itself, growing, strengthening, until we know we can make life beautiful, leaning on each other.

I love you, Craig.
Merry Christmas
Ann

"Wow, Annsy," he said. "That has to be about the best Christmas present anyone ever gave me. You know, though, I think that this strength you say I give you comes from the confidence I gain from having you with me, supporting my ideas."

"Really? Then our life together really is a circle. You're there for me and I'm there for you."

Craig nodded. "I think that if I'd not met you I'd be like a vegetable somewhere—no purpose or direction. I'm so glad I found you."

"Me too."

"I love you, Ann. I've opened my eyes to a lot of new things since I met you. You show me the simple beauty in the world around us."

I twisted on the sofa so I could see his eyes. I opened my mouth to speak, but he silenced me with a warm finger crossing my lips. "Hear me out. Every time I see you sad, it hurts me a little. When you cry, it's like sticking a sword in my gut. When you're happy, there's no way I couldn't be happy with you. There's a beautiful spark of sunshine in your smiling eyes.

"Sometimes I wish I could be that happy. You lift me out of my dark moods when I've had a bad day at work. If it wasn't for our goals and dreams, our life together, there wouldn't be much reason to be here on Earth."

"The baby," I said.

"Definitely something to brighten a gloomy day. I'm looking forward to seeing you and me in our baby. That will be a reward for both of us. At the same time, I feel so helpless during these months of pregnancy. I wish I could help you bear some of the burden and be more aware of the life which we created. I kind of get obsessed worrying that something will go wrong again and I miss out on those little special moments."

"I worry too."

"How so?"

"I've had a few spells over the last week or ten days where I feel really dizzy. And sometimes I think my ankles are swelling again."

"You haven't mentioned this before."

"Well, I want to believe everything is all right. Just when I get full of dread, the baby moves or kicks, as if he—or she—knows I need a little sign that all is well. So I put it out of my mind. I'm sure the next month will bring lots of tense feelings, but we just have to hang on to those little signs."

Early the next morning, I woke in a cold sweat. A thin wail of despair escaped my lungs into our dark bedroom. Craig stirred and reached over to me, clasping my hand in his. "You okay?"

"I think so. Just another nightmare."

"C'mere. He pulled on my far shoulder and we rolled toward each other. We weathered the remainder of the night cuddling together.

The bright morning sunshine dispelled the rest of the night's dread.

Craig returned to work early in January, leaving me home alone. "Good morning, Baby," I said. "How about some Thoreau today?" I reclined in the sofa and propped my feet on the piano bench in front of me.

I read from *Walden.* "'Regularly at half-past seven, in one part of the summer, after the evening train had gone by, the whip-poor-wills chanted their vespers for half an hour, sitting on a stump by my door, or upon the ridge-pole of the house.' Hey, Baby, I can hardly wait until you're here, discovering the world. Maybe someday we'll hear whip-poor-wills too. Maybe on a camping trip. Your daddy and I like to go camping, you know. I'm really looking forward to watching you discover the world."

On the seventeenth day of January, Craig took the day off. I stayed home from school. We didn't talk much over breakfast, but by mid-morning, he had gathered his house plan sketches and we piled into our car for an appointment to talk to a loan officer at the bank about building a house on our acreage.

The interview didn't go well. He gathered his carefully drawn house plans, scrunched them together and stormed out of the bank. I waddled after him as fast as I could. He sat in the driver's seat of our car and slammed the door. "Well, I guess this was the wrong day to find out about a loan," he snapped as I joined him.

"Do you think the answer would have been different tomorrow?"

"No. It's just that... I thought some exciting news would help us get through the day."

"That would have been nice on the first anniversary of Gabrielle's birth."

He nodded. "I didn't dream they would deny funding. They're trying to tell us what kind of house we can build. That I can't build a house unless I do it the way they want me to."

Craig raised the plans he still held, ripped them in two and tossed them into the back seat.

"Well, I'm starting over. I'm going to prove to everyone—including myself—that I can build the house we choose. If we want solar panels, we should have solar panels. Truly, I think that's going to be the way of the future." He started the car and we headed home.

"How can we do this without money?" I asked.

"We'll save our money until we have enough for each step. I'll draw up plans for a simpler house, one without a basement. I know how to build foundation forms, and we can do it ourselves."

"It'll take longer."

"Yes, a lot longer. But we've got the trailer, so it's not like we'll be losing money on rent somewhere. Your dad's offered to mill us some lumber at his summer sawmill."

"You're saying we'll build the house just like we built the garage and the well house?"

"Sure. Why not? And we can put up a wind mill, and use solar panels, and have a wood-burning stove."

"And be totally independent, in harmony with nature."

"We can salvage used lumber from old houses, and store it in our garage until we have enough for the next step. Nobody can tell me we can't build a house the way we want to. Especially not today. Today's hard enough without that kind of news."

We drove up our driveway and Craig parked the car at the east end of our tiny mobile home. He reached for my hand.

"You feeling any better today?"

I shrugged. "About the same. My feet feel tight and swollen. It seems like my heart starts racing for no reason every now and then. I get dizzy several times a day so that I have to sit down."

"Baby still kicking?"

"Yes."

"Let's go in and check your blood pressure."

We made our way to the trailer. Craig took my coat and settled me onto the couch.

"Look!" My face lit up as I gestured toward the window. He glanced across the room. On the table in front of the window, one of the plants we had received a year earlier in sympathy for our loss had burst into bloom while we were gone. "It's a sign. God's telling us that everything will be all right. Don't you think? Why else would it bloom today?"

He nodded. "I'll take it as a good sign," he said and hustled to retrieve the blood pressure cuff from our small bathroom.

8
A BROKEN RAINBOW

Three weeks later, Craig asked if I would go on a grocery run with him.

"No, you go ahead."

"Sure you don't want to come along?"

"I'm kind of tired. I'll just wait here and lock up the chickens when they go in."

"Okay then."

"Don't forget milk and flour."

"Frozen peas and tomato sauce." He recited more of our grocery list.

"You have the list." I smiled and waved him off.

Half an hour later, evening deepened into twilight. I threw a jacket over my shoulders and headed to the chicken house. The last hen lingered outside, pecking at a speck on the ground. I chased her into the hen house and secured the door against night prowlers. Then I made my way heavily back to the trailer house.

Inside, I turned on our small television and relaxed on the sofa. A few minutes later the baby kicked hard. It was hard enough that the blow seemed to lift me off the couch a couple inches.

"Whoa, Little One," I said, my eyes widening. "Take it easy." Baby answered with some normal stirrings. "That's better."

A few minutes later, I stood and turned toward the bathroom. The instant I was upright, a flood of clear, warm liquid gushed from between my legs.

"Oh, my God." I said. "That wasn't you, was it? I think my water has broken."

A labor contraction circled my belly. "Oh, my God." I said again. "Craig, hurry, please."

I bustled to our telephone and fumbled with the directory. Here it was, after six. The doctor's office wouldn't be open at this time. I called the Winfield hospital. When the evening operator answered I said, "I think my water just broke."

"I'll connect you to Labor and Delivery," she said.

After a brief description of the kick and the water gush, the obstetric nurse said, "You better come on down."

"Right now?"

"As soon as you can get here."

"My husband went to the store."

"Let's hope he doesn't linger too long."

I headed to the bathroom to clean up and change clothes. Pulling a daypack from my closet I stuffed some clothing for inside. I added a hairbrush and toothbrush and set the bag by the front door. Contractions continued to squeeze my abdomen but they weren't at regular intervals yet. I paced the length of the trailer, wide awake. "Hurry, Craig. Please hurry."

Finally I saw the headlights of our little car turn into the drive. I threw the coat on, picked up my bag, and met him, ready to go.

"What?" he said after one look at me.

"We need to go to the hospital."

He threw the groceries in our refrigerator and we left.

The labor and delivery team wasted no time settling me into a room. They connected me to a fetal monitor. Craig and I smiled at each other. We watched the reassuring blips and numbers. Everything looked normal.

"Five centimeters," the nurse said. She grinned at me. "You aren't going back home. Not without a baby."

"So this is it? But it's still five weeks early."

"This is it, honey. There's no stopping this now. Baby's in a bit of a hurry."

I caught my breath as the intensity of another contraction grew.

"I'll call your doctor." The nurse whisked out of the room and passed another who entered with a clipboard.

"Have you decided on a pediatrician for the baby? We'll need to let him know when the baby is born."

"We haven't given it much thought yet," Craig said. "Can you tell us about the local doctors?"

She named a few, giving a brief review of parental reports after each name. "What do you think, Sweetie?" he said.

I shrugged and began to breathe purposefully as another contraction built.

"How about Dr. Smith?" he asked. I nodded.

"I'll note Dr. Smith here on your chart," the nurse said.

The entire team seemed motivated by the intensity of contractions. Between concentrating on my breathing and watching the hospital team bustle around, I watched the blips on the monitor. Baby's heartbeat—normal. Excitement grew.

"I can't believe it. Can you?" I asked Craig. "We're really going to have a baby in just a little while."

"I know. I can hardly believe it myself." His blue eyes sparkled.

The doctor breezed into the room. "Let's check you and see what's happening," he said. Assisted by the labor nurse, he checked the dilation progress. "Time to go to the delivery room." he announced.

Contractions continued and intensified on the way. "I don't want you to push yet," he said.

It was all I could do not to push with the contractions. Finally settled in the delivery room, he gave the go ahead. "Okay. With the next contraction, push."

The flurry of activity seemed to freeze. Everything was now in slow motion, with great effort. As if from a long distance away, I heard several voices encouraging me to push. Push! With every ounce of strength I could muster, I was doing just that. "I can see the head," Doctor announced.

Then one of the beeps on the monitor blipped to a steady buzz. Baby's heartbeat had flat-lined on the screen.

"Forceps," the doctor said. A moment later he added, "Call Dr. Simpson."

Something was wrong. This couldn't be. I turned my attention to a new contraction. Its intensity dwindled and my entire body wilted. I felt mushy. My energy, and that of the contractions, seemed spent.

The specialist breezed into the delivery room and glanced at my wilted state as he headed to the end of the table. With one quick tug, he delivered the baby and rushed our son to a nearby table. For a short eternity, the team concentrated on reviving him while Craig and I clung together, terrified.

A few moments later, Dr. Simpson asked our Doc softly, "Are you going to call it?"

Doctor nodded.

"No, no," I said in a hoarse voice. "Don't give up. Please don't give up."

The doctor stepped toward us. "I'm sorry. There's nothing we can do now. Your baby has died."

A nurse brought the little bundle to me. "Do you want to hold him?" she asked. I nodded. She laid our baby boy on my chest. He was still warm, and oh, so limp. I couldn't see him well at that angle, but I gently caressed his head, and fondled his tiny ears. He was damp with birth residue. I wanted to sit up and hold him, squeeze him and cuddle him, but I couldn't.

"We need to get you to surgery," Dr. Simpson said. "You have a bad tear. I need a surgical team to repair it."

I looked at him but said nothing. I didn't care what they did to me. I didn't care about anything anymore.

The next few days blurred in a haze. We stumbled through them automatically. We'd done this before so we knew what to do now. A precious snip of the baby's hair was sealed in an envelope, tucked securely in my purse. Early in the morning before the graveside service, we traveled the countryside with our cameras, searching for scraps of beauty that would dull the pain in our hearts, an artistic expression of the unutterable sorrow that lodged there. The collage, a collective photo of love for our son West Carl, included shots of angry water, ice creeping up on new life, and shadows surrounding a life that once was.

"You're awfully quiet," Craig said when we turned toward the cemetery.

"I don't know what to say."

"Me either."

"I just really don't know. Is there something wrong with me that kills our babies? This is so unfair."

"Nobody ever said life would be fair."

"Do you remember when we first thought of the name West?" I asked.

"Yeah. I think it was our backpack trip in Colorado."

"Lost Creek, I think it was. The name was your idea."

"I remember we hiked only part way and pitched our tent on a grassy hillside."

I nodded. "We sat at the campfire and talked about having a boy someday and calling him West. We tucked that idea away until now."

"We can use it again someday," Craig suggested.

"I don't know. I don't think I can do this again."

"Maybe I should get a vasectomy."

"That seems so final," I whispered.

"Or maybe not," he said softly and squeezed my hand. "We could adopt. Let's adopt a child."

"I don't know. I don't want to think about that right now. I just want our babies. Our own babies."

"I hear you, Annsy. But I feel we are destined to raise a family, so maybe we should consider adoption."

"West isn't even buried and you're already talking about adopting. I can't. I just can't think about that. To think we'll never again see a little one that is you and me put together." I choked on a sob. "I'm so angry."

"Angry? You don't look angry."

"Well, I get mad quietly, on the inside."

"Who are you angry with?"

"The hospital. Sometimes I'm mad at you. I'm furious with myself, my body. It has let me down big time."

Craig closed his eyes and shook his head, as if to clear similar feelings from his mind.

"I'm mad at the baby."

"The baby?"

"I know. It's crazy, isn't it? I don't want to believe it myself. How could I be mad at the baby—for dying on me?" Craig squeezed my hand with both of his.

"At God," I added. "I'm mad at God."

He nodded.

"I don't want to lose West," I said. "I don't want to forget our little baby boy. The thing that really bothers me is that you didn't get to carry our baby to the nursery. I didn't get to see your face light up. I have been robbed—we have been robbed. This just isn't right. It can't be. Everything was so different. The kicks. The flower. It just can't be."

Craig stood at my side on the lonely hilltop, hands in his pockets. I threaded my arm through his and leaned against him as our pastor spoke at our son's graveside. Inside the pocket of my plaid dress coat, a folded envelope stowed a precious lock of West's hair. The memorial locket holding his sister's hair hung around my neck.

Here we were, at Gabrielle's grave, with a second tiny, satin-covered casket. A large bouquet of blue and yellow carnations covered the lid. A sprig with red and white carnations and baby's breath stood at the name plate which marked Gabrielle's grave.

Our parents stood nearby in a loose circular pattern. Muffled sniffs of the grandmothers echoed my sentiments.

"I honestly don't know why this has happened." The pastor said. "I honestly don't know what part God played in this. Somehow I resist saying that God has made this happen, or even saying that God allowed this to happen. I really can't think of a good reason. I can honestly say, however, that I am confident God's love is with us and with West Carl, and that in this moment and forever, God's love will be with us and in us and will see us through. May you be aware of God's love and presence in your lives. Amen."

Reflections
In memory of Baby West

9
ALIEN TO MY OWN KIND

Blood is softer than water.

I discovered that in my warm baths. Following doctor's orders, I soaked in a hot bath every day to hasten the healing of the delivery tear. I could tell by feel when part of the film of draining blood was released. Soft and slick, like a wet mushroom, the blood felt different than the bath water. When I stood and opened the drain, red fragments and tendrils floated in the water. They gyrated in terrible contortions in the direction of flow. Down the drain. Pieces of what once held the life of our son floated helplessly and uselessly down the drain.

"I am still dying the death," I whispered.

After all those positive signs, why did he have to die? I couldn't understand. Maybe God didn't speak to us after all.

Sometimes I felt that I was two completely different people. One of me was weak, angry and reclusive. I resented families that had babies. I could easily grow to hate children out of jealousy. I decided to purchase a children's book for the library as a memorial gift thinking it might be the last thing I would ever do for a child. Then I could recede into my forgettableness and wallow in misery, anger, and self-pity for the rest of my life.

The other part of me sought activity and involvement. I cared. I did care very much about people, old and young. I wanted to share life with children, not just our lives but all the life on earth. I believed we would be good parents. What good was life if we couldn't share it? Why celebrate Christmas? Or Easter? Birthdays? Thanksgiving? Why celebrate at all without children? Why develop our own family traditions if we would never have a family?

The day arrived when I headed back to my classes. Jenny, another education student who had become a good friend, greeted me with an intense gaze, as if she wondered when I was going to lose my cool and break down into a blathering mess.

"How are you doing?" she asked, her voice oozing concern.

"I don't know. I had to get out of the house."

She nodded. "Let me know if I can help."

I turned to the crowded classroom and worked my way toward an empty desk. Once seated, I closed my eyes. I caressed the two pendants hanging on my neck, holding wisps of the hair from my two babies. *I can do this. For them I must do this.* The tiny lockets gave me strength to meet each day, and courage to move forward.

A month later I sat limply on the extra chair in the exam room of our weekly clinic. The doctor said, "You've healed well. You had a really bad tear, but Dr. Simpson did an expert repair job."

Okay. My body is healed. My heart is still broken.

"I got the autopsy report a few days ago," he went on. "The boy had the same congenital problems as the little girl. Major issues with the heart. He had essentially a single ventricle, as did the baby girl."

"The same thing? How could that be? Everything felt so different."

"Well it was the same thing. Evidently they both developed to the point where their own hearts would normally take over much of their bodies' circulation. Before then, the mother's heart—your heart—pumped blood through the placenta."

I shook my head.

He continued, "The boy had quite a bit of edema, swelling commonly found with heart failure."

"This is all in the autopsy report?"

"Yes.""I want to see it. Send it to me."

"Usually the autopsy is sent to physicians. There may be medical terms—"

"Send it to me. Who would need the information more than the parents? And we're still waiting for the photo you promised would be taken on February 11."

"Yes. Well, I was meaning to tell you. Apparently, the hospital did not get pictures after all."

The news stabbed at my heart like a knife. "You promised!" Acid dripped from my voice. "Why would you tell us that photos were taken if you didn't know they had been? I can't believe you would do that to us twice."

"There may be some photos of the infant boy along with the autopsy from Wichita."

"Then you will get them for us," I said in a no-nonsense tone.

"I'm not sure that's a good idea."

"I want the pictures of our baby and I want the autopsy report."

He sighed in resignation. "I'll see what I can do."

The return address on the large manila envelope was that of my physician's office. Multiple stamps plastered the top. The whole thing must have weighed a pound. I slid the day's mail from our rural mailbox and held it to my chest as I walked up the driveway.

Once inside, I carefully released the clasp, broke the seal, and slid a stack of papers onto our dining table. There were at least fifty sheets in the report, a collected summary of findings from multiple medical facilities beginning with the Winfield hospital and ending with a geneticist at the University of Kansas Medical Center.

Two pieces of cardboard, three inches by eight inches, were taped together. A note on the outside indicated that its contents were to be returned to a Wichita hospital. I broke the tape and slid out a 35mm color slide, the only photo in existence of either one of our babies. It was a post-autopsy slide, a gruesome view of our son with bloody gashes spaced around his body where a coroner's knife had entered. Considerably swollen, partly from the heart failure he had incurred, but also partly from post-mortem processes, he was far from a pretty sight.

I gasped. A vision of crass, methodical, unloving hands violating his tiny body consumed my mind. I slid the photo into its cardboard sheath and vowed never to return it to the medical community. No one, save his loving parents, needed that photo. I turned to the sheaf of medical findings.

A summary page listing "Final Anatomic Diagnoses" stood out. Its outline format seemed fairly straightforward. However, point number two lost me quickly. "Anasarca" topped a list.

"Right pleural effusion, serous.

Left pleural effusion, serous.

Peritoneal effusion, serous.

Univentricular heart, situs solitus"

It was a completely different language. Discouraged that I couldn't even understand the information, I decided to take the report to the public library and find an unabridged dictionary.

An hour later, I stood at the library's copy machine. Unwilling to mark on the originals, I planned to make all kinds of notes and explanations on the copied pages. I slid the originals back into their mailing envelope and headed to the stand which held a huge unabridged dictionary of the English language.

Slowly and methodically I looked up the technical terms. A grisly, tortured image began to form in my mind. "Right pleural effusion, serous" translated to the observation that the membranes around the right lung were flooded with a watery substance. The same was true of the left lung and abdominal cavity. There was marked under-development of the lungs, which essentially meant there were no alveoli. West Carl's heart was a two-chamber heart, missing both the left atrium and left ventricle.

In short, our baby boy suffered almost the exact same developmental problems which had killed his sister. Neither baby could have lived, had they ever made it to our world.

How could that be? It made no sense. He was so much more active than little Gabrielle. Why? Why? Why? What did that mean for us? Were we never to feel the joy that parents feel for a healthy newborn baby?

I turned to the genetics report. No consistent abnormalities in the DNA were observed. West Carl was a chromosomally normal male child. I turned to a clinical correlation page. The summary paragraph indicated that the abnormalities did not fall into any common category such as Down's Syndrome. "This conclusion tends to buttress the view that the anomalies described in sibling fetuses are either genetically multifactoria, teratogenic, or a combination of the two. Every effort should thus be made to exclude a teratogen."

Teratogenic. Teratogen. Sounded ominous. I wondered what that meant. I had never seen or heard the terms before. I turned the dictionary pages to find the definitions.

"Teratogenic: tending to cause developmental malformations and monstrosities.

"Teratogenesis: production of monstrous growths or fetuses."

I coughed out a lungful of air. My stomach churned. I felt like someone had just punched me in the gut. I couldn't breathe. Seconds after I read about the production of monsters, I grabbed my scattered papers and staggered to my car. Hardly able to see through the tears swimming in my eyes, I collapsed into the driver's seat and wept long and hard.

That evening Craig studied the autopsy report.

I took a deep breath. "Our babies weren't monsters. They were just little babies, trying to get born."

Craig wrapped me in his arms. We swayed gently back and forth.

"I'm going crazy," I continued, through gasping breaths. "In my mind, I imagine horrible things—ghastly things that must have happened to West and probably to

Gabrielle too—the swelling and circulatory problems and tiny blood vessels bursting. I can't imagine how it wasn't painful—and I was helpless to relieve their suffering. I guess it did hurt to die."

"I don't know," Craig said. "Maybe their nervous systems were delayed too."

I shook my head. "I didn't even know it. How could I not know? And the picture—I can't stand it. I wish we hadn't approved the autopsy."

"Why?"

"I have visions in my mind of our baby being cut apart by knives in the hands of cold, uncaring people, people who didn't care that he was once a person. People who thought he was a monster. It makes me sick to think that something he and I had worked so long to build was cut apart irreverently in an hour or two. You may think I'm crazy, but I got this repulsion to eat meat for the same reason. How could I so calmly cut apart something that took so long to grow in another mother's womb? The world is a cold, cruel place."

Craig reached for a kitchen towel and dabbed gently at my wet cheeks. "There are still beautiful things, Annsy. You've got to look for the small miracles."

"I feel like such a freak. Like I don't even belong to the human race. I'm not a real person since I can't produce what normal people do. I'm not totally human. But I'm not anything else either. I'm just a misfit. If I was a cow, they'd have butchered me by now."

"Well, you're not a cow."

"Do you think we'll ever have a family?"

"Of course we will. We're destined to raise a family."

"I don't know. I'm not sure any more."

"Somewhere there is a little baby or a child who needs a mommy and a daddy. We've just got to trust that God will bring us together."

"I don't want somebody else's child right now. I just want the two we already had." I slumped against Craig's shoulder.

"I know, Annsy, I know," he said softly. I felt his tears fall on my cheek.

10
INCHING FORWARD

"We should adopt a baby," Craig urged.

I shook my head.

He lifted my chin until I had to look into his eyes—eyes that were, like mine, stricken with a chasm of sadness. I knew action helped him deal with our losses. He filled his days with frenzied activity.

"You know how long my cousins waited for their baby," he said. "Years. I just think we shouldn't waste any time."

"Craig, you are always in a hurry." Lacking the energy to take any steps toward an uncertain future, I drooped.

He hugged me gently, then pushed me away and sought my eyes again. "Hurry every chance you get. Think about it a minute. Only two agencies handle infant adoptions in Kansas, Lutheran Social Services and Catholic Social Services. We know that the Catholic agency handles more adoptions. And that they favor Catholic families for the placements."

I nodded.

Craig went on, "So let's join the Catholic church."

"I don't know. I just don't know. That seems so extreme, so foreign to me."

"What harm could come from it? We're on a quest, a search for our child. We've got to do whatever it takes and that would give us something to do."

I could think of no response. I had no energy to protest.

"Anyway, I called the priest in Augusta. We have an appointment to see him tomorrow evening."

"You did? We do?"

"Just try it. Come with me. We'll simply ask him about joining the Catholic church. Please?"

I shrugged my shoulders. "I don't know. I don't want to go somewhere and end up crying in front of a stranger."

"Let me do the talking. Will you at least think about it?""I'll think about it."

Weekly meetings with the priest began the following evening. He listened as Craig explained our interest in learning more about Catholicism. He welcomed our interest, answered a few basic questions and gave us each a hardbound catechism book to study.

"You seem pretty quiet today. Subdued maybe," the Catholic Father observed one evening late in March.

I nodded. "Today was the day our baby should have been born." Craig squeezed my hand. We sat together on a couch in the church office.

"A tough day." The priest nodded.

I blinked back tears.

"Do you want to talk about it?" he asked.

"I don't know if I can."

"Take your time. Obviously both of you loved your child very much. How are you dealing with the loss, Craig?"

"I have moments. I try to stay busy so my mind doesn't dwell on death. But sometimes something will kick in, a little something that reminds me of the pregnancy, and all the little signs of life the baby gave us."

"What signs of life?"

"The little kick during the sonogram. The wiggles and bumps on Ann's tummy during the La Maze classes. The flower that burst into bloom on Gabrielle's birthday."

Father looked at me as I shrank miserably into the couch. "I'm sure you also noticed these signs?"

I nodded. "I am so confused. I thought all the signs were sent from God to assure us that everything would be all right. That this time was different. And then it wasn't. Maybe God doesn't speak to us after all."

"Oh, I think He was speaking to you."

"What bothers me is that I was helpless to do anything. I wonder if the babies felt any pain. I imagine they did, and I could do nothing to help them." I stopped to swallow a sob.

"Have you ever thought that God was indeed speaking to you? Those signs, those little messages are very true. Everything is well. The babies are with God in heaven."

After a moment I said softly, "No, I hadn't thought of it like that."

Craig said, "But neither baby was baptized. I thought Catholics believed you had to be baptized to get into heaven."

Father waved his hand in a twisting motion and bobbled his head. "I think God loves your babies even more than you do. A loving God could not condemn an innocent child that had no chance at life."

"So you think the babies went to heaven?" I asked softly.

"Most definitely. Went up like a skyrocket. That's what I believe," he said.

My dear baby West,

Here it is, May, but winter refuses to go. It lingers with nighttime fingers urging us to cuddle under the covers. Our furnace continues to run until mid-morning. We wear coats until nearly noon, and put them on again before the sun has set. Denver is buried under snow. No snow here, but cold damp winds whip from the north and chill me to the marrow of my bones. Our garden grows slowly. Sweet potatoes remained dormant until the last of April. Trees didn't bud out until this first week of May.

The killdeers have finally returned and frogs are waking up. Spring will soon be here. But it is an empty spring, little West. You're missing out on the warming season. Instead of bringing life, this spring harbors death. Winter struggles to stay. It's as if the whole world knows there is something amiss. Time refuses to go on. My wholesome earth can't stand to continue without you.

Baby West, I miss you. I will always miss you. I cannot jump into the wind. I haven't the strength. I cannot fight for our future and our future child. I don't want time to pass. I want it to back up, to right what is wrong, to gather what is amiss, and bring you along with us into the future. I love you, my child.

"Greg told me about a square dancing group starting up in town. Let's join," Craig said in June.

"Square dancing?"

"Yes. We haven't been dancing for a long time, you know."

"But, square dancing? I don't know how to square dance."

"They're having lessons. We could learn. It'd give us something to do. Shall we sign up?"

"Sure."

Summer passed quickly. We stayed busy with our garden. Craig's new house plans met with the loan officer's approval and we found a general contractor to manage the construction. Our project was scheduled early in the following year. We relaxed in Minnesota for a two-week vacation in July. We composed a letter about our desire to adopt a baby and sent it with a photo of ourselves to agencies across the country as well as all our distant friends. Most of the responses brought dismal news. No babies here. No babies there. Check with someone else. When we did receive useful information, we followed every lead and acted on every tip.

By the end of August, I had enrolled in another semester of education courses. Classes started before Labor Day, so I stayed busy with studies. Without fail, I carried or wore my precious lockets daily, to give myself a symbol of courage. For the children, I would forge ahead. Still, at times, the despair of our double loss overwhelmed me and I struggled to maintain a calm exterior. My biggest fear was to create a scene in public, so I guarded all my emotions in secret.

Ma and Pa with garden produce

One day over supper, Craig mentioned, "One of my co-workers at Boeing told me today that we should check with hospitals. Wesley in particular delivers so many babies they might give us some ideas of doctors or lawyers to contact."

"I guess we could take our letter to the hospitals in Wichita."

"Wesley for sure."

A few days later I took our information to Wesley Hospital. I was directed to their social services office and found a familiar face. Ruby Gentry, from our square dancing group, sat behind a desk.

That evening I told Craig about her.

"Really? Ruby works at Wesley Hospital?" he said.

"Not only works there—she is their social worker."

Craig grinned, infected with my excitement. "So what did she say?"

"She was real nice. She wasn't too encouraging, though. She said it is rare that a baby is born at Wesley with no prior arrangements, but sometimes a mother will leave a baby in the hospital's care. Then she has to find a home for the child. She put our information in her file. Our names are on the list."

"I suppose it's a long list, too."

"Yeah. And we're way down at the bottom. But it's neat that we actually know somebody."

The spring semester began in January. This would be my make-or-break college experience. I was scheduled for student-teaching in an urban high school setting this semester. I couldn't afford to let myself become distracted by personal issues. The anniversaries of our losses came and went, and we remained distracted with frenzied activities. Ground-breaking for our house started in February. Through daily conferences with the contractor, Craig managed the construction of our new home.

I struggled with my teaching activities. It seemed that I was nearly alone in my own small universe. The high school students fought and complained at nearly every opportunity. Supervising teachers complained when I overlooked a few housekeeping chores. Yet they never stopped to explain what their expectations of me would be.

The experience of student-teaching became a mountain of stress for me. I missed seeing Jenny on a regular basis. I dreaded the visits from my college instructor. And yet I persevered. Bolstered by the thought that this would all be over by May, I dragged myself to school early every morning.

11
THE FIFTH DAY OF MARCH

"Bye, Sweetie," Craig leaned over for a quick peck. He sprinted into the steady stream of foot traffic filing into Boeing for first shift.

"Bye. Have a good Monday," I called after him. He turned and gave me a thumbs-up.

The previous weekend held a hint of promise. Work started on our basement foundation in front of the trailer where we lived. I managed to grade all the papers and tests from four different classes I student-taught. Craig worked overtime on Saturday, but was able to get our non-starting car towed to a repair shop. And now it was Monday.

I drove to the corner and returned to the bypass. The Wichita High School where I taught four classes required another fifteen minute drive through heavy morning traffic. My school day proceeded as usual. Before the starting bell, I collected my notes, reviewed plans, and gathered the papers to return to the general science class. A second-hour planning period gave me time to prepare for the rest of the day. Physiology class followed. In the middle of returning the previous Friday's tests, my supervising teacher popped into the room. "You've got a phone call from the boss," he said.

"Which boss?" I asked.

"You'll see. I'll finish handing these out. You take the call."

I slipped into the science office and picked up the receiver. "Hello?" I said tentatively.

It was Craig. "Hey, come get me." His voice crackled with fire.

"What?" My mind raced ahead, reviewing the day's classes. "You want to have lunch? I've got a long lunch break in about forty minutes."

"No—I mean now. Right now."

"Craig?"

"I just got a call. From Ruby Gentry. She has a baby for us."

"You're kidding." There was no response. "No, you're not, are you? A baby." Chills ran along my arms.

"We have one hour to decide if we want to keep her."

"Her? A little girl. One hour? Oh, my."

"She was born Friday and she's healthy. Healthy, Annsy. Her mother is white and her father is black."

My heart raced. A baby. For us. As I listened to Craig describe his conversation with Ruby, I paced across the tiny office. "She's ready to go home today," he said. "And Ruby called us. Come get me."

The supervising teacher walked into the office.

"I have to go," I said.

When I pulled the car into a parking space at Boeing. Craig dashed out, opened the driver's door and scooted me over. His blue eyes sparkled. He was in full dimple mode.

"What do you think?" He asked in excitement.

My mood matched his exactly. "I don't see how we can say no."

"That's what I thought you'd say." We embraced awkwardly, twisting on the front seat. "I think we've got us a baby."

"Why would there even be a question?"

"I guess because of the mixed race background. Remember all the agencies that insisted on placing a biracial baby in a black family?"

"Well, she's half white too."

"That's exactly what I thought. Let's go tell Mom and call Ruby."

Craig's mother listened, speechless, as he spilled the news. She grasped one of both of our hands in each of her own, and squeezed, hard. "Oh, you two. We've been waiting so long for this grand baby."

Then tears flowed down her cheeks and she reached for a tissue.

"We need to call Ruby," Craig said as he reached for the phone. A few minutes later, he looked up. "She's not in the office right now. We'll try again a little later. This is so sudden, Mom. Of course, we've still got all the baby stuff, but I don't know how we're going to manage the days. Ann's got another six weeks of student-teaching."

"Don't you worry. I'll help out however I can."

"I want to call my folks. May I use your phone?" I said.

"Of course."

My mother was also overjoyed. "Let me help. I could come stay for a while if you want."

"Sure, Mother. We'll need lots of help for a while."

"Happy day."

"Very. I haven't been this excited in years—maybe never. I can hardly stand it. I think I better go. We need to go get our baby. Talk to you soon, okay?"

I turned to Craig as I hung up the phone. He nodded and reached for my hand. "Ready?"

"I'm ready."

We smiled at each other. In spite of the drizzle, the sun shone in our hearts.

"Out to lunch. Back at one o'clock." The sign on the hospital social services office door informed us. Craig looked at his watch. "We've got about forty minutes. Let's get some lunch too."

"Hospital snack bar?"

He nodded.

The snack bar offered a variety of sandwiches and fresh fruit. We made our selections and ate quickly. Then we wandered into the gift shop.

"Oh, look. Baby clothes."

We wandered among the gift items, fingering tiny outfits tenderly.

"What do you think we should name our new baby?" Craig asked.

"Hmm. Well, this is all so sudden. Any ideas?"

"We could name her for a song bird. Remember how we liked the name Phoebe?"

I nodded. "Phoebe. How about Phoebe Dawn, because she brings a new day into our lives?"

"Phoebe Dawn. I like that," he said.

"Let's get her a little outfit. What about this yellow one? The color of sunshine."

"A happy color. Let's get her mother a card too, and thank her and wish her well."

We browsed through the cards. There were so many baby cards, but none seemed appropriate for a mother in her situation. "Congratulations. Congratulations.

Sentiments on what it means to have a new baby. These just won't work." I shook my head.

"Well, what about this one?" Craig pulled one from a different area. "'And then for a moment the sky stood still while a new star was born.' It's blank inside. We could write our own message."

"She will definitely be a star in our lives. That's good," I said. "What time is it?"

"Five 'til one."

After we purchased the yellow dress and the star card we ran to Ruby's office. Back from lunch, she met us with a smile. "Have you decided?"

"Yes. We want her," Craig said with no hesitation. I nodded in agreement.

"Then let me be the first to congratulate you on your new baby."

"When can we see her?" I asked.

"A couple hours, maybe more. But we have lots to do in the meantime."

"Can't we see her?" Craig was disappointed.

"No. Not until the legal side is completed. But let me assure you she's a beautiful baby. She has the prettiest eyes. She looked right at me and held my gaze for a few moments when I was in the nursery this morning."

"A couple of hours?" I said.

"Seems like forever, doesn't it? But it'll pass quickly. She's ready to go home with you today. Let me call the attorney I know and he'll get the ball rolling. Please have a seat."

Ruby spent a few minutes discussing the situation over the phone. She glanced our way with a reassuring smile now and then.

"He's sending an assistant to the courthouse in El Dorado with the proper paperwork. When it gets back here, we're free to proceed. Now I'll call the mother."

Craig and I looked at each other.

"Hello. This is Ruby Gentry at Wesley. I just wanted to let you know I have a family for your little girl. The couple has no children. They live in a neighboring county. They're very excited and happy to welcome this darling baby into their home. I know the parents personally and I'm certain they'll make excellent parents for this child."

After the phone conversation ended, she said to us, "The mother was quite relieved that someone wanted her baby. Have you thought about a name?"

"Yes," we both said.

"We thought we'd call her Phoebe Dawn," I said.

"It's lovely. And it fits that precious girl perfectly."

The next hours were a whirlwind of activity. "You have a lot to do this afternoon," Ruby said. "First off, you need to stop by the attorney's office. He has papers for you to sign before he can approach the court in El Dorado. No time to waste there. Then, there are things you need to think about."

"What things?" Craig asked.

"Well, for starters, do you have a car seat for Phoebe? You must have an infant car seat before I can release her to go home with you. You need clothing for a baby girl. What about diapers? And formula. You'll need something to feed her. Let me call the nursery to find out what they recommend."

A few minutes later, we headed out armed with a list of baby items for our shopping spree. We found the attorney's office in downtown Wichita and hurried in to sign the papers. "That was fast," Craig said as we returned to the car. "Now where?"

"There's a department store near the college. Let's go there," I suggested.

We parked the car in the crowded store parking lot and hurried inside. The baby section was easy to find. Deciding on the best car seat was not so easy. "There are so many. How do we know which one to get?" I asked.

"I guess we just go with our gut and pick one," Craig said.

With the car seat in our cart, we perused the aisles, studying the items offered for infant care. Diapers and plastic pants. "Sure you don't want disposables?" Craig asked.

"Just what would we do with disposables out in the country?" I raised my hands, palms up. "There's no trash service. We do, however, have a washer and dryer."

"Good point."

"Here's the Similac they recommended."

"What about lotions? Shampoo? A little comb?"

"Bottles, blankets, bibs…"

"We'll probably need those too."

A shopping cart full of baby items later, we checked out and headed to the car. I wrestled the baby seat into its place on the back seat, while Craig filled the trunk with supplies. Then he came around to the other side to give me a hand strapping the infant seat securely in the car.

"That should do. Anything else?"

I shrugged. "I don't know. Hopefully we're good for a day or so. Let's go back to the hospital."

At six in the evening we sat once again in Ruby's office. She waved a paper in the air and looked at us. "Here's the custody order. Let's go get Phoebe."

My heart raced as we all walked to the elevator that would take us to the newborn nursery. I slipped a trembling hand into Craig's. He squeezed it and looked at me, smiling broadly. The elevator moved much too slowly. But it finally opened onto the ob-gyn floor. Ruby ushered us to the nurse's station and introduced us. "Here are Craig and Ann Darr, the proud parents of our little girl in the nursery."

We followed the nurse to a small room adjacent to the nursery, craning our necks as we walked past to look for our girl. It was impossible to know which baby was ours. "Please have a seat," the nurse said. We sat in the cozy arm chairs and she disappeared. Ruby smiled. After a moment the nurse was back, holding a tiny bundle. She brought the baby to me and laid her in my arms.

What a perfect child. Asleep at the moment, she wiggled her tiny fingers. Her chest rose and fell as she breathed. With a trembling finger, I gently stroked her beautiful tan forehead. Wisps of fine black hair curled over her head. I gently smoothed them with my hand.

Tears welled in my eyes, so that Phoebe's face blurred. I blinked them back quickly and looked at Craig.

"...and we have a couple little educational filmstrips for you," the nurse was saying. I jolted into awareness, wondering what else she had said. I hadn't heard a word.

"Let's check her diaper. We'll go through a basic diaper change. That will probably wake her up."

It did. She began to cry as we struggled with the diaper. We learned ways to fold cloth diapers, ways to mix and feed formula, ways to bathe an infant. Phoebe, now awake, fussed through much of our parent training. I was so preoccupied with soothing her, sharing her with Craig, and just soaking up our daughter's vitality, I heard very little of the instructions, and could not have told anyone what the filmstrips were about.

"Are you ready to take your daughter home?" Ruby finally asked.

Phoebe Dawn, a ray of sunshine

12
HOME SWEET HOME

Ruby waited in the hospital with Phoebe and me while Craig brought the car. When he arrived, she helped us secure Phoebe in the infant carrier. "Good luck to you," she called as we left.

Our hearts soared as we pulled onto Hillside Avenue. I waved and watched Ruby disappear into the hospital. I smiled at Phoebe in the back seat.

"We've got to run by Mom and Dad's," Craig said. "They're probably wondering what happened."

His parents threw open the door as we drove onto their driveway. We carefully extricated Phoebe from her protective cocoon and Craig proudly carried the precious bundle to their porch.

Clarice beamed at us. "She's adorable."

"What a beautiful baby," Lenny agreed. "Come on in. Have a seat."

Clarice accepted her new granddaughter from Craig's arms. He and I sat together on their living room sofa. "What are you going to name her?" Grandma Clarice asked, rocking the baby gently.

"We thought Phoebe. Phoebe Dawn," Craig answered.

She nodded. "Hi, Phoebe Dawn. Welcome to the family."

A moment later, Phoebe whimpered. Grandma transferred her to my arms and I pulled a bottle of formula from our new diaper bag.

"They said she would eat about every two hours," Craig informed his mother.

"That sounds about right," Grandma agreed.

Phoebe was soon placated. I played with her tiny hands while the others chatted.

"How are you going to handle the day care?" Grandma asked.

"I was meaning to ask you about that," Craig said. "Tomorrow, I'm going to take the day off work. Ann still has to go teach, but she will have spring break in a couple weeks. So, in the meantime could we bring Phoebe here? At least part of the time?"

"Sure," Grandma said, smiling.

"Look—did you see that? She just smiled at me," I announced.

"Sure she did," Grandpa Lenny teased. "Probably just gas."

"No, I swear. It was a smile. Her first smile."

Craig shook his head. "Whatever you say, Annsy."

Half an hour later we walked back to the car and fastened Phoebe carefully in her seat. Craig and I took our daughter home.

A hearty wail emanated from the tiny room where Phoebe lay in the crib.

Next to me in our bed, Craig nudged me with his elbow. "I hear her. I hear her," I said. "I'm awake."

"Have you gotten any sleep at all?" he asked.

"Not much."

"How many times did you check on her?"

"I don't know. A few. I was afraid I wouldn't hear her if she woke up. Then afraid there was something wrong. That she had quit breathing."

"Well, she's finally hungry. You going to feed her this time?"

"Yup." I crawled over Craig in our crowded mobile home bedroom and headed for Phoebe's room down the hall. Cradling her in the crook of my arm, I mixed formula and then sat to feed her until she was content. "Five o'clock? Geez, girl. You slept nearly all night."

I changed her diaper and brought her back to our bedroom. "Here, Craig. It's almost time for me to get up." I laid Phoebe on his chest and crawled back over him. Phoebe quickly went back to sleep. We three cuddled until the alarm rang.

The next few nights followed a similar pattern. Craig and I took turns feeding the baby in the middle of the night. Then we brought her to our bed and cuddled. When the alarm shattered the early morning stillness, we dragged ourselves up and hustled through the morning routine which now included packing supplies for Phoebe and carting her to Grandma's for the day.

One afternoon, I arrived at her house. "Come here," Clarice said. "I want to show you something."

Laid on her bed was a prim, lacy infant gown. "It's lovely," I said.

"That was my baptism gown. Maybe you'd like for Phoebe to wear it at her baptism?"

"That's a precious idea."

We had Phoebe baptized at church on her third Sunday. My parents came for the occasion and Mother stayed to watch Phoebe the following week. After that it was spring break in the Wichita schools. Finally, I could be with my daughter around the clock.

Tuesday afternoon Craig returned home from work sporting a black patch over his left eye. Strapped around his head with a narrow elastic band, it fit closely over his eyelid under his eyeglasses.

"What's with the pirate patch?" I asked.

He mimicked a pirate swaggering onto our doorstop, stumping as if with a wooden leg. "Ahoy, me maties!" he yelled.I giggled. "No, seriously. What's up? It's nowhere near Halloween."

"I don't know," Craig said. "It just seems like my eyes won't focus together. All of a sudden I'm getting double vision."

"Maybe you should go see the doctor."

"I have an appointment with my eye doctor Thursday." He changed the subject. "How are things shaping up for tomorrow's home study?"

"Okay, I think. I've been cleaning all day. Do you think the trailer looks good enough?"

"Yeah. Much as I can see with one eye, anyway."

"Thank God our house is going up. The social worker can see we'll be able to move into a bigger home soon."

The following day, Craig arrived home early for the appointment. Freshly bathed and dressed in her festive yellow dress, Phoebe was the picture of a perfect baby. Two-thirty came and went. The licensed social worker missed the appointed hour. I paced our tiny living room, bouncing the child with each step. Craig sprawled on the couch.

"What do you think they do in a home study?" I asked.

"I don't know. Study our home, I guess."

"That makes me kind of nervous. What if this social worker doesn't much care for our home?"

Two-thirty-five. Still I paced.

Two forty-two. Finally a car turned into our driveway and rolled to the graveled parking pad east of the trailer. A man in a three-piece suit carried an attaché case to our front stoop.

I let him in. Craig shook his hand and apologized for the patch over his eye. "I think I have a lazy eye muscle or something. I've got a doctor appointment tomorrow to find out."

The man introduced himself as a good friend of Ruby Gentry's. "Please, relax," he assured us. "My goal today is to learn about the two of you and what you have to offer this child. It's kind of a legal formality in the adoption process, but one that must be done in every Kansas adoption."

"Have a seat," Craig said.

"Would you care for a glass of iced tea or water?" I asked.

"Sure. Water's fine."

I transferred Phoebe to Craig's arms and headed to our small kitchen. A few seconds later I returned with glasses and a plate of sliced banana bread.

"Now tell me, how did you two meet?" The social worker asked the first of a thousand questions.

Two hours later, he stopped scribbling and placed his notes in the attaché case. "That completes our interview." He rose to his feet. "I'll draft a report to give the Butler County judge. I think you have a lot to offer a child and the two of you have a solid relationship. Just a word of advice, though. Never make the mistake of thinking you're doing this child a favor by adopting her. She's doing you a favor. I know a dozen families who would love to have a baby like this. Ruby chose you for Phoebe. But it's not like there were no other options for her. I think Ruby chose well when she selected you two. There'll be challenges along the way, but you can handle them."

He extended his hand to shake both of ours. "I'll take my leave now and wish you well."

Thursday afternoon, Craig arrived home from work a half hour later than usual, still sporting the eye patch. "How was your eye appointment?" I asked.

"Okay, I guess." He sounded exhausted.

"What did he say about your double vision?"

"I don't think he knew what to say. He set me up for a CT scan on Monday." Craig looked at me with his one lusterless eye.

"You okay?"

"I'm really beat. And I have a headache."

"I'm sure everything will be fine."

"Yeah. But right now all I want to do is make like a potato and head for the couch."

"Why don't you take some aspirin and stretch out while I finish fixing supper?"

After our meal and an hour of television, Craig went to bed early. I played with Phoebe a while longer, fed her and put her to bed before I joined him.

He didn't sleep well that night. He fought with the covers and never found a comfortable position. About three o'clock after Phoebe's nighttime bottle, he sat up and reached for the door knob as I crawled back in bed.

"What's up, Craigie?" I asked groggily.

"This damn headache won't go away. I need some more aspirin."

"Maybe Excedrin?"

"Maybe."

The throbbing in his head had not abated before the alarm rang at six. "I don't think I can work today. Would you call my supervisor?"

"Sure. And I'll get you more Excedrin."

"It's not helping."

I brought some anyway, along with a glass of orange juice. I sat on the bed, cradled his head on my lap, and gently rubbed from his forehead across the crown to his neck.

"Feels good," he mumbled.

About eight, Phoebe stirred and cried. I disengaged from Craig's head massage and headed down the hall.

"Bring me a pan," he called after me. "I feel sick."

I brought a large bowl, set it next to him on the bed and tended to Phoebe's morning ritual. Twice during her diaper change and morning bottle, I heard Craig retch in our bedroom.

He stumbled to the bathroom to empty the bowl and vomited again in the toilet. Back to the bedroom, he collapsed on the bed. Daisy jumped up beside him and stretched out. She rested her chin on his chest and watched his face. Craig slowly reached up to pat her a couple times.

After settling Phoebe on a blanket in her corner of the living room, I hurried to his side. "What can I do?"

He shook his head. "This headache is killing me."

"It must be a migraine."

"I guess."

He swung out of bed and lunged for the bathroom. He didn't make it beyond the doorway before he heaved. His stomach contents flew across the tiny room to splat in the bathtub.

"Craig, I'm going to call your doctor."

He shook his head. "No, don't."

His headache intensified through continued bouts of violent vomiting. By ten o'clock, he was ready.

"Call Dr. Varden."

"Not your eye doctor?"

"No, Dr. Varden."

I quickly summarized Craig's symptoms to his general physician. "Double vision, severe headache, projectile vomiting—get him to the hospital now," Dr. Varden said.

"He's got a CT scan scheduled for Monday."

"We won't wait until Monday. We'll do a scan today."

I bundled Phoebe into her car seat and returned to the living room for Craig. He leaned heavily on me as I helped him to the car. After leaving the baby with a grandmotherly neighbor, we headed toward Wichita and Wesley Hospital.

Two orderlies unloaded Craig into a wheel chair and whisked him away while I moved the car to the parking garage. I found him again in the radiology department, lying on a gurney to await his scan. He gave me a half grin. "I guess that's one way to move up your scan appointment," he said. I squeezed his hand and stayed with him until they rolled him to the tubular machine.

An hour later, Dr. Varden met me in the lobby where I paced from window to window. "There's a mass in the center of Craig's brain. He has a tumor of some sort."

My stomach flipped. "A tumor?" *This couldn't be. Not Craig. Not us.*

"We're going to admit him and call in a neurosurgeon," Dr. Varden continued.

My knees became jelly. "I have to sit down." I groped for the wall as my legs buckled and I slumped to the floor.

13
THE FIGHT BEGINS

"The mass is about the size of an egg and is located here, at the base of the brainstem." The neurosurgeon pointed to the knot on the scan which appeared in stark contrast to the rest of Craig's brain. "What has happened is that the mass is blocking the flow of spinal fluid. The build-up of fluid in his skull is causing his severe headache."

"And the double vision?" I asked.

"Indeed. The double vision as well. The optic nerve to his left eye is affected."

"What do we do?"

"Our first step is a relatively simple procedure to relieve the pressure in his skull. I'll insert a shunt to drain the spinal fluid through an alternate pathway. Craig's headache will be immediately relieved."

"A shunt?"

"It's a special tube. I surgically insert it through the top of the skull and thread it up and over the skull, under his skin. The spinal fluid will be absorbed into his body. The pressure will be relieved. It's a minimally invasive procedure."

"You don't try to remove the tumor?"

"Not at this stage. Our first priority is to relieve the pressure in Craig's head. Then we decide what to do next."

"When will you do the shunt?"

"First thing in the morning."

The nursing staff had Craig ready by six o'clock the next morning. His transport team arrived eight minutes later and transferred him and his tubes to a gurney. We headed to the elevator. Craig eagerly anticipated the end of his persistent headache. I held his hand as we moved along the hallway and he offered me a tiny smile.

In the elevator, he whistled. I soon recognized the tune "You Are My Sunshine." I smiled at him and squeezed his hand.

The aide moving his transport chuckled. She sang along with Craig's whistling. "You are my sunshine, my only sunshine. You make me happy when skies are gray..."

I tried to join in but my voice broke.

Later, the neurosurgeon met me in the waiting room. He smiled, "Everything went well. Craig should notice an immediate improvement."

"Good. Then what?"

"Well, I think we'll do some non-invasive testing. We need to pull together a team to decide on the best treatment. We'll give him a couple days to recover from this procedure. Our next step will be to determine the nature of that mass. We'll attempt to find out what we're dealing with through an arteriogram and a biopsy, if that is needed."

"What happens today?"

"Today Craig pulled through the shunt procedure in good shape. He's in recovery now. When he's alert enough, he'll go back to his room and I'll be up to visit with both of you."

An hour and a half later, we were in his room. Our eyes met. "Hi," I said softly.

Craig waved from his hospital bed.

"How are you feeling?" I asked.

"Pretty good, really. Just sleepy."

"No headache?"

He shook his head. "No, much better."

"That's great."

"Where's Phoebe? I've been thinking about her."

"She's with your mom right now."

"I sure miss her."

"I know. I wish there was a way to bring her for a visit, but I don't think that would be such a good idea."

"She's a month old today, isn't she?"

"Yes. Her first month."

"You going to have a party?" Craig asked.

"I don't know. Maybe."

"I think you should. Take a cake to Mom's this evening when you go."

"But it wouldn't be right without you."

"I'll be there, in spirit."

"Okay, then. We'll celebrate. One month. It's been a helluva month, hasn't it?"

"Ann, you don't talk like that."

"Not usually. You have to admit though..."

Craig nodded and wrinkled his nose. "Yep. True. One helluva month."

That evening on his rounds, the neurosurgeon shared more about Craig's condition. "Any kind of mass is serious when it's in the brain, whether it's malignant or not. It can affect nerve centers by pressing on critical areas."

"Like the double vision?" I asked the neurosurgeon during his visiting rounds the following morning.

"Yes, like vision problems. And there's no place for the mass to go—no soft tissue that would allow for expansion, due to the rigidity of the skull."

"What do you do about it then?"

"Some tumors can be surgically removed. In Craig's case, that plan is problematic due to the location of the tumor. It's very deep, you see, right at the top of the brain stem where all the nerve transmissions pass through to all parts of the body."

"Are you saying there's nothing you can do?" I searched his face for a glimmer of hope.

"No, no. Our plan is first to gather as much information as possible. I'm going to schedule Craig for a brain arteriogram."

"What's that?" Craig asked.

"It's an x-ray procedure where the radiologist injects a special dye into an artery that supplies blood to the brain. The pattern of arteries will then show up on an x-ray. Malignant tumors have an intricate network of arteries feeding them. Anything else will not."

"Hello, you two." Ruby Gentry peered around the door and stepped into the room. Craig and I looked at each other. We had been dreading this moment. Was she going to tell us she had found another family for our baby? A healthy family?

"I heard Craig was here. Thought I'd drop by to say hello. How's that beautiful baby?"

With the back of my hand I swiped across my cheek. *Here it comes,* I thought. But I managed to say, "She's fine. She's with Grandma Clarice today."

"I bet you both miss her immensely."

I nodded. "I'd bring her in to visit Craig, but I'm worried about the exposure risk."

"Well, you should check out the courtyard. Craig could walk to the courtyard and meet Phoebe there for a while."

"You mean the garden between the parking garage and the hospital?"

"Yes."

"I didn't know he could go that far away."

"He can walk anywhere on hospital grounds. Keep active. Get some fresh air."

Craig smiled. "We'll check it out."

"Have you heard any more from the attorney about finalizing Phoebe's adoption?"

"Not yet," I said. "But we've not been home much for a few days."

"Well, I have some news for you. All the paperwork is in order. So you can proceed with the final step as soon as you can schedule a trip to El Dorado."

I caught my breath. "You mean—I thought—I figured you were here to tell us you found a different family for Phoebe."

"Heavens no. That baby girl is yours. Why would you think I'd place her in a different family?"

"Well, since we don't know yet what Craig is facing. There's no guarantee he'll be around."

"You can rest easy. I wouldn't dream of disrupting your placement. If you think about it, there are no guarantees any of us will be around for any length of time. That baby is yours, in sickness and in health."

I inhaled slowly and deeply, overcome with gratitude. "Thank you, Ruby. I was afraid we'd lose her because of this."

Ruby stretched her arms toward us. Craig and I each clasped one of her hands in ours. She smiled. "Why don't you go find that courtyard? And remember to let Grandma know she can bring the baby there to meet you."

That afternoon, I wrapped a robe around Craig's hospital gown and helped him into slippers. We headed out for a walk. The nurse in charge insisted we take a wheel chair in case Craig didn't have the strength to get back. He pushed it along the halls. His IV bottle swung from a tall hook attached to the chair, a silent third party on our walk. At half past two, we stepped into the fresh air and wandered along the landscaped walkways in the hospital courtyard. We found Craig's mom and Phoebe waiting for us on a little bench.

Craig sat next to his mother and eagerly reached for the baby. "Hey, Munchkin," he greeted her. "Goo-goo. Ga-ga." As he played with her tiny hands, her fingers curled around his. He bounced Phoebe on his knee.

We chatted with Grandma Clarice about the planned arteriogram. "When will that be?" she asked.

"Tomorrow, I think," I answered.

"Yeah, tomorrow. I can't have anything to eat after supper tonight," Craig added.

Forty-five minutes later, Craig handed the baby to me and I cuddled her for a few moments before handing her to Clarice. We reluctantly said our farewells.

"We'll do this again sometime," Grandma promised. She helped Phoebe wave a tiny hand and they returned to the parking garage.

Phoebe visits her daddy in the hospital courtyard

Twenty-four hours later, Craig lay immobilized in his hospital bed after the arteriogram. "I need to sit up," he said.

"Not yet," I reminded him. "They said you shouldn't move for a couple hours yet. You don't want to re-open the artery they used to insert the dye."

"I know. But, I've got this itch."

"Let me scratch it for you. Where?"

"Down on the top of my right foot."

"Here?" I scratched his foot.

He nodded. "Now the other one."

I scratched for him.

"Now my shoulders."

I chuckled. "You're milking this for all you can get."

"Darn tootin'."

The surgeon entered the room. I crossed my fingers and held my breath.

"Hi, Doc," Craig said.

"I've reviewed the arteriogram," the doctor said. "The blood flow pattern indicates that the mass in your brain is well-supplied."

My heart sank.

Craig's smile faded. "It is cancer then," he said.

"That's what the results indicate." The surgeon laid his hand gently on Craig's knee. "I'm sorry."

"What now?" Craig asked softly, more to himself than to anyone else.

"I think next we would recommend surgery, for two reasons. First, to try to remove the tumor, or as much of it as possible. Second, to get tissue for a biopsy so we can determine what kind of brain tumor it is. There are several kinds of malignancies and they each have different characteristics."

"Surgery?" Craig asked. "On my brain?"

"Yes. Obviously there are significant risks involved, given its location adjacent to your brain stem."

"Brain surgery scares me to death," Craig said.

"It is not something to attempt without carefully considering all the risk factors."

"Do you think you can remove the tumor?"

"That is doubtful, given its location. The procedure is extremely complicated. If you want to think about it for a while, I think that would be wise. We could dismiss you and let you go home for a couple days to give it some thought. Anyway, I'm sorry the arteriogram didn't have more favorable results."

After the doctor left, the room was absolutely silent. I picked up Craig's right hand in both of mine and rubbed it. He would not meet my gaze. When at last he spoke, there was no life in his voice. "I want to go home," he said.

The next morning, the back seat of his parents' Buick was filled with inflated balloons when Craig's dad arrived. We piled into the front seat. I held Craig's hand and leaned against his shoulder all the way to his parents' house. Though we were silent, Lenny chattered the whole way across Wichita.

When we arrived in their driveway, the edges of Craig's mouth curled ever-so-slightly into a tiny smile. More balloons festooned the front porch, framing a huge paper banner that shouted to the spring morning, "Welcome Home Craig."

Inside, Clarice handed Phoebe to her daddy and he rocked her until she dozed. He rocked her through the nap, silent, while his parents and I discussed progress on the construction of our house, cute things Phoebe had done, and plans for the adoption finalization.

"When?" Grandma Clarice asked.

"Monday."

"This coming Monday?"

"Yes. That's what our attorney set up. We need to go to El Dorado and be at the courthouse by ten."

"Can we come along?"

"I don't see why not. I think my folks want to come too. Time for a party, right?"

During Phoebe's afternoon nap, I talked Craig into a walk along the dry creek that meandered through the neighborhood.

"Look, Craig." I dropped his hand and waved toward a small tree twenty feet away along the wooded draw. "A bluebird."

He nodded. His eyes sparked to life as we walked. "I've always enjoyed exploring this creek bed. Always find something exciting."

"You'd never know this was right across the street from your folks' house."

"In the neighbors' back yard," he said.

"I can hardly wait until Phoebe is old enough to go exploring with us."

"Yeah, that will be fun. For you, anyway." His smile dissolved and a wall rose between us.

"You, too, Craigie." I encouraged him. "You're going to beat this and live a long time."

"I don't know, Ann. I think I just want to go home and take what time I have left and be master of my destiny."

"Please don't give up."

"I'm so afraid that the brain surgery will do something and I'll be left a vegetable, not knowing anything. I'd rather take my chances at home and just let nature take its course."

"But, you can't just give up. You've got to fight. After all, look what you've got to live for. We have a baby, a daughter. She needs her daddy. Our house is going up."

"I know. It's just—there are so many risks. I don't like the idea of someone in my brain with a knife."

"You'd rather just play the hand you've been dealt?"

"Yeah. I think I would. At least I have a little time I can enjoy. I feel pretty good, now that the headache is gone."

"Oh, Craigie. Please. You can't... *die*." I managed to say the word out loud. "What would I do without you?"

We stopped walking. My eyes brimmed with tears. Craig would not look at me. "I don't know, Ann," he said with no inflection in his voice. "That will be up to you."

We didn't speak of death again. It remained a specter that shadowed us and dogged our steps. I turned my energy toward activities that I hoped would re-awaken in my husband a will to live.

Construction continues on the house

We spent a sunny day at our little home where Craig checked on the progress of our wall studs. He walked the floor plan, checked each corner and room of the house he'd designed, peered into the basement opening and turned to me with a smile on his face. He carried Phoebe as we walked the boundary of our twenty-acre home site.

The lilac bushes we planted along the driveway sprouted new leaves.

"Look, the peas are up." I showed him our garden.

Sunday evening we headed back to Wichita to spend the night at his folks' house. My parents met us there. Monday morning we drove together to El Dorado. "We'll wait here." Clarice spoke for all of them. "This should be your moment."

After Craig helped me out of the car, I gathered Phoebe into my arms. He grabbed the diaper bag. The three of us walked across the vast courtyard into the judge's chambers at the El Dorado courthouse. Our attorney was already there. We chatted for a few moments before we signed the documents. Phoebe Dawn was our daughter, unquestionably, and forever. Nobody would take her away from us now.

After a celebratory steak dinner, we returned to the house in Wichita. Craig stretched out on the guest bed with Phoebe on his chest. They both had a nap. A couple hours later they emerged from the room, refreshed. He propped himself on his elbows beside her on the living room carpet and helped her manipulate rattles and squeeze toys. "Goo-goo. Ga-ga," he said to Phoebe.

At home that evening, he looked at me across the supper table and said, "Okay. I'll do it. I'm ready to go back."

I perked up. "Yes?"

He nodded once. "Yes. I'm ready to fight this thing." He tapped the side of his head. "I want to be there when Phoebe grows up."

I reached for his hand. "You know I'll be with you all the way."

14
THREE STEPS FORWARD, TWO STEPS BACK

An aide settled Craig into a wheel chair at the hospital admissions desk. He waved as he rolled away. I remained to complete paperwork. Fifteen minutes later, I headed up to his room on the oncology floor. Already dressed in a hospital gown, he looked ridiculously strong and healthy in the spare garment. He paced the room. When I stepped in, his eyes met mine and he flashed one of his ornery grins.

"What?" I looked around.

He grabbed my hand, pulled me to the middle of the room, and reached for the television control.

"Look what I found." Country music floated into the sunny room. "Want to dance?"

I smiled. "Sure."

He swung me into his arms and we began a lively two-step. The music changed and slowed to a dreamy waltz. Craig gathered me closer and we swayed to the music. As we passed the door, he pushed it shut. We danced and danced. On the eve of the most frightening day of his thirty-two years, we danced in the hospital.

The next morning at precisely six thirty-two Craig's surgery transport team transferred him to a wheeled gurney. He reached for me and I leaned over for a quick hug and kiss. He pressed a piece of folded paper into my hand. We left the room and proceeded toward the elevator. He still held my hand.

I smiled at him in the elevator, but he didn't smile back. There was no whistling or sunshine on this journey. The aides rolled him into the surgical suite and I settled into a chair in the waiting room. I opened the note he gave me.

Well, Ann, as much as I don't want to I decided to go ahead and write this. I want you to read it while I'm in surgery. You probably are going through a lot of personal turmoil too. I guess I've never consciously faced death before. I want you to know that I love you. Truly I do. I will love you until I can't do it anymore. I admit we aren't perfect in our love for each other but it's as perfect as I need or ever want. I don't want to leave you. I wish there was a way for us to leave this earth together. The comforting thing is that someday we will be together in heaven. We'll have that simple life with family and pups and all those things we treasure.

From now on in our life together, I ask if you will remind me what I have to be thankful for. I love you, Sweetie. Kiss. Kiss. Stick with me through this difficult time for both of us. I feel bad for you because you are suffering for you and for me. Maybe Phoebe can help you remember you have a bright future. If I am not to continue further into this bodily life, I will surely be an angel for you. Watch for little hints from heaven. I love you, Ann.

Craig

Late that afternoon, he returned to his hospital room, his head wrapped in a turban of gauze bandages. He was conscious, but barely.

"Hey, Craigie." I searched his eyes for some glimmer of recognition, the tiniest sign that he was still there, and I squeezed his hand.

"Hi, Ann," he answered.

Yes. My Craig was there. The surgery had not stolen him away from me.

Though the surgeon checked on him once that afternoon, it was the next morning before we visited in depth about the intricate surgery.

"I was able to retrieve some cells for a biopsy, but I barely managed that."

"What do you mean?" I asked. Craig lay in bed, listening. He let me do the talking.

"The tumor was so deep that I had trouble even getting to it. I was not able to remove any of the mass other than the biopsy cells. To do so would have damaged healthy brain tissue and created many neurological problems for Craig."

My heart sank. "So it's still there?"

"Yes."

"What now?"

"Now we pull in an oncologist. The next step may be to dose the tumor with radiation that will kill some of its cells and slow its growth."

"I'm sorry, but won't that damage healthy brain tissue also?"

"The radiologist can direct a beam to very specific locations, so extraneous damage is minimized. We'll let Craig recover for a few days and then set up his treatment schedule. I imagine most of that can be done as an outpatient."

"What about the biopsy? What did it show?"

"The biopsy indicates Craig's tumor is a low-grade astrocytoma. These are fairly slow-growing tumors, as tumors go. Still a serious situation, given the lack of space in the skull for expansion of any sort."

"How many different kinds of brain tumors are there?"

"That's difficult to say. Each tumor is individual and may take on characteristics of more than one type."

"Astrocytomas are fairly good, though?"

"As far as tumors go, an astrocytoma is the one to have. If you'd like to read up on brain tumors, stop by my office sometime and I'll loan you a book."

After the doctor left, I turned to Craig. "Astrocytoma," I said. "The slowest-growing type of brain tumor, Craigie. I'll take that as a bit of good news."

"We need some good news," he said.

The following Sunday was Easter Sunday. I held the hospital menu and read to Craig from the list. "Do you want oatmeal, eggs or pancakes tomorrow?" He slumped in the recliner beside the room's window, and I sat on a straight chair next to him. A nurse aide named Linda bustled about, changing bed linens.

"Oatmeal," he said.

"With toast?"

"Yes."

"Orange, apple or tomato juice?"

"Apple."

"For lunch, do you want meatloaf or roast beef?"

He didn't answer.

"Craig?"

Still no response. His eyes busily moved from side to side, as if he were actively watching a basketball game.

"Craig... Craig!" I grew frantic.

Linda came around to his chair and watched his eyes for a few seconds. She reached to his shoulders and squeezed them slightly. "Craig?"

No response.

She looked at me. "It's like he just went somewhere else."

"I know. What do we do?"

"I'll get his nurse." She stepped into the hall.

"What did you say?" Craig was back.

"Oh—what happened? We were filling out tomorrow's menu and you kind of disappeared."

"All the people moving around in here distracted me."

"People? It was only Linda and me."

"No. The room was full of people."

"Seems like you're hallucinating or something."

"No, I swear, there were lots of people scurrying around."

"Okay," I conceded. "Well, meat loaf or roast beef?"

"Roast beef."

An hour later I suggested we go to the hospital's chapel for the Easter worship service. "I don't think I can walk that far," Craig said.

"I'll push you." We swung through the courtyard after the service and stopped at the snack bar for milkshakes.

Back in his room, lunch awaited. After lunch, I helped him into bed. "Do you want to try that imaging idea?" I asked.

"Imaging?"

"You know. When you relax, think happy thoughts and consciously release some of your body's natural defense mechanisms to battle the cancer cells."

"Oh. Sure. Couldn't hurt. How do we do that?"

"I brought some music. Some Beethoven, the Pastorale Symphony. I'll put it in this little tape player and coach you through the imaging process. All you have to do is relax and let your mind follow my cues. Ready?"

"Ready."

"Close your eyes then." I started the music.

"Okay. Now take a deep breath and relax. Feel the tension in your shoulders work down your arms and out your fingertips."

I paused until Craig wiggled his fingers.

"Now imagine yourself to be in your favorite place. Minnesota, maybe?"

He nodded.

"Imagine we have just crossed Clitherall Lake in that boat and we walk to a green, grassy meadow. The sun shines warmly. Birds sing in the trees. Small waves lap at the beach nearby."

I paused.

"Now sit down and take it all in. Soak up every sensation of this beautiful place."

The symphonic music floated around us, painting the idyllic scene in my mind. A few moments later with music filling the room, I continued describing each step of the disintegration of the tumor.

When the imaginary tumor had disappeared, I closed my eyes and let the symphony run its course. I glanced at Craig. His breathing was slow and regular.

"Craig?"

No answer. He had fallen asleep.

Half an hour later, my mother arrived. "I'll sit with Craig if you'd like to run home and check on things," she said.

"Where's Phoebe?"

"She's with Clarice. She's fine there. Why don't you take some time for yourself?"

I looked at Craig again. He slept soundly. I glanced out the window at the perfect spring afternoon and nodded. "Thanks, Mother. Call me if you need me. Otherwise, I'll be back about dark."

At home, I surveyed the progress on our house. A pallet of shingles had arrived, along with the stove pipe for our wood burning stove. I called my sisters. Daisy and I hiked the perimeter of our twenty acres. In the garden, asparagus shoots had erupted from their hidden crowns. I harvested a batch of asparagus.

When I brought the asparagus into the kitchen, the phone was ringing. I dashed for the receiver. "Hello?"

It was Mother. "Craig has taken a turn for the worse. I think you need to come back."

"What do you mean?"

"I think he's having seizures, like grand mal epileptic seizures. There are a lot of people in here working with him. They told me to call you."

"I'm coming." I grabbed my bag and jacket and ran for the car, leaving Daisy alone again in the locked trailer.

The car would not go fast enough. I was a good fifty minutes from the hospital. *Why did I leave?* As I drove, I convinced myself that Craig must be dying. I would never see him again.

Twenty minutes into my frenzied drive, the car's radio blared "Somewhere My Love" from the movie Dr. *Zhivago.*

I sang along, thinking of my husband. I imagined him seized with tremors. "Someday, we'll meet again, my love. Someday... You'll come to me, out of the long ago—"

My voice broke. My vision blurred but I did not slow the car's speed. I had to get back.

I whispered the last words of the song. "God speed my love, 'til you are mine again." Somehow I arrived safely at the hospital. After parking the car, I ran to the entrance, then to the elevator. The door opened and Linda stepped out, headed home at the end of her shift. She took one look at my stricken face, grabbed both of my hands in hers, and got back on the elevator with me.

"Linda, what's going on?" I choked on the words.

"Craig's had several seizures, accompanied by convulsions. He gets a code blue each time. He's had one about every thirty minutes for the last two hours."

"Oh my God. Why?"

"They aren't sure why. They're trying to figure out why he started seizing now and what medication will control it."

Craig had been moved as a result of the seizures. She guided me to his new room. He looked fairly normal. He caught my eyes and gave me a little smile. "It's been kind of exciting around here since you left," he said.

"I guess so. You okay?"

"I'm sore. But otherwise, I..." His voice trailed off. Suddenly his eyes darted sideways in their sockets repeatedly. Then they rolled upwards and froze.

"Here comes another one," a nurse yelled. She turned to me. "Stand back please."

I shrank against the wall beside my speechless mother. Craig's legs thrashed. His arms and fingers tensed into rigid sticks and jerked around. He yelled in a guttural, unintelligible way.

Unable to watch, I closed my eyes.

"Valium!" the nurse yelled.

Another nurse brought a syringe. After administering the drug, Craig settled back into a normal, relaxed pose. He dozed.

"The seizures are exhausting," Linda explained softly at my shoulder.

"Do you think he was having a little seizure this morning when he quit talking?"

"Very possible."

A medication called dilantin prevented further seizures. A few days passed as he recovered and gained strength. Consultation with a neurologist, an oncologist, a radiation specialist and Craig's general practitioner developed a treatment plan that included a series of radiation sessions. Brain tumors, we were told, did not respond well to any known chemotherapy so the radiation was our best hope for a remission.

Craig's first radiation treatment was scheduled for one o'clock the following Wednesday. I spent the morning at home to check on the construction progress and re-connect with Daisy. Neighbors had been taking care of our place since the first hospital dash. Phoebe was with her Grandma.

I found Sunday's asparagus still waiting to be cleaned in my kitchen sink. It was a little limp, but not too bad. More stalks waited in the garden. After cutting another batch, I washed and steamed it. Then I wrapped it in foil and placed the package in a thermos. I locked the trailer and headed back to the hospital. Having received a special parking permit for the radiation clinic, I entered the outpatient door with our precious asparagus.

An aide with an empty wheel chair ambled slowly down the hall toward the elevator. I hustled past her, pushed open the stairwell door and bounded up four flights of stairs, two at a time. I ran to Craig's room. With a flourish I presented the year's first asparagus spears to him. We grabbed them one at a time with our fingers and snarfed them down. We had just popped the last spears into our mouths when the aide I passed four floors below knocked at the open door.

She settled Craig into the wheelchair and we all went back down the elevator. The radiologist consulted scans and scrutinized Craig's bare head. She measured from ear to ear and from forehead to first cervical vertebra. With a purple marker, she drew matching squares on the sides of Craig's head above and a little behind his ears. Then she drew an X in each box.

Craig lay on a flat table with instructions to remain absolutely still. The radiation team and I retreated to watch from behind thick glass.

Straightforward and painless, the treatment lasted only a few minutes. Craig was dismissed as a patient that afternoon. He continued the radiation treatments as an outpatient, thrice weekly for several weeks. During this time, I managed to return to my student teaching obligations. A few days after I returned, I arranged to bring Phoebe in for a visit. The once-hostile students warmed up to the baby, cooing and admiring her perfection. Though previously I had sensed a mountain of resistance to my presence, now I felt gentleness, and an undercurrent of kindness, even empathy. The tension at school had evaporated.

Craig again managed the progress on our house construction. Dr. Varden filled out paperwork to start federal disability compensation. Requirements for government disability were that the condition causing impairment either was permanent or terminal. By mid-May, we received word from Social Security that his disability claim was denied.

"Well, Craigie, they must think that you're going to beat this," I said.

"Yeah. I guess so. I guess it's time for me to go back to work. No more radiation or surgeries. I'm working on our house. So I guess I can go back to work."

I finished the semester and came home to be with my baby girl. Finally.

15
THE LAST CAMPOUT

By mid-summer, it became clear that Craig's reprieve would be short-lived. After his seizing in April, the state pulled his driver's license. Increasingly, the responsibilities in our little family which he had handled with competence fell on my shoulders. His daily medications caused his body to retain fluids and he puffed up. His face took on a very youthful, cherub-like appearance. His left arm hung almost useless from his shoulder and his left foot dragged along the ground as he walked.

He experienced growing confusion. He became disoriented easily and could no longer recognize familiar landmarks. He was slipping away from me, no question about it. I began to feel like a single parent of two small children.

Further consultation with Dr. Varden and a new CT scan convinced us all that any shrinkage of the egg-sized tumor from radiation had disappeared. Dr. Varden assessed Craig's mental acuity in a simple interview. He related to Craig with warmth and compassion, and detained me briefly at the end of Craig's appointment.

"This man should not be working," he insisted to me rather angrily.

"But, the disability—"

"I know. It's absurd that they denied his claim. I'll file it again."

This time, the claim was approved. Rallying to support him, his department at work set up collection baskets to help with our growing expenses. They knew he was unfit to work. Now the government admitted that fact as well. Though I bravely persevered, Craig's deteriorating condition took its toll on me.

The hopeful little family
Photo courtesy Butler County Times-Gazette

Toward the end of July, we painted rooms and finished trim in our new house. It was time to move in. Moving day brought a dozen of our family, friends, and Craig's coworkers. We emptied the little mobile home in just a few hours. After the moving crew left, my mother brought me a *Reader's Digest* magazine.

"There's an article about a promising new treatment for brain cancer," she said. "You might be interested."

Dr. Vincent Klassen of Philadelphia's Misericordia Hospital had designed an experimental chemotherapy which targeted brain tumors. The process showed enough promise to receive national attention. Consultation with Dr. Varden helped us decide to contact Dr. Klassen.

Since there was nothing more Wichita could offer us in the way of a life-sustaining treatment, Dr. Varden gave the nod for experimental treatment. We contacted Klassen's office. Wichita sent Craig's file and scans, and we were soon scheduled for the first week-long treatment of the methotrexate. The last day of July, Craig and I boarded a TWA flight in Wichita, passed through Chicago's airport and landed in Philadelphia. Craig's dad had friends who met us at the airport and dropped us off at Misericordia. An imposing brick building adorned with Catholic statuary, it was surrounded by a security fence. As we entered the fortress, my heart pounded in my chest.

Craig's hospital room was in a sunny nook on the oncology floor. Dr. Klassen's patients filled one whole wing. A second bed for me was squeezed into the room's darkest corner. Like us, most of the brain cancer patients and their companions came from a long distance.

The head nurse, a Catholic nun, bustled into the room to brief us on the treatment. "There are some important guidelines for you to follow during Mr. Darr's treatments," the nurse informed me. "First, the MTX only works in an alkaline system. As of right now, Craig's intake of acidic foods is forbidden until his physician says differently."

She continued with the treatment requirements until her list was complete. "One more thing. Don't ever walk off hospital grounds."

"Oh?" I said, surprised.

"You are not from Philadelphia. This neighborhood isn't safe. Everything you might need can be found in the hospital."

She whisked out of the room.

I recalled the wrought-iron fence surrounding the hospital.

What might I need during my husband's stay in a hospital a thousand miles from home? Food, certainly. Shelter, check. A place to lay my head at night. Yes. How about freedom? Friendship? Somebody to talk to? Food for my soul? Such things were in short supply. The wrought-iron fence soon became prison walls to me. I longed to go for a morning walk, but I could not escape. There was no place to go.

One morning I leaned on the windowsill and stared into the sunshine outside. People bustled along the street outside the vicious-looking fence. I held a letter from my mother. She had sent news from Phoebe, writing us a letter from our precious girl with details of their daily lives. I read and re-read the letter. Then my mind wandered out the window back to home.

"What are you doing?" Craig broke into my reverie.

"I'm just sorting thoughts."

"Why are you ordering socks? Are your feet cold?

I smiled and turned to him. "No, silly. Not socks—thoughts. I'm sorting thoughts. I'm thinking."

"Oh. What are you thinking about?"

"Phoebe. I really miss her."

"I know. Me too. We'll be going back home soon won't we?"

"Yes. Day after tomorrow. Do you think she will be much different?"

"I don't know. What do you mean?"

"A week in the life of a baby is a long time. We're sure missing a lot of her first year."

"I know. I'm sorry. I wish things were different."

I walked to the chair beside Craig's bed and sat down. "You know that tree you saw fall in the rain forest of Mexico?"

He nodded. "I haven't thought about that for a long time."

"Well, this time away from Phoebe, and her growing up without us—that's our tree falling in the forest."

"I don't follow you."

"She's growing and laughing and crying even though we're not around to hear her. When we get back, she will be different. Changed. The 'tree' made a noise, even though we weren't there to hear it."

"When we get back, we'll have to celebrate with her," Craig said.

"How about a campout? Labor Day weekend, let's go camping."

"At the Darr pond? Then we could go fishing too."

"Let's do it. Phoebe's first camping trip for her six-month celebration." Just thinking about it lifted my spirits.

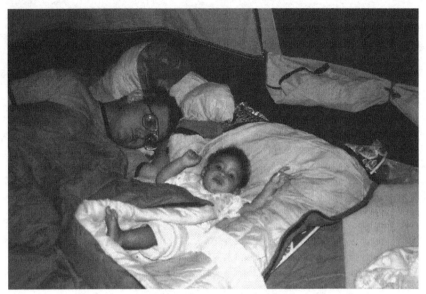

Labor Day campout

Friday afternoon of Labor Day weekend, we rolled under the shade trees at the Darr family retreat in Harper County. I unloaded the tent and picnic supplies. We began to set up our camp. Craig had a few problems with the equipment.

"We've only done this about a thousand times," I said. "Can't you find the curved pole that joins those two long ones together?" My voice carried a bite with it, but Craig didn't notice. I bounced a restless Phoebe while he pawed through the stack of tent poles. His face held a bemused look. He picked up one aluminum tube after another, turned each one around in his pudgy hands, and tossed them back to the ground. It was as if he'd never seen them before.

Daisy bounded joyfully through nearby brush, hot on the trail of a squirrel. In my arms, Phoebe suckled noisily on her bottle. Her hunger had interrupted my tent-pitching activity. I watched Craig's bewilderment from a lawn chair set up three yards away.

"There. There it is," I spotted the missing tent stake from where I sat.

"Well, I can't do this." He threw the last pole onto his discard pile and scratched his head. "Sorry, Annsy, I'm not much help."

I sighed. "It's okay. Can you get a blanket out of the car?"

He turned toward our vehicle and shuffled in its direction. His left leg dragged noticeably as he walked. Phoebe finished her bottle and I rose to follow him, swinging the baby onto my left hip so my right arm was free. This was how we'd laid out our camp equipment so far. I balanced a baby on my left hip, tugged and straightened the ground cloth opposite Craig's efforts, spread our nine by ten foot tent, and hammered tent stakes with my right arm.

He pulled a folded comforter from the back seat of our car. "This?"

"That will do. Let's lay it out over here and let Phoebe roll around on it. I need both hands to raise the tent.

With Phoebe content to scoot around on the comforter, I busied myself at the tent. We had pitched this tent together countless times in previous years. Today I pretty much had to do it alone. Finally it was up. I stood back to assess our weekend abode, and collected Craig's left hand in mine.

"There," I said. "It looks pretty good, don't you think?"

"Yeah. Sure." His voice was flat.

I stepped forward, unzipped the doorway and peered inside. "Home sweet home. Hey, let's get the sleeping bags in and go for a walk."

We toted the sleeping bags and other camping gear from the car. Then I swept Phoebe up. I picked up the comforter and handed one corner to Craig.

"Hang on, Craigie." I shook a few twigs and leaves off the blanket, tossed it into the tent and zipped the door. "Ready for a walk?"

We set out up a dry creek bed. Daisy trailed along. "Let's check out the Seven Springs," I suggested.

Progress was slow, but eventually we arrived at the location where some prior occupant had dumped seven bed mattresses years ago. Now only bare bed springs remained. Grass and shrubs grew through the coils.

An hour later we returned to the tent. "You want to go fishing while I get supper ready?"

Craig agreed. I helped him pull his tackle box and fishing pole from the car. With a lawn chair slung over my shoulder, Phoebe, Daisy and I walked to the north pond with him. After he settled on the bank we returned to the tent. I let Phoebe explore the camping quarters while I spread the sleeping bags. She cooed and burbled.

I collected cooking equipment from the car along with food supplies for the evening menu. With the camp stove set up on a picnic table, I started heating a pot of water for macaroni. After returning to the tent, I lay down with Phoebe on the sleeping bags. Together we rolled around. I laughed. She laughed. Camping was such fun.

A few minutes later, I rose to check on the pot of water. It was nearly boiling. I glanced up as I tore open a box of pasta. Craig headed toward our campsite. He slogged slowly, staggering wildly from side to side, dripping water as he walked. Soaked from head to toe, wet fronds hung from buttons and snaps on his overalls.

I ran to him. "Oh my God—what happened?"

"I don't know. I fell in. I guess I lost my balance. I was trying to get my line. It got tied up in the reeds."

I looked in his eyes. They lacked luster and expression.

He continued. "It was really hard to get out too. The reeds acted like they wanted to tie me up."

"I'm so sorry. Let's get you changed."

Our little camping trip to celebrate Phoebe's first six months had become an ordeal. Everything was up to me. I no longer had a partner for my adventures. I had two children to care for, worry about and keep safe. Camping didn't seem fun anymore.

16
CONFUSION AND CHAOS

The wind picked up. I grabbed Phoebe's hand and tugged the pre-school child along the trail a little faster. She whimpered in the chilled air. Snowflakes danced through pine trees along the mountain path. In moments, the air swirled white. I could hardly see the trail.

I knelt to my daughter's height so that our eyes met. "Hey, Kiddo," I said, as calmly as I could. "We need to get off this mountain. Quickly. Let me carry you a while."

She leapt into my arms and I stood, swaying slightly under her twenty-five pounds. I headed down the trail. Each step was powered by desperation as the snow fell thicker. What had started as an idyllic Sunday afternoon walk on a mountain trail above Telluride, Colorado, became a frantic flight for our very lives through an autumn mountain blizzard. The temperature plummeted. Wet needles became snow-covered and icy. My feet slipped with each step.

I stumbled to my knees. Phoebe screamed. With difficulty, I managed to keep my hold on her. "It's okay, Baby Girl." I tried to soothe her through my own panic.

Out of the swirling snow a dark figure took shape and approached us. "Bear!" I thought. As it neared, I saw it wasn't a creature of the wild, but a man.

I called to him. He made his way to the spot where I knelt with Phoebe in my arms. He assisted me to stand with a strong lift on my elbow and forearm.

"Follow me," he yelled over the howling wind. I didn't know who this man was, but I sensed he was a friend. He turned off the path a hundred yards down the mountain and climbed upwards through the pines. I struggled to keep up. Every few feet he glanced over his shoulder to make sure I was still there. Fifty feet later, he turned back and was at my side in two strides.

"May I carry her?" he asked.

"Where are we going?"

"An old miner's cabin at the top of this ridge. Let me carry her. We'll get there faster."

I nodded. We transferred Phoebe to his arms and he swung her onto his back. She clung to his chin and buried her face in the top of his hat.

Up the hill we went. In the graying whiteness, I could make out a dark wall ahead. An old log cabin lay squarely in our path. Its door sagged. Snow drifted across forest litter on a roof that showed clear signs of decay.

Our surprise friend—a hunter, perhaps, or maybe a forest ranger—kicked in the heavy wooden door after three explosive jabs with his right foot. We tumbled inside. He swung Phoebe to the floor and leaned into the door with his shoulder, pushing mightily to close it against the storm. I joined him, my shoulder ten inches lower along the door's edge. Slowly, the door creaked shut, and the howl of the wind stilled.

"Hold on a minute. I'll find a lamp," our benefactor said. He groped in a corner and came up with an old-fashioned oil lamp. A quick flash flared as he lit a match.

Then a soft warm glow lit the inside of the rough-hewn cabin.

"Firewood in the corner," he said. "Hand me some kindling and I'll get a fire started."

Phoebe and I toted arm loads of firewood to the hunter who knelt at the fireplace on the cabin wall opposite the door.

"You know this mountain well," I said. "Thank you so much. I don't know what we would have done if you hadn't found us."

He smiled a handsome grin and nodded. "You're welcome. I grew up on these mountains. I've spent many a night holed up in this cabin and another on the peak across the valley. Seth. My name is Seth."

I introduced Phoebe and myself.

Seth's dark brown eyes sparkled in his face. He removed his hat and a thick mop of black hair bushed up on top of his head. He nodded again. "Ladies," he said in greeting. He studied me closer. "I think I know you. Aren't you the piano player at the Silver Mine Bar and Grill?"

"Yes," I said. "You go there?"

"Every Friday night."

The three of us curled comfortably in front of a roaring fire. Outside the wind whipped snow around the cabin. Its walls shook against the cold blasts. The cabin trembled.

"Ladies and gentlemen, this is your captain speaking. We are on our final approach to Philadelphia. Please return to your seats. Fasten your seatbelts. Return your seats to their upright and locked positions. Return your tray tables to their upright and locked positions, and stow any personal items underneath the seat in front of you."

Dang. It was just a dream. The cabin vibrated around me, but it was not from the icy wind of a mountain blizzard above Telluride. Vibrations emanated from the powerful jet engines and thrummed through the 747's passenger cabin. I opened my eyes. Neither Phoebe nor the dream hunter Seth sat beside me. Craig did. We returned to Misericordia for his next round of chemotherapy.

I pushed the button on my seat to bring it back to its upright position. Then I turned to him.

"Craig, sit forward." I reached for the button to raise his seat.

Motionless, he stared straight ahead.

"Craigie, sit forward, please." Still nothing.

"Craig." I put a little more emphasis in my voice. "Would you please lean forward? We need to get ready to land."

Finally he looked at me. "Oh. I thought you said 'Shit forward.' I was trying to figure that one out."

His confusion struck me humorously and I laughed.

The following morning though, nothing seemed funny. "I'd like to talk to the doctor," I said. "I need to know what's going on. I have questions and we need answers."

"Yes, Mrs. Darr," the nurse said calmly. The pin on her uniform identified her as Ellen. "I have relayed your request. Dr. Klassen's staff is aware of your concern."

"Why doesn't anyone answer my questions? We've been here more than twelve hours and you just now brought Craig's ID bracelet. The ice in the cooler melted long ago and you're just now bringing more. I don't understand why it was so important last month and now it's not."

"Please, Mrs. Darr. We're very busy and short-staffed today with a lot of patients. I'm sure the doctor will be in at some point. I just don't know when." Ellen slipped out of the room.

I took a deep breath and turned to Craig. Asleep, he was completely unaware of the events occurring around him. I felt frustrated to the point of tears. *Woman lonely. Woman alone. My dear Craig. Please come back to me. I miss you so much.*

I killed time making lists. Daily schedules, lists of holiday plans, lists of people who supported our desperation through prayer or monetary donations. So many gifts had flooded in through Craig's co-workers at Boeing, or friends from around the entire country, the flights to Philadelphia and back had so far cost us nothing.

It had been weeks since I was able to muster a prayer for his health. I couldn't find the right words. But I felt comforted to know so many people across the continent had put him on prayer lists. Their faith sustained me and cradled Craig in love.

I had questions, lists of questions. What was the radiologist's interpretation of Craig's latest scans? When could we expect to see results from the chemotherapy? How long should we keep coming with no apparent improvement? Why couldn't an oncologist in Wichita administer this treatment?

I desperately needed answers.

I began to log all the details of Craig's experimental treatment on the slim chance that if I could share the specifics, maybe Dr. Varden could arrange to have future treatments administered in Wichita. I also needed something to do to help pass my time inside the hospital's wrought-iron fence.

"What'cha doin?" Craig said when he woke from a short nap that afternoon. I wondered how long he had watched me scribble notes in my spiral notebook.

"I'm just writing in my journal."

"What are you writing?"

"You know me... I've got to write everything down. I've got some ideas." I faked a smile.

"Like what?"

"I'm keeping notes about your chemotherapy. Maybe someday I'll write a book about our trials and tribulations with cancer. We could tell the world how bravely you fought and never gave up and finally conquered the disease. Then maybe they'll make a movie about it which will warm the hearts of America."

Craig was silent for a moment before he said, "It might sadden the hearts of America since we don't know how it turns out." He twisted the sheet in his hand. "I thought of something I want to tell you."

"Okay. Shoot," I said.

"I'm glad I had you and I think I had true love."

"Me too, Craigie. Me too," I answered softly.

"I think this might be the end, you know."

"The end?"

"Yeah. I don't like to think about it. I don't like to think about dying. I'm going to fight with all I've got."

"Okay," I whispered.

"There's so much to live for."

A week later we were home again, waiting through the next few weeks until another treatment.

"See you soon," I said to Craig's mother and hung up the phone. I turned to Phoebe who sat in her high chair playing with a pile of Cheerios on the tray.

"Here, Kiddo. Want some fruit?" I placed a small bowl of apple bits within her reach. She grabbed three and stuffed them into her mouth.

"A little help in here." Craig's monotone voice wafted thinly down the hall.

I sprinted to the bedroom and stopped short when I saw him. His sweatpants twisted a quarter-turn at the waist. His eyeglasses bow rested inside his left ear. His face looked catawampus. His shoes were on, but the left shoe tongue had doubled back and bunched up on the top of his foot.

I couldn't believe the shirt. Its neck opening stretched tightly across his chest. The entire shirt was twisted. One sleeve turned inside out. Both arms threaded through sleeves, but everything was twisted and tight. Craig managed to make a straight-jacket from his comfortable sweatshirt.

"How did you do that?"

"Don't know. Just trying to get dressed. Can you help?"

"Sure. Have a seat." I pressed down gently on his shoulders. His knees buckled and he perched on the edge of the bed.

"Now let's see." I worked with his good arm, bending the elbow and straining to pull the shirt off. I worked a good five minutes with no progress.

"I don't see how you got this on." I grew more astonished by the minute. "I think I'll have to cut it off, Craig. Stay here while I get some scissors."

"I'm not going anywhere."

I dashed to the kitchen. Phoebe happily played with her breakfast as she sat in her high chair. I found scissors in the utility drawer and sprinted back to the bedroom. After a few strategically placed snips, his arms slipped free from the binding sleeves. I dropped the shredded shirt to the floor and helped thread a fresh shirt over his head and arms.

"I still do not see how you managed that one. I didn't think I was talking to your mom that long. Oh, by the way, she's coming out this morning to stay with you and Phoebe."

"Why?"

"So I can tune a piano."

Craig looked at me blankly for a moment. "You're going to paint tuna cans?"

I giggled. I pulled him to his feet and gave him a big hug. He stood listlessly like a giant rag doll and offered no reciprocated squeeze.

"Yes, dear, I'm going to paint tuna cans."

17

A Long Dark Tunnel

Filled with hospital routine, the days of our November treatment week passed slowly in Philadelphia. By Thursday, I mustered a little excitement in anticipation of two things. First, Dr. Klassen would be back from a conference the next day. Since we hadn't seen him all week, surely that would mean a productive consultation about Craig's deterioration.

Second, Craig's dad flew into Philadelphia on a business trip. He planned to stop at the hospital for a visit.

Lenny Darr's smiling face peered around the door frame as he knocked on the open door Friday morning.

"Hello," I said. He entered the room and walked to Craig's side. He gripped his son's trembling hand.

"Hi, Dad," Craig said thinly. He managed a lopsided grin.

"When will the doctor be by?" Lenny asked me.

"I don't know. We haven't seen him at all this time. He's evidently out of town."

"What's up with that, I wonder?" Lenny said. "We'll have to see about it." He pulled Craig's call light.

A minute later, the nurse arrived. "Yes?" she asked.

"I need to see Dr. Klassen. I've been trying to set up an appointment to talk to him for weeks."

"Dr. Klassen has a very tight schedule."

"Well, I need to see him. I'm only here for a short time. I might never have another opportunity to talk to him about my son's treatment."

"I'll mention it to his office." She left.

"Don't get your hopes up," I advised. "We don't see Klassen very often."

"You don't? Isn't he Craig's doctor?"

"Well, yes, but..." I shrugged and shook my head.

"I would have thought you'd see him daily. Doesn't he do rounds?"

I repeated, "We don't see him very often."

"Well, how do you like that?"

Lenny left to attend a business lunch. At two he returned. "I've got to head back to Wichita tomorrow afternoon."

"I bet Klassen isn't even here on the weekends," I said.

"Then today is all I've got." He paused a moment and looked at his son. Craig stared listlessly at the wall. Lenny took a deep breath. "What do you say about you and me just going over to Klassen's office and paying him a visit, appointment or no?"

"Now?"

Lenny nodded. "Right now."

Vincent Klassen, in contrast to Lenny's stature, stood barely taller than my own five and a half feet. His facial features defined his temperament, angular and sharp. He scowled. "My schedule is full. I have no time for this."

"I've tried to make an appointment in your busy schedule for more than a month." Lenny jogged his memory.

"I just don't do that."

"You don't have time to talk to me about my son, one of your patients? It's not like I can come back any time. I fly out of here tomorrow for home—a thousand miles away."

Klassen glared at Lenny.

"Look, all I want is to find out how you think my son is doing. Surely you've got a couple minutes for that."

Klassen nodded once and we followed him into the office.

After we were seated Lenny asked, "How do you think he's doing?"

Klassen glanced through a stack of files and pulled one out. He skimmed the documents inside it.

"It appears Craig is holding steady in his responses to the neurological tests my assistants administer. The latest scan shows reduced swelling in his occipital lobe."

"So you think he's getting better?"

"I think it's clear the treatments are working. Reduced swelling in his brain tells me that."

I gasped. "Why does he keep getting worse then?"

"Worse? What do you mean? The scans clearly show Craig's swelling is down."

"But he can barely walk. It's harder and harder to get him through the airports."

"He's probably just weak. Muscles atrophy from lack of use."

"Then why don't you have him on a physical therapy plan?" I burst out. "I've been asking for that since last time we were here."

"That is not my concern."

"You don't care that he can barely feed himself?" I asked in disbelief. "Or that his entire left side droops? His left leg drags along the floor when he walks? Why would you not want him working on motor skills and exercises?"

"If the man is dying," Klassen said coldly, "why bother him with little exercises? Again, it is not my concern."

Astonished, I could think of nothing to say.

Lenny said, "It's not your concern that by all outward appearances, your patient is in a rapid decline? That we have seen no signs the treatment has had any effects? That—"

Klassen interrupted Lenny's tirade. "Look. I'm sixty years old, nearing retirement. I don't need or want all the patients who come to me. I didn't ask you to come here, you asked me. So, if you don't want to bring Craig, don't bring him. This interview is over. I've got things to do."

He dismissed us with a wave of his hand.

I stumbled back to Craig's room blinded by tears. Lenny walked at my side, his arm across my shoulders. Back at the room, we gazed at Craig, sleeping again. Lenny grabbed a tissue and dabbed his own eyes. "I'm so sorry, Annie," he said.

"I don't know what to do," I said. "It's heavy. It's so heavy, the responsibility for taking care of Craig. I guess it's all on me and I really don't have a clue what to do now."

Three days later, we were home again, the hiatus between November and December treatments. Phoebe's first Thanksgiving approached, and I couldn't feel less thankful this year. What should have been a joyous occasion loomed bleakly ahead of us. Desperate for an upward swing in our moods, I planned a holiday trip across the state where my family would congregate for the traditional turkey dinner in Hays. We arrived late Wednesday morning.

After lunch and an hour's nap, Craig, Phoebe and I headed to Marvin's house. We entered up the ramp in the back. Marvin hadn't seen us for a year. He questioned us about our experiences as parents and our trips to Philadelphia. Craig relaxed with his long-time friend and mentor, and carried on a fairly lucid conversation.

After a few minutes, Phoebe pushed away from me. She slid off my lap and crawled toward a chair across the room. She pulled up to it and fingered its flowered upholstery. Her unsteady legs wobbled. Tight curls on her head bobbed up and down.

"She'll be walking soon, won't she?" Marvin said.

"It won't be long," I agreed. "She pulls up to everything already."

"How old is she now?"

"Nine months in a couple more weeks. I was walking at nine months. For most babies, it's a little longer though."

"What about you, Craig? Do you know your age at your first step?"

Craig looked at Marvin a moment with a blank expression on his face. "Can't think of it. Guess you'd have to ask my mom."

Phoebe dropped to the floor again and took off to another corner.

"Looks like she wants to explore," I said. "Maybe I'll show her your porch and backyard, Marvin. You two can visit for a few minutes."

I swept the squirmy child into my arms and headed to Marvin's screened-in-porch.

"Bye, Snickelfritz," Craig called after us.

We stopped to see the artwork on the porch. I set her on the seat of Marvin's battery-powered wheel chair. She soon discovered the buttons and levers which operated the chair. "Okay. Enough of that," I said. I lifted her off the seat. She squawked.

We walked down the ramp. Marvin's flower garden grew along its sides, now dormant with brown autumn foliage. I swung Phoebe onto my back so she could look over my shoulder and gave her a quick tour of the stone sculptures in Marvin's backyard, gifts from a sculptor friend of his.

When we returned to the house, we found Marvin alone in his living room. I raised my eyebrows in surprise and glanced around.

"He's in the bathroom."

I nodded and set Phoebe down again. She crawled across the room toward Marvin.

"How are you holding up?" he asked.

"About as good as can be expected, under the circumstances."

He nodded. "It's hard to watch a loved one fade away, isn't it?"

"Boy, you got that right."

"Craig seems to have accepted his condition. He's prepared for the end."

"You were surprised to see how much he's slipped, weren't you?"

"Yes. You've told me in letters and over the phone, but I couldn't imagine it until I saw him myself. He's very open about his feelings and concerns."

"That's good. But it's also rare. He talks nonsense most of the time."

"Phoebe sure is growing. She must be a ray of sunshine in your life."

"I don't know what I'd do without her. I think I would just give up."

"Craig seems to doubt that the treatments in Philadelphia are doing any good."

"I wonder that myself."

"When do you think it will be time to stop going? He indicated that time was near."

"It may be. But when do you give up? I don't know. One of the other ladies there told me that it would be us wives who make that decision. When we do, we pronounce a death sentence."

"Maybe you should let Craig decide."

"He told me he wanted to fight to live."

"He may be ready to change his mind. When he decides he doesn't want to go for any more treatments, no one should try to talk him out of it."

There was a moment of silence while that advice settled upon my heart.

"That's wise, Marvin. But so hard."

"I know, Annie."

"I dread that moment because I'm afraid I'll have a big fight with his folks and his brother. They probably won't want to give up. But life like this is no life at all. I feel so trapped. It's like a prison with only one way out and I'm not sure I'm ready for that yet."

The bathroom door clicked open. Craig shuffled down the hall. "Ann?" he called.

I jumped up. "In here, Craigie." I stepped toward the doorway. "He gets lost easily," I said to Marvin as I passed him.

I turned Craig around and guided him back to the living room. He collapsed onto the sofa.

"What were you guys talking about?" he asked.

"Same thing you and I were," Marvin answered. "Philadelphia. Treatments. How long to keep going."

"Oh," Craig said. "I don't know if I'll go back too many more times. I'm not afraid."

"Not afraid?" I said.

"I'm not afraid to die. I have the easy part. The rest of you have to keep on living."

The next morning, as he sat on the bed, Craig asked, "You know where the electric box is?"

"No. Why?"

"I think there's a defect in the wiring. I should go fix it."

"What do you mean?"

"Well, see that light? It seems to come on every day at the same time and then it comes down and cuts your hair."

I raised my eyebrows. "Really? Cuts your hair, huh?"

"Yeah. I should probably go fix that. It's defective."

18
THE FINAL PHASE

Clarice volunteered to accompany Craig to Philadelphia for his December treatment. I couldn't face another trip east, to the horrid wrought-iron prison and stone-faced medical staff. When they returned, she shook from the trauma of a harrowing journey with a disabled man through the airports. He was irritable too, and spoke with slurred speech. *Like a drunkard*, I thought.

The next morning he appeared to be in a better mood. His speech had cleared up. He was agreeable about getting dressed and did his best to help. As I knelt to slip house shoes on his feet, he asked, "Do Kay and Gary wear underwear?"

I looked up at him, chuckling. He appeared intently serious.

I answered, "Yes, I suppose they do. I really don't know for sure, though."

"Well, do they have one of those machines that tell you what to wear and when to get dressed?"

"A machine? I don't think so, Craigie."

After breakfast, he played with Phoebe for a long time, longer than he had for weeks. He even was able to pull her into his lap as he sat in his favorite easy chair. That afternoon we decorated for Christmas. I placed a tree on a small table inside Phoebe's playpen. It was safely out of her inquisitive reach. We hung our favorite ornaments on the needled limbs for our daughter's first Christmas. *And probably Craig's last,* I thought. Phoebe bubbled with delight. Craig helped for a few minutes and then watched from his chair while I finished. He seemed pleased with the results, though he said nothing.

That evening, at bedtime, I helped him change to pajamas. As he stood unsteadily beside the bed I wrapped my arms around him. His knees bent and his legs collapsed. He bounced on the mattress.

He looked into my eyes. "I'm not going to Philadelphia again."

"Okay, Craig," I whispered. I tucked him into bed and dashed to the bathroom. I closed the door, leaned against it and slid to the floor. The day had arrived. Craig had made his decision. I shook with silent sobs from the impact of his choice. We were giving up.

The following evening Craig's brother Alan arrived at dusk to sit with him while I whisked Phoebe away to the Christmas pageant at church. My heart could not have felt less merry but I went through the motions. After all, it was her first Christmas. I couldn't sing without crying, so I didn't even try. There was little joy in my world this holiday season.

The program over, I gathered Phoebe into my arms. We joined the crowd spilling from the sanctuary to fellowship hall for refreshments. Calls of Christmas cheer came from all directions. I selected a cookie for Phoebe and we headed to a festive table.

Someone tapped on my shoulder. I turned around to find the pastor. Though smiling, his brow was also furrowed. "Your brother-in-law is on the phone," he said over the holiday hubbub. "There's been an incident with Craig." He beckoned me to follow.

A friend standing nearby reached her arms out to Phoebe. "Let me take her while you get the call."

I passed Phoebe to her waiting arms and hustled to the pastor's office. He closed the door. The joyful sounds of Christmas died. Pastor handed me the telephone receiver.

"Hello?"

"Hey, Ann." Alan's strong voice boomed from the receiver. "There's been a little incident. We were having a nice little conversation here a few minutes ago and Craig just stopped. Then, well, he's had another seizure. It was pretty intense. I called for an ambulance and it's on the way."

"Ambulance? From where?"

"They're taking him back to Wesley."

"He's on the way to Wesley?"

"Not yet. The ambulance is on its way here. Now don't worry. He's all right. Just had a pretty severe seizure, but it's over now."

"I should go to Wesley, not home?"

"That's where Craig and I are headed. You should probably get Phoebe home for the night shouldn't you?"

"Phoebe? I don't know. I don't know anything anymore."

There we were, back in Wesley Hospital where it all began.

How much worse could a person get before the body's systems shut down? *Lord, help me. Help us. If Craig is going to get well, please let him get well. And if he's going to die, please let him die. I can't stand this any longer.*

Clarice peeked into the room. "It's time. Dr. Varden is in the conference room."

I nodded to Craig's parents, his brother, and the doctor as I entered and pulled the door closed behind me.

Lenny dabbed at his eyes with a handkerchief. "Will he have to stay in the hospital now?"

"Not necessarily," Dr. Varden said. "Let's go over the critical decision. We'll see about it." He looked at me and smiled, but there was sadness in his eyes. He motioned me to a seat.

"I called you all in here because you are the key players in Craig's life and you need to make a decision for him. I think you all realize by now that Craig is going to die. There's no miracle cure in existence that would restore his former life."

Lenny sniffed loudly.

Dr. Varden continued, "Do you understand that?"

Murmurs of affirmation came from the rest. Unable to speak, I simply nodded.

"The time has come for a decision. It's a tough one, but we can't let his suffering continue with the dim hope of a miracle cure." He raised a sheet of paper and held it loosely in front of his chest. "I have a form. We call it the 'Do Not Resuscitate' or 'No Code Blue' form."

"What would that mean for Craig?" Lenny asked.

"We'll do everything possible to keep him comfortable, but we'd stop all treatments that would be designed to keep him alive, or that we hope would provide a cure."

"Where would he be?" Clarice asked.

"If we contact a home health service, I see no reason he can't go home. There's no need for him to stay at the hospital."

There was a moment of silence. Alan spoke first. "I say we sign this form. The life he's got right now is not the life my brother would want. If there's no chance for him to get better... we shouldn't prolong his suffering."

Lenny choked. "Well said, Son." Craig's father wilted into sobs that shook his broad shoulders.

"I will sign," Clarice said softly. "He's worse after every trip to Philadelphia." Her voice ended in a strained whisper.

Dr. Varden turned to me. A lump in my chest threatened to explode with my first word. I struggled to control my breathing, and to stem the deluge of tears that threatened.

After a few seconds of silence, Alan spoke, "So far, we're all in agreement, but I'd like to hear what you have to say, Ann."

I took a deep breath and opened my mouth, but no words came out of it. A strange pain in my throat strangled my words. I shook my head. Finally, I managed to whisper hoarsely, "Oh, you guys." I clutched at my throat with rigid fingers.

"Ann, surely you don't want Craig to have to live like this," his mother implored me.

"We've got to give him back to God," Lenny said. "I can't stand to see him like this. How can you?"

I shook my head again and opened my mouth. The pain in my throat pinched off words. Craig's family talked at once, arguing with what they perceived as my dissenting opinion.

My chest heaved with anguished breaths. *Oh, the irony. And I thought I would have to convince them to let Craig go, to free his spirit.*

Finally, I made a conscious effort to relax the muscles in my neck and shoulders. I exhaled forcibly and managed to moan, "No—you don't understand. I'm not disagreeing with you. I—just—can't—say—it." I fought to get the words out. My trembling hands clutched awkwardly at my throat.

There was silence in the room again. Dr. Varden nodded somberly. "So we're all in agreement?"

Every head in the room nodded. Every eye filled with tears.

Dr. Varden handed me the form. "Ann, as Craig's representative it's up to you to sign. But it's good you all agree." He gave me a pen. And I signed the paper.

19
PASSION FIRST MEANS SUFFERING

Craig remained in the hospital for three days. Dr. Varden's office arranged round-the-clock home nursing care. Finally I was able to take him home. We arrived with Phoebe four hours ahead of the first Licensed Practical Nurse. It was a precious four hours, the last we were to savor as our own little family unit, together and alone.

When the first nurse arrived, our beautiful home was quickly transformed into a makeshift care facility. I was a stranger in my own house, and I hated every minute of it. Craig became less and less communicative and more and more belligerent. He knew. On some level, he knew why there were strangers in our house.

His physical care became the responsibility of the nurses. That much was a relief to me. The mental care, the love, and emotional support, was my territory. A hospital bed arrived and our double bed was moved to the basement. I insisted on having a twin bed brought up so I could remain at Craig's side during the night.

The male nurse on duty questioned my decision. "Are you sure you want to do that? You'll rest better in a room of your own."

"Yes, I want a bed in there for me. That is *our* bedroom. We still hold hands at night. I know that's important."

"Okay. We'll move the bed." He threw up his arms in mock surrender.

Not only were there nurses at our house, we hosted family guests for Christmas as well. My folks arrived to offer assistance wherever it was needed. My dad spent hours in our shop to sort, organize and put away tools Craig had accumulated while we built our little homestead. "I have a better understanding of Craig after cleaning his workshop," Dad related to me one evening after supper.

"What do you mean?" I asked.

"I wonder if he didn't have some kind of premonition that his time on earth would be short. He just pushed himself to do more and more, and never had the time to put things away in an organized fashion."

"Maybe you're right. 'Hurry every chance you get' was his trademark."

"Always in a hurry?"

"That's my Craig."

"I feel badly that he won't be able to enjoy life here with you and Phoebe."

"Not without a miracle," I said softly.

Christmas morning, Phoebe crawled into our bedroom. I closed the door to dress. Craig lay helplessly on the hospital bed, but his eyes were open. I lifted Phoebe to his side. "Hey, Phoebe, shall we wish Daddy a happy Christmas?" She cooed and burbled. Then she crawled all over the bed, crossing Craig several times in her explorations. He reached an unsteady hand to her curly head and said, "Hi, Snickelfritz."

By mid-morning, Craig sat in his favorite living room chair. Gifts were opened. The day nurse headed to the kitchen to prepare his medicines. His mother worked on

Christmas dinner. Grandpa and Uncle Alan took Phoebe outside to look at the chickens and gather eggs.

When I knelt in front of Craig, he looked into my eyes. We connected. He brought his right hand to my cheek and stroked it gently. He looked at me with tenderness and a great sadness. Tears brimmed to my eyes. *Craig, dear Craig, how I love you. I know I've had true love too.*

I awoke very early on the first day of a new year. For a few moments, I couldn't pinpoint what had roused me from sleep. I strained to hear something. Was it Craig? Was he still breathing? Yes. I could clearly hear the rasping sounds in his throat as air passed in and out of his lungs.

The baby maybe? Had Phoebe stirred and cried in the night? I listened hard, but could detect no unusual sounds coming from her room.

The call of a coyote filtered through the window. Its song rose and wavered in the stillness. It poured its passion into the winter night, perhaps right under my window. That must have been my waking call.

As I listened, a second coyote joined the chorus from a distance. A third canine voice chimed in from a different direction. I rose and tiptoed to our bedroom window thinking that I might catch a glimpse of the nearest vocalist against the snowy backdrop. No. I could see nothing dark against the starlit snow to the west.

I padded barefoot to the living room. The third-shift nurse peered anxiously out the front window.

"See anything?" I asked.

"No. But it sure sounds close. Did it wake you?"

"Something did. Guess it probably was the coyote."

I moved to the window and leaned against it, pressing my nose against the glass. All I could see was a white wasteland.

"*Doctor Zhivago*," I uttered softly.

"What?"

"This looks like a scene from *Doctor Zhivago*, don't you think? Do you know that movie?

"Yes. It's been a while though."

"A frozen winter wasteland and a coyote howling eerily. This is a scene right out of the movie."

I returned to the bedroom and listened to Craig's labored breathing. "Somewhere, my love," I whispered to him.

I'd been reading the book that inspired the movie. "Passion," wrote Boris Pasternak, "First means suffering." *Perhaps the two are inseparable.* Certainly my life paralleled parts of the story line. It was filled with passion, with the beauty that accompanies pain and tragedy, as well as love and happiness.

Marvin called sometime in the afternoon on New Year's Day. I filled him in on Craig's condition and the events since Thanksgiving. "It was his decision, Marvin. Like you said. He flat told me he would not be going back to Philadelphia again. Nobody has tried to change his mind."

"How's he doing?"

"Worse than ever. He hardly ever speaks anymore. When he does, he makes no sense. Here lately, he has started spitting out his pills. I don't know why. Maybe he's had enough and thinks the end will come faster if he stops taking the pills. Maybe he just can't swallow them. I don't know."

"You have nursing care around the clock?"

"Yes."

"How's that going?"

"The nurses drive me crazy. I feel like... like they have stolen Craig away from me. I wish they'd just go away and leave us alone. But I guess that's not possible."

"You sound distressed."

"Oh, Marvin. You don't know the half of it. I can hardly sleep at night. I keep listening for Craig's next breath, wondering if there will even be one. I can hardly eat. I'm always on edge. My hands shake whenever I'm awake. I want to tear my hair out."

"You certainly have a lot on your plate right now."

"Yes. And I'm failing. I'm failing at everything. I can't even cry when I'm supposed to or not cry when I shouldn't. It's crazy."

"Annie, I'm so sorry. I wish there was something I could do to help."

"Just talking to me helps a lot."

"Have you thought about what you'll do after it's over?"

"I haven't given that too much thought. Daydreams, mostly."

"Just remember, every ending makes a new beginning.

Happy Birthday, Dear Craigie. Today, January 10, is your thirty-third.

You will never read this letter or even know I've written it. In a sense I already write to you as I wrote to our babies, from my heart to heaven. I hear your labored breathing as you sit in your favorite chair. Your congestion seems worse all the time. It has been days since you said anything to me that made sense. You have kissed my hand and rubbed me across the shoulders and patted me as if to comfort me. I know your love is still there. A little while ago, you gave me a full kiss on my lips. It was the first real kiss in many days. I wonder if it will be our last?

I try to feel what you must be feeling inside, to imagine what you may be experiencing. All I come up with is uncertainty. I imagine you dream a lot. Your waking moments, I would guess, are filled with confusion when we try to talk to you.

"Craig?" I might say to get your attention.

"Huh?" you respond as if suddenly we reach the same frequency.

"Are you hungry?"

And then you mumble about the rooms, the ceilings, a vague reference to another person—one of the nurses, maybe?—or something completely incomprehensible.

I imagine that your waking moments are filled with love, too. Love that is complete and unconditional for me and Phoebe and your mom, dad and brother. And love for God. Perhaps you feel close to Him now. He can reach you even if no one else can. He carries us through difficult times.

Whatever marriage has been for us, it is almost over. I have many doubts about myself. I've failed miserably. I failed you. I didn't find the medical treatment that would restore your health. I failed Phoebe when I put our own desire to have a child above her welfare. I selfishly clung to her when she could have found love in a complete family. After all, what is a baby without a daddy? You would have been a far better parent than I will be. I'm so weak and insecure. And daddies are so special to little girls. What have I done to this baby in my selfish desperation?

She is walking now. Maybe you know that. If not, I wish you could see it.

I cannot bear to think of a future without you. What am I to do? I have decades of loneliness ahead of me. I just can't stand it.

Happy Birthday, my dear Craig. Since Jesus was thirty-three when he died, it looks like you may have that in common with Him.

20
ANGEL'S BLOOD AND TEARS

Craig's physician knocked on our door. "Come in, Dr. Varden. I didn't know doctors still made house calls."

"We don't very often." He smiled and squeezed my hand as he stepped inside. "I wanted to see Craig and didn't want you to have to get him out in this weather."

"Thanks. That would have been impossible, I think."

"This gives me an opportunity to see your arrangement and to talk with your nursing service."

His attention turned to Craig in the living room easy chair. "Hi, Craig." He pulled some medical instruments from a bag and conducted a gentle examination. Occasionally, he asked a question of the evening nurse. Then he studied the written chart for a few minutes.

"He's having trouble with meds?"

"More and more," the nurse said.

"Let's start grinding them and administering the powder in applesauce. Do you have a mortar and pestle?"

"Yes. We all carry them."

"Do you have applesauce?" he asked me.

"I'm pretty sure we do."

"Let's give that a try." He turned to his patient. "Craig, we're going to administer your pills in applesauce now. You won't have to worry about trying to swallow any more tablets."

Craig stared blankly ahead.

"May I see the hospital bed and sleeping arrangements?"

"Sure."

In the bedroom, Dr. Varden glanced around and nodded his approval. He turned to me. "I wanted to talk to you a little bit where Craig couldn't hear," he said in a low voice. "Even though he doesn't respond, it's very likely he can hear and understand what is being said around him. You might keep that in mind."

I nodded.

"Based on what I observed this evening, I don't see how he can last much longer. The end is very near."

I squeezed my eyes shut.

"It's likely that the swallowing problem will get worse. My concern is that he must have the medicine to control his seizures—for your sake. If necessary, we can administer his meds through suppositories. For now, hopefully the applesauce will do."

"Okay, Doc," I whispered.

"Hang in there, Ann. Please call me any time—day or night—if Craig's condition changes." He handed me a card. Three different phone numbers were listed on it; his office, his home phone, and an answering service.

Two days later, I argued with the weekend nurse. "You can't just let him lie here all day, hour after hour."

She recorded his urine output on the chart and emptied his catheter bag. "But what's the point?"

"Look, I know about bedsores. I know a person needs to be moved every few hours. This is Craig's home. Whether you like it or not, he benefits from a daily routine."

"We can turn him in the bed."

"No. We'll move him to the front room. He can be part of the household there. He enjoys watching Phoebe play."

"He can't help with the move. It's like moving dead weight."

"That's why we have a wheelchair and a Hoyer lift. You don't need to lift him by yourself. I'll help. But he needs to be moved."

The nurse relented. We worked the straps around Craig, hooked him to the lift and moved him to the wheelchair. In the living room, we settled him in his chair. Phoebe and my mother played with a shape puzzle on the living room floor.

"I need to prepare his meds," the nurse said.

She disappeared into the kitchen. I joined Phoebe on the floor and played hide-and-seek with a star and a triangle. She giggled when she found them under my hands. I pulled her to her feet and helped her take a few unsteady steps.

"Let's go see Daddy."

I tugged her hand and pulled her gently toward Craig. When she arrived she grabbed his knee and shrieked with delight. Craig stared straight ahead, not seeing either of us. But he brought his right hand to her head and patted her curls.

The nurse returned. "Here are your morning meds, Mr. Darr."

She spooned applesauce from a small dish toward his closed mouth.

"Open your mouth, Craigie," I said.

He didn't respond. I pulled gently downward on his chin. He opened his mouth and she spooned in three bites of applesauce.

Ten minutes later, he drifted off to sleep.

We moved Craig several times through the course of the day. We wheeled him to the table at lunch time. He ate very little, even with assistance. Early in the afternoon, I spread a comforter on the carpet and he joined Phoebe there for a nap. The second shift nurse arrived to relieve the day nurse. She helped move Craig to the dinner table. After dinner, we moved him back to his favorite chair again.

About nine o'clock, the nurse prepared Craig's evening medications. Together we went through the drill. I helped him open his mouth enough to accept a spoonful of applesauce. One. Two. Three. Then it was gone.

"Do you think he swallowed?" the nurse asked.

"I think so. I saw his throat move. There, it moved again."

"I saw that. Good."

Fifteen minutes later, I tucked Phoebe into bed and returned to the living room. "Think it's time to move Craig to the bedroom?"

Before she could answer, Craig gurgled. He opened his mouth and gasped for air.

I looked at the nurse. "He can't breathe. What do we do?"

Craig's distress intensified. He gagged. His good arm flailed in the air, groping for a hand hold on something. I reached to him to offer support. His hand whipped past mine.

"What do we do?" I shouted.

The nurse took my hands gently in hers. Quietly, in stark contrast to the chaos screaming in my head, she said, "I don't think we're supposed to do anything."

She was right. This was it. I gasped. My whole body tensed as Craig's distress grew.

Every fiber of my being—all that I had or would ever be—yearned to do something to help my husband in his final moments of life on earth. Yet, I knew she was right. I knew I had signed the paper. I knew none of his family wanted to prolong the miserable existence that his life had become. But I also knew that if I'd waited until that very moment to make the decision, it would have been different. I wanted to help him, to place every ounce of strength I could muster into an effort to ease the moment's trauma. I wanted to fill his lungs with air again. But I could not.

I wrung my hands and paced the floor. "Maybe he didn't swallow that applesauce after all," I said, shaking my head.

"He's going fast. "Perhaps you should call his folks. If they want to be here, they need to come."

I lunged for the phone and punched in their number. Clarice answered on the first ring.

"Craig can't breathe. The nurse said if you want to be here, you better come." I hung up without waiting for a reply and turned back to the living room. Mother stood two steps behind me, her arms open to offer me a hug. I brushed her hand and rushed back to the living room.

Craig's gasps seemed to last an eternity. In reality, it could only have been a few minutes. He thrashed in the chair and fought for breath. Bloody mucous dribbled from his nostrils. Then he shuddered and grew still. It was over. His whole body relaxed. He sprawled in the chair, limp.

The nurse quietly removed his catheter and disappeared. I knelt beside his body. Tears washed my cheeks. Mother brought a chair from the dining table. She offered me a handful of tissues. I dabbed at my eyes. Oblivious to the rest of the world, I sat beside Craig. With a trembling hand, I reached the tissue upward and tenderly wiped the drips of blood from the tip of his nose. I gently stroked his cheek with the back of my hand.

Beloved face that I will never see again as long as I live. I dabbed more of the bloody drips from his nose. Then I reached to my face and mopped my tears with the same tissue.

I lifted his right hand and squeezed it. His fingernails already held a bluish tint. The skin paled. *Beloved hand that I will never hold again as long as I live.*

And I wept. I dabbed at my cheeks and I dabbed at Craig's nose. I sat beside my husband, the best friend I'd ever had, and held his hand for the very last time. And his blood, the blood of my angel, mingled with my tears in a lingering farewell.

Part III
Forty Days in the Wilderness

"Keep close to Nature's heart, yourself, and break clear away, once in a while, and climb a mountain or spend a week in the woods. Wash your spirit clean..."
John Muir

The Farm

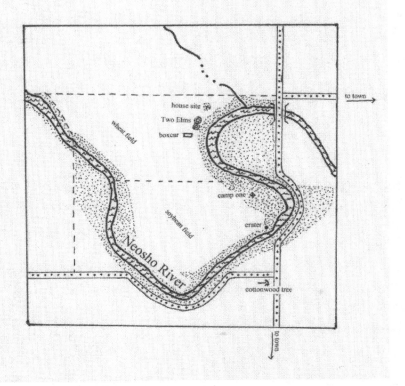

21
THE DUST OF DEATH

"My pain is like a river of tears, so full it fills up the four oceans."

Thich Nhat Hanh

I pulled the bright Mexican shawl tightly around my shoulders. It took the edge off the bitter breeze that played in my hair. A gift from Craig long ago, the shawl reminded me of his devotion. Born on a wave of grief, I stumbled to the tent erected over the gravesite. A crowd of friends and family surrounded me.

Adjacent to a country Lutheran Church, the small cemetery overlooked the farm of his maternal grandparents. Since that farm and his grandfather had provided Craig's first love of nature and a home for his heart, this location seemed right for him in many ways.

I collapsed on a chair reserved for me. Phoebe was handed down over my shoulder, bundled warmly in a snow suit. I drew her into my arms and wrapped the warm shawl around both of us. Tugging an edge of it over my head, I bent forward to hide from the crowd. The two of us sank into our own bleak and lonely universe.

I glanced up as the eulogy was spoken, though I didn't hear the pastor's words. A heavy sailing rope encircled the basswood casket crafted by my father. A massive spray of flowers adorned its simple, dignified lid.

Words floated to me on the wind as if they originated a great distance away. They held little meaning. I fixed my gaze on the casket which held the body of the love of my life. I tried to visualize him inside, relaxed and peaceful, his smooth cherub cheeks soft and cool in his sleep of death.

Then his eyes opened. He gazed in confusion at the dark surroundings. He raised his right hand to push tentatively at the lid. When it didn't budge, he pushed harder and began to claw at the satin sheet. "Help," he squeaked, very softly at first. Then, louder, "Help me, Ann! Help! Help!"

I woke with a start in the darkness of our bedroom, the horrific image lingering in my mind. Heart racing, I flung myself up to run to his aid. But there was nowhere to go. I sank back to the bed and sobbed.

When would the nightmares cease? I knew Craig had died. I was there. I knew we hadn't buried him alive. Yet I couldn't shake the notion I'd failed him when he needed my help the most, when there was nobody else left to help.

I glanced at the clock. It was half past five and still dark. I recalled the date. The eleventh day of February. This was the second anniversary of our son's birth. And death. In the darkness, a new wave of remorse swept over me. Preoccupied with Craig for months, I'd not given our two lost children more than a passing thought.

"I forgot you," I whispered. "How could that be? How could I forget my own children? Why did all this have to happen?" I slid to the floor and sobbed.

The dream where Craig woke confused and frightened in his casket recurred often in my long nights.

It was as if he was calling for my help from beyond the grave. With no other recourse, I began a flurry of church-related activities. When an event at my church was scheduled, I was there. Outwardly, I sought to become a model of piety. Inwardly, my heart ached with grief. I found myself questioning the existence of God. But in order to take care of Craig now, he needed God. My whirlwind of activity at this point became a ridiculous attempt to insure there was a supreme being, that Craig would be fine. And just in case there wasn't, I would make a god by my actions.

Gradually this notion became a folly in my mind. It was absurd to think I could create God. I cut back on the church activities and fell into a weekly attendance pattern, drifting further away. One day blended with another. Every time I passed the photos of our happy little family on the day when Phoebe came to us, I caressed the smiling faces. If only we could return to that day and start again. If only I could stop the forward march of time and turn the clock backward.

Time, however, proceeded forward, minute by lonely minute. In defiance, I stopped all my clocks and hid my calendars. I sought to lose myself in unmeasured time by selecting each day's most memorable event to identify entries in my journal. The "Day of Phoebe's First Birthday Party" came and went with a bittersweet celebration. Grandparents and neighbors arrived for cake and ice cream. But Daddy was absent.

Winter ended not on March 21, but on the "Day Daisy was Challenged by a Coyote Crossing our Brome Pasture."

The "Day I Found the First Asparagus Spear" shooting up toward the sun was the day I decided

Phoebe and I should take a vacation together. In my mind, our little honeymoon would cement my commitment to her. I packed her up. We flew to Kauai for a week in our symbolic renewal as a family of two.

When we returned, I was convinced that I needed an extended retreat to find myself and my purpose in life without Craig. We headed to Hays for a visit with my parents and with Marvin.

"My life is a big question mark, Marvin," I said to him. I slouched in a flowered wing-back chair in his living room.

"Uncertainly prevails," he said.

I nodded. "What do I do now? How long will it be before I can grieve for Craig, my husband and friend?"

"Craig, the man."

"Right now, I feel relief that his suffering is over. But I don't want to remember him as the helpless, confused shell of a person he became. How do I deal with this?"

"Give it time, Annie."

"Time. That resource which ran out on Craig. How much time? Hours? Days? Months? How long do I cower under the specter of a grim future? It weighs so heavily on my shoulders. Will there ever be joy again?"

"You'll find it. I'm certain."

"Right now, the fates are winning. I'm a little bird, trembling with fear in a storm. Craig once told me how a bird has to face the wind and leap into it in order to fly. The winds of my life have been like a tornado. And Craig was my rock, my shelter. Now he's gone and all I can do is hang on for dear life. I don't have the strength to jump into the wind."

"You will. You may not think so now, but you'll find your way. Have you been writing any poetry? Your metaphors sound ripe with meaning."

"I can't write, Marvin. I don't know where to begin."

"I recall a few times in my life where I felt drained and without direction. Try doing some purposeful relaxing, deep breathing. Let the tension drain from your mind."

"Meditation."

"Yes. It helped me."

I sighed. "I'm almost afraid to relax. I have these nightmares almost every night. I dream about Craig—that we buried him alive and he wakes up, confused and alone, calling for me. And I'm not there."

"Annie, I really believe that it helps to talk with someone who understands feelings or aspects of grief that hurt and don't go away. Loss and grief are possibly the hardest emotional struggles we go through."

"Counseling?"

"Think about it. A counselor, a minister."

I smiled weakly and leaned forward to tap Marvin's hand. "Talking to you helps. You can be my counselor. I do need to find a way forward."

"Remember the essay you showed me? 'Corners.' Events in life cause you to round a corner and head in a new direction until you complete a circuit and come back to the point of origin, completely defined. You have turned another corner in your polygon of life. Are you starting to feel defined?" Marvin asked.

"I guess you could say that," I said. "But that analogy seems flat to me now for some reason."

"Are you suggesting that life has more than two dimensions?"

"Don't you think it does? There is a depth to life also."

Marvin nodded, but he said nothing.

I continued, "When I was a geology student, one class we had to take was mineralogy. Minerals are classified in several groups of crystalline structures. Their basic components give each mineral a capacity to grow into three-dimensional crystals."

"Like diamonds?"

"Yes," I said. "Or rubies, or emeralds, or amethysts. Under the proper conditions, many minerals become beautiful gemstones."

"And you think that life is more like a gemstone than a hexagon or an octagon?"

"Possibly. Maybe each of us is born a rough gem. As we get older and experience life, we end up polishing one facet of our diamond-in-the-rough, so to speak."

"I see where you're going," Marvin said. "Life is a process of gaining experience and wisdom."

"It's more than just turning corners. Sometimes it's hard work. The stone can be very rough and have many faces. Before we die, we need to polish all of them."

"You'll end up with a thing of beauty before you die," Marvin said.

"And just like there are many different minerals with countless variations, our rough stones all carry different potential. But in the end they can sparkle with our polishing efforts."

"I like that analogy. I think life is more than a flat experience."

"The way I see it, I've got some work to do now, polishing several facets of rough grief."

"Do you have a plan?"

"Of sorts."

"What do you have in mind?"

"I think I need a retreat."

"A retreat." He pondered the idea.

"Forty days in the wilderness like Jesus when he turned thirty. You know how Craig and I bonded through nature. I've always felt comforted by the wild side of life—the beauty of a sunset, wind blowing in my hair."

"You do love nature," Marvin said. "I remember. And I remember the sunsets we chased a few summers ago."

"Don't you see how this would be right for me?"

"Yes, I can see where you'd think that. But to isolate yourself at this time in your life might have repercussions you don't expect. Many people need the companionship of others to help the healing process."

"I've thought about that. I also think that every loss is different and means something different to every survivor. There are probably as many ways to grieve as there are people grieving. And as many ways to heal. Don't you agree?"

Marvin said nothing.

"I really need you to understand," I said. "I think someone or something is telling me to do this. The timing is impeccable."

"I can agree that everyone is likely to experience grief differently. But that won't stop me from worrying about you."

"Noted, Marvin. But everyone has to find their own way and this is mine."

"I enjoy talking to you, too. But don't discount the guidance a trained professional has to offer. Many people seek professional counseling when events in life overwhelm them," Marvin said.

"That may be what they need. But I think we all need to follow the direction our hearts lead us. I'll soon be thirty. After my birthday, I'll follow Jesus into the wilderness. I have a hunch he found more there than we know."

"Sounds like you've given this a lot of thought."

"Perhaps. I found mention in forty different Bible verses of Jesus heading off into nature, away from people. That's one verse for every day in my retreat. I think he found God in nature, as I have in the past."

"Forty days in the wilderness. What will you do with Phoebe?"

"I need to figure that out. Guess I'll go talk to my dad."

From Marvin's, I walked two blocks to the campus and headed toward Albertson Hall on the far side of the picturesque square. As I walked, I considered my forty-day plan. Where should I take this retreat? Colorado was a possibility. I had always loved the mountains in our neighboring state. Alaska presented another option. I had fallen in love with the forty-ninth state during a visit there fifteen summers previously.

Somehow, neither of these options felt right as I considered them now.

There was the land which belonged to our family. With the Neosho River running through it, a native forest beckoned in my own backyard. It was every bit as isolated as any national forest area further west. And I knew it better. At various times throughout my childhood, I'd helped my grandmother or my father pick nettles for a green vegetable. We'd harvested wild grapes and made jelly. We'd picked small white peaches from a wild fruit tree, and once or twice, my dad helped me locate the ripe fruit of small pawpaw trees that grew in the timber.

"Pickin' up pawpaws and puttin' em in my pocket," he'd sung as we scavenged.

I knew I could find wild food on the Farm.

I recalled a story my grandmother once told me, about the call of the Farm to the hearts of our family members.

"The last time Lester was home from the Navy," she'd said, "he sat on the porch and just looked and looked. Then just before Charley entered the hospital and died, there was a time when he just sat and looked and looked. It was almost as if they knew they'd never see the Farm again and they couldn't get enough of it."

The land had called to them and it was calling to me now. I had not grown up on the Farm, like my father and his father before him, but I felt that somehow, if I headed to the woods on our family's land, I would re-connect with their hearts. It made sense to return to my roots. From them I could find my new path. My wilderness destination would be the Farm, which now belonged to my father.

A few minutes later, I tapped lightly on his office door and peeked around the corner. He sat at his desk, writing notes for his next lecture in soils class. "Well, hello," he said when he saw me. "What have you been up to?"

"Just talked to Marvin," I said.

"How is he?"

"He's amazing. He has this way of making me feel like my life matters. While I was there I kind of fleshed out an idea I've been pondering."

"What's that?"

"My plan to search for a direction in my life. The thing is, I would be away from Phoebe for several weeks. And it has to happen soon. This summer is the only time in my life when I could do it."

"Then do it. I have great faith in your ideas."

"Don't you even want to know what it is?"

He raised his hands, palms up. "Just do it."

"What about Phoebe?"

"We'll help with her. I'm sure there are others who'll lend a hand. She's a good little tyke. Hardly ever cries."

I smiled. "She is amazing, isn't she? Kind of independent though. Gets into everything."

Dad chuckled. "That's a toddler for you."

There was a moment of silence. Our eyes met and the warmth of a father's love passed from him to me. "You do what you need to do," he said again.

22
FAREWELL ADVICE

*"We are Nature, long have we been absent,
but now we return."*

Walt Whitman

"Maaaa—maaa." Phoebe's familiar voice woke me from a light sleep. I rolled out of the twin bed across the small bedroom from her toddler bed. I lifted my fifteen-month old daughter and gave her a squeeze. We groped our way in the dim light to a rocking chair in my sister's living room.

We cuddled together, rocking back and forth. I hummed quietly to calm her. In minutes, she slept again. I tucked her back into bed, drew the covers up around her chin, and leaned over to kiss her forehead. I couldn't go back to sleep.

This day would be the first day of my forty-day quest. After an early breakfast with my sister Kay and her husband, I packed my overnight items into my Plymouth Horizon. Daisy pranced around the car, eager to begin our adventure. I peeked one last time at Phoebe. I smoothed an unruly curl of black hair on her forehead while she slept. She didn't stir. I tiptoed toward the car.

"Here—you might want this." Kay handed me the toothbrush I'd left in the bathroom.

"Thanks. I hope I haven't forgotten anything else."

We hugged in farewell before I drove onto the county road. Daisy settled onto her special seat to watch the scenery. Drizzle smattered the windshield as we headed north and west toward the Farm of my father's childhood. The rain stopped before we reached Emporia. A few minutes later, I pulled into the driveway of my parents' retirement home. They stirred under their towering oak trees, cleaning up after the rain. Daisy and I headed to their lush vegetable garden.

"Headed to the Farm?" my dad asked.

I nodded.

Mother asked about Phoebe.

"She was still asleep when I left."

"Have you thought what you'll do for drinking water?" Dad asked. "I doubt the old well can be used."

"I brought a couple gallons from home in jugs. I figure I'll head to town for a re-fill when I get low."

He nodded. "In a pinch you might be able to get some spring water. When I was in boy scouts, we'd look for a damp spot above the river. After digging a hole in that spot, it would eventually seep full with spring water."

"I'll keep that in mind."

After hugs all around, Daisy and I drove into the nearby town of Americus. We found my grandmother sitting in her wing-back chair. She combed her long white hair to re-braid and pin over the top of her head, a daily morning ritual.

"Now, what you doing?" She chuckled when I peeked in the front door.

"I'm going up to the Farm. Going to spend some time there."

"I heard you was going to camp in the timber a while."

"Yep."

"Well, just watch the river. If it starts coming up, you high tail it out of there."

Grandma Georgia had lived through two floods and a tornado in her decades on the Farm. Twenty years previously, she'd had the house moved to a lot in town. Nobody had lived at the Farm since. "Okay, Grandma. I may stop by from time to time."

"I'll be here. I don't expect to go no wheres."

"Tell me the story again."

"What story?"

"About Smoky and the flood."

She laughed. "You want a story?"

"I love the stories you tell."

"Well, it was the summer of fifty-one. Maybe fifty-two. No, I think it was fifty-one. We'd had lots of rain, almost fifteen inches in one day, I think 'twas. The river was out of the banks and got into the barns and the house. When the rain stopped, we had us a chore."

"Mama—Mama! Your chickens!" Paul hollered as he dashed into the farm house.

"What is it, Paul?" I asked.

"They're floating away down the river."

Sure enough, several piles of soggy feathers drifted by on the flood waters. Some of the layin' hens flapped against the current. Others were already limp and lifeless as they disappeared into the trees on the riverbank.

"We can't do anything for them, Paul. Just let 'em go," I says.

"But Mama, they're fixin' to drown."

"Some already have, I 'spect. Now grab that broom and help me sweep the water out of here."

Paul helped me swoosh water towards the doors. Charley couldn't do much as he got winded easy. By dusk, most of the water was out of the house. We tramped around in our boots to check all the corners.

"I guess that 'bout does it," I says. "Think we can turn out the fryers yet? Why don't you check the yard."

Paul peeked out the kitchen door and went out onto the stoop. "Maybe. The water's still goin' down." He glanced at the sky when more thunder rumbled. "I'm so sick of rain. Looks like more's a-coming."

"Guess we can leave the fryers in the closet overnight," I says. "Help me get the beds spread now so we can turn in."

After dark the wall telephone rang. Five long rings meant there was an emergency and all parties should pick up. I rolled out of bed and stumbled to the telephone. All the neighbors had already picked up. "What? What is it? The dam? Oh, my! Charley—Paul, the dam at Council Grove broke! Another flood wave is comin' our way. Be here in 'bout twelve hours!"

At first light, we's up. We roll the mattresses and stuff them onto the tops of the wardrobes. We gather as many small things as we can and head up the ladder to the attic.

"Bring the little dog, Paul," Charley says.

"What about Smoky?"

"Smoky can come in the house. But he's too big to carry up the ladder."

"Get the photo albums. Your school work. A radio. A clock. I'll fix some lunch for us," I says.

In the Shadow of the Wind | **215**

We move around the house, making sure everything is on the table or counter top. The kitchen cupboards are stuffed full. I slap some sandwiches together from the last of the bread I baked two days before. Charley helps as much as he can. I finally tell him to go on up the ladder to the attic, and wait for Paul and me there.

"I might try to go get a load of cobs so we know we have some dry fuel for cooking," I says. I head toward the barn where we store corncobs and firewood. It's slow-going. I slog through the mud and water left from the day before. Before I can get back, a wave of water three feet high swells over the ridge to the north of the house.

"Hurry, Mama! The water's coming!" Paul yells to me.

I take one look, drop the cobs and lunge for the house, a-slipping and a-sliding all the way there. Paul and I cling to the attic ladder and watch the water rise. It flows under the doors and seeps in through the windows. "Get on up there, Paul!" I says.

By noon, the rushing sound of water below dies down. I get out the sandwiches and as we eat, Smoky starts howlin'. He makes such a ruckus, I says, "You better go see what's wrong with Smoky, Paul."

Paul's gone a long time. Charley and I hear him sloshing and half-swimming through the water below in the front room. Finally, his head pops through the attic opening. Smoky howls in the background.

"What's up, Paul?" Charley says.

"Smoky's all right. He's down there, sittin' on your bare bed springs, just a-howlin' away."

Her story done, Grandma Georgia chuckled. I laughed with her.

"You going to look for some arrowheads?" she asked.

"Might. I'd sure like to find one. Where was that Indian village exactly?"

"You know that low rise due west of where my house used to be? In the valley beyond the rise is the best place to look. I think it's where their lodge was."

"I'll check it out."

After a farewell hug, I headed to my waiting car.

"Remember to watch the weather, now," she called as I backed out of her driveway.

23
FUGITIVE AND VAGABOND

I am a fugitive and a vagabond,
a sojourner seeking signs.
I cannot cause light; the most I can do is try
to put myself in the path of its beam.

Annie Dillard

Roughly parallel to the Neosho River, the gravel county road led along a twisting, diagonal path for seven miles. We arrived at the elm tree that marked the entrance to the Harris homestead. I drove slowly along the dirt track and parked around the bend, out of sight of any passersby. The Two Elms which we dreamed would shelter our wedding ceremony nearly eight years ago beckoned with a friendly shade. A railroad boxcar sprouted in the middle of a wheat field fifty yards west of the elms. The only structure left on the homestead place, it had been brought in years before by my grandfather when the local branch of the Katy rail line had closed and sold its surplus equipment. The boxcar now stored items for several family members.

"Here we are, Daisy Pup." She bounded out and raced to the nearby wheat, snuffling busily. I surveyed the loaded car and set our camp supplies on the ground. The tent and ground cloth, sleeping bag, foam pad, handmade velour comforter given to Craig by a couple of

Mennonite friends, half a dozen water-filled canteens, an empty bucket, a backpack of spare clothing, the Peterson *Field Guide to Edible Wild Plants,* binoculars, writing journal, camera and accessories, camp stove, fuel and matches, and a pack of emergency food items would go to the camp.

Additional clothing, towels, extra food supplies, two plastic gallon jugs of water and a botanist's plant press would stay with the car. Using two of my half-dozen army surplus straps, I tied the sleeping gear to my backpack and hoisted it to my shoulders. I clipped the canteens to my belt. My Olympus camera hung around my neck. I picked up the tent and staggered a step or two away from the car.

I briefly considered dividing the camp supplies and making two trips from the car to the campsite. "Nah. I can do this. Come on, Daisy."

We proceeded slowly along the farm road that paralleled the river's edge. We passed the wash which held the rusting remains of a discarded piano. A second wash held my Uncle Paul's old car and a couple of household appliances. I knew these items were strategically placed to slow the process of top soil washing into the river, but they seemed an unnatural intrusion into my wild acres.

At the end of the half-mile road, the river curved eastward. The field acreage swept after it. The wheat field broadened into a wider stand of new soybean sprouts. I followed the rows of beans to the eastern edge where the timbered area extended in a thinner stand with ample space between trees.

Grandma Georgia once told me she'd discovered a circular disturbance of fresh earth when she walked the timber in this area years ago. "It looked like God had just reached down and pulled up a tree by the roots," she said. She figured it could be the site of a fallen meteorite. Somewhere in these trees I hoped to pitch my tent beside the cup-shaped depression framed by a low mound of black soil.

Before I found the meteorite site, I found a small clearing near a narrow path.

"Look at that, Daisy, a deer path. This could be a good camp site. Maybe we'll get lucky and see some wildlife."

I stomped the undergrowth in a twelve-foot circle and laid out the tent's ground cloth. I staked and raised the little orange tent. The door faced east, toward the deer path. I spread the sleeping bag inside and left the extra clothing in a corner. Then I looped a couple straps together and tossed one end over a low branch to hang my food container near the tent.

Camp One

The sun finally peeked through the clouds and the air warmed. I shed my long-sleeve shirt, turned the bucket upside-down, and sat for a moment at the edge of my camp clearing. The orange tent issued an invitation, but it held bittersweet memories. Visions of backpacking trips, honeymoon nights, and a camping trip on the rim of the Grand Canyon floated through my mind. The tent had accompanied me on many adventures. Without Craig, it felt hollow and desolate.

"Come on, Daisy, let's go."

I swung my day pack to my shoulders. We retraced our three-quarter mile hike to the car and drove toward town.

Five miles up the road, I parked the car behind a shed at the home of a family friend. A loaded mulberry tree hung over us. For thirty minutes I picked mulberries while Daisy explored. After I tied the bag of berries to my backpack, we set out on foot north and west, back to camp. To preserve my solitude, I shied away from the road. We trekked along the edge of the trees that followed the river's meanders. The winding course easily added a mile to the five-mile trail.

After an hour, we encountered the first of three eroded draws. A well-established side stream blocked our direct path along the river bank. Twelve feet separated us from the other side. Water ran in the bottom of the draw. I had no idea what the depth of the creek was. Daisy jumped in. She soon swam, so I knew it was deeper than she was tall. If I waded across my things could get soaked.

I headed up the stream. The draw narrowed within a couple hundred yards. A few yards further, a tree branch hung over the muddy trickle in the draw. At the edge of the draw I took one sideways step downward. In spite of the waffle tread on my boots, I slid one long muddy track to the trickle of water.

"Whooaa!" I threw my arms out for balance and bent my knees. My rump glanced along the muddy bank. Wet muck soaked through the jeans.

Straightening, I sprang forward to cross the narrow creek. Grabbing hold of a tree anchored on the other side, I pulled myself up to the field.

"I made it, girl," I said, stomping to dislodge some of the loose mud on my boots. With a stick, I scraped mud from my backside. We moved on.

A little later, the timbered area along the river broadened into a park. We stepped into the woods and found the river's edge. A fire pit, a weathered picnic table and a crude tree house presented idyllic images of happy family outings. In my mind, I heard a child's voice and saw a happy family out for a Sunday picnic. They could have been Phoebe, Craig, and me in another life. Thoughts of my happy-go-lucky toddler put a sad smile on my face. "What do you suppose Phoebe's doing right now, Daisy? I wonder if she's down for a nap. I bet she'd really like this playhouse."

Several logs surrounded the fire pit. I sat for a few moments to enjoy the private park. Daisy plopped at my feet. I briefly considered the possibility of crafting a raft for a river float trip during my sojourn.

I began to feel buggy. Something crawled on my neck. I reached up and removed a tick. "Hello? What have we here?"

I unsheathed the hunting knife and squashed the little blood sucker with the sharp tip of the knife. "So there," I said to the small carcass on the log next to me.

"Wait, what's this?" A second tick navigated my left forearm. "Time to go, Daisy." She bounded from her resting place before I could straighten my legs.

The next draw we came to was much deeper and wider than the first, a regular tributary stream. We followed its banks searching for a way to cross. At length, we came to a fallen tree which spanned the width of the stream. Other debris piled against the larger tree. The whole mass of tangled limbs offered a bridge. I stepped out on the trunk and tested each foothold before transferring my weight. Step by step I moved across the draw.

Daisy decided to swim this one too but the current swept her downstream as she approached the center. She paddled frantically as she neared the broader and deeper Neosho.

My heart pounded. I imagined her overwhelmed by the current, unable to get across. "Come on, Daisy—you can do it," I called. Her white snout and brown ears bobbed downstream as she paddled faster. The current slowed at a small curve. She broke free from its hold. She bounded to the top of the opposite bank in two leaps and shook. River water sprayed around her.

We trudged onwards. In mid-afternoon we saw the old farm house across the road from the entrance to the Farm. "We made it, Daisy."

Along the lane, a broken tree at the edge of the timber moved with slow swells, in and out as if it was breathing. I stepped toward it for a closer look. Dozens of tan butterflies clung to the tree's rough bark. They slowly flexed their wings. The tree came alive with the bark of waving wings.

Hackberry emperor butterflies

Back at the campsite, I added the mulberries to my food items and deposited the backpack in the tent. The dried mud stiffened my jeans. I decided to rinse them. I grabbed a couple of the green army straps, a change of clothes, and my bucket. We headed to the river's edge near a large sycamore tree that leaned over the water. I removed my boots and socks, looped the knotted straps around the tree, and wrapped the straps around my hands. Backing away from the anchoring tree, I lowered myself ten feet to the water's edge.

I hadn't seen a living soul since I left my Grandmother earlier in the day. I slipped out of the muddy jeans, t-shirt, and my underwear, and piled the clothing on a piece of driftwood. Though alone, I felt uneasy, as if some hidden eyes watched me. I looked over my shoulders. Still nobody. A ray of sunshine broke through the forest and I stood naked in the sun for the first time in my life.

I closed my eyes. Slowly, my uneasiness disappeared. I became less self-conscious and felt confident that no judging eyes would find me here. The sun imparted friendly warmth. United in spirit with God's natural world, I felt at peace.

A few moments later I opened my eyes, tightened my grip on the straps and stepped into the river. With the straps in my hands, I felt secure. I could pull myself to shore if the current proved strong. The bank sloped steeply toward the middle of the river so that five feet from the water's edge, I floated. Only my head remained above the surface. The frigid water took my breath away and I was instantly refreshed.

Allowing my legs to float in the current, I kicked and splashed for a few seconds. When the cold numbed my feet I pulled myself from the river. I stood barefoot on the driftwood and rinsed the mud from my jeans. I wrung them out and draped them over a tree branch higher on the bank.

I tied a strap to the bucket handle and cast it into the river. After it sank, I tugged the bucket toward my feet and pulled it from the water. A sunbeam blazed in the green undergrowth of the timber. I pulled myself upwards away from the river's edge until I could stagger barefoot toward the inviting stream of light. I stood in the sun to dry. A pair of beetles traversed the leaf litter on the ground. They crawled up and over my big toe, without straying from their path. I stood tree still. The insect feet tickled as they crossed my toe and moved back to the forest floor.

"Hey, little bugs. I wonder if you have ever met a human before? Were you impressed?"

I felt awed to think that billions of creatures lived their entire lives without ever encountering a human being. Within the universe, I remained an insignificant speck. I hardly mattered in the larger scheme of things. The thought humbled me. I hoped to represent humanity favorably in the natural world during the next few weeks.

Dressed in fresh clothes, I gathered the straps, the rinsed clothes, and the bucket of water. Daisy and I headed back to camp where I fed her a cup of dog food. While she ate, I filled my bowl with mulberries for my evening meal.

The breeze grew still as the sun settled on the western horizon. When mosquitoes appeared, we retreated to the tent. I stretched out on the sleeping mat and watched the deer path until the evening light dimmed and the undergrowth became too dark to see. We saw no deer that day.

The loneliness of the day weighed heavily on my heart. With darkness, doubts entered my resolve. For months now, my evenings had been times of intense loneliness. Nighttime often ushered in nightmares. Doubts about my forty-day plan assaulted my awareness. My conviction wavered, already, after just one day.

"I am a fool, Daisy." I drew the dog closer to my chest. "Craig, I miss you so much. My rock. My shelter. My leader. My friend. I don't know if I can do this."

I was a helpless little bird. The winds of my life had been a gale for the last few years, a series of whirling events that uprooted any and all shelter I could find. I didn't exactly fly here. I was blown on a tornado and deposited in a completely new and strange life. My Oz. How would I face the winds of my life? How would I turn myself around and leap into the wind to take flight? How would I find my way home again?

"I haven't the strength."

I heard birds, insects, and a squirrel. They chattered and sang into the evening hours. It mattered not at all to my wild neighbors whether anyone was around to hear them, but they sang their unique songs regardless. The thought intensified my loneliness. Though I followed my own heart into this sojourn, I felt abandoned. Nobody knew where I was. Did they even care? Did I want them to? Or did it even matter? "We are all alone in this world after all, aren't we? In spite of what we may think, we all travel the road alone."

Craig had finished his road alone. My future belonged only to me. What I had not realized before was that we were alone even when we had each other.

"I can't stand it. I will end up crazy after forty nights like this," I said to no one.

Gradually the chorus in the nearby trees became still. There was no sound, only ominous silence. Sinister and primeval, total darkness descended in the moonless night. Daisy slept soundly beside me, and I wrestled alone with my musings. I silently recited the prayer of St. Francis and added my own plea.

Lord, make me an instrument.
If it be Your will, use me as Your pen.
Make my mind like a blank piece of paper
And write upon it Your truths and Your wisdom.
Lord, make me Your instrument.

Show me the way, God.
Show me how to live the rest of my life.
Show me how to fly.

24
ONE WITH THE LIGHT

At night make me one with the darkness.
In the morning make me one with the light.

Wendell Berry

Would this night never end? The stillness of nighttime on the river bank screamed in my ears. No sound tickled my eardrums. I tossed.

"Maaa—Maaa," Phoebe's young voice cried.

Awakening from a light sleep, I listened intently. Nothing. I kicked inside the sleeping bag, rolled over and returned to a light sleep.

"Ann, help me!" Craig called.

My eyes popped open again to utter darkness. I squeezed my eyelids shut, as if that would stem the flow of waiting tears. If only I could control the dreams and hasten the return of daylight. I drifted off to sleep.

My maternal grandmother held two infants, one in each arm. She smiled at me from a long flight of stairs that ended in a fluffy cumulus cloud. My own arms felt heavy, weighed down by emptiness and all of the world's injustice. My shoulders ached with excruciating tension.

Once again, I woke in the darkness.

Was every night going to be like this? How could I make it through the next thirty-nine days?

Daisy stirred next to me. I rolled over, scratched her familiar soft fur, and pulled her toward my heart. We cuddled together and she eased the ache of my latest nightmare. I heard nothing except her breathing and my own blood rushing through my vessels. I dozed again.

The next time I woke, the tent was filled with a dim light that signaled the approach of dawn. As the sky brightened, creatures of the forest stirred. A limb snapped in a tree south of my tent. I heard another snap. The rustlings of my wild neighbors came from every direction.

The unmistakable sound of something crunching dog food came from just inches outside the tent. Daisy perked up her ears and growled softly. I twisted by inches until I could peek out the door of the tent. A raccoon sat at the dog dish, eating Daisy's leftovers. He brought fistfuls of the hard kernels to his mouth while his eyes behind the mask darted back and forth.

Daisy barked. The raccoon grabbed a chunk in each forepaw and ambled casually away.

Songbirds awakened. They called bright greetings to each other. The whine of a mosquito joined the day's symphony. Another mosquito hummed, and then a third. Soon the air buzzed with insect tones. Each whined in a different pitch. I opened my eyes and looked to see if there were any mosquitoes inside the tent. One fluttered against the roof. I reached up to swat it. It was outside, but its shadow played on the surface above me.

Daylight crescendoed steadily. Though no mosquitoes entered the tent, hundreds whined in the outside air. Their miniscule shadows bombarded the roof of my nylon tent adding tiny pops to the morning chorus.

"They must be hungry, Daisy. I don't want to get up."

With the whole timber awake, a ray of sunshine broke through the forest canopy and found my tent. The air inside warmed and I threw off the covers. Daisy whined and squirmed.

"You need to go outside, girl?"

She jumped up and pranced on my outstretched legs, her stumpy tail wagging fiercely.

"I get it. Me too. It's time to get up, I guess." I unzipped the lower edge of the door. Daisy shot outside. I crawled onto the flattened plants at the tent door, stood, and stretched. As the sun rose in the sky, a little breeze played through the trees. Fortunately the mosquitoes retreated with the arrival of the sunshine. The night was over and a bright day stretched before me. I turned to the supply bag suspended from the tree limb east of my tent. After serving up a new portion of dog food for Daisy's breakfast, I headed for the bag of mulberries hanging at the rear of the tent. It wasn't there.

Bits of the ripped bag fluttered across the ground. Yesterday's berry harvest was gone.

"Damn raccoon." My heart sank. I resisted the urge to break open my emergency rations. There would be no breakfast for me until I found something to eat.

I crawled halfway inside the tent and grabbed my boots and daypack. Sitting cross-legged on the mashed plants, I pulled on the boots, and winced as pressure returned to yesterday's blister. I glanced into the pack. Edible plant guide? Check. Hairbrush? Check. I grabbed the brush and ran it through my long hair, quickly parted the locks and wove two long braids.

"Come, Daisy. Let's go see what the Neosho River Pantry has to offer this morning."

With a vague notion that I might easily find another mulberry tree, a ditch full of cattails or a stand of some edible greens, I headed deeper into the woods. We angled south roughly parallel to the river bank. I waded through knee-deep brambles, watching for edible plants that I could identify with confidence. Ten minutes later, I circled westward toward the edge of the cultivated field. The border area between timber and soybeans was thick with undergrowth. I plowed through it and jumped to the cultivated furrows of young plants, heading north.

I scanned the edge of the timber, but breakfast eluded me. I turned a complete circle, searching further. My gaze was drawn to a shrub a hundred yards north along the edge of the timber that stretched east and west. Its branches bowed under thick clusters of brilliant white blossoms.

"Elderberry?" I trotted toward the blooming bush. When I reached the shrub, I pulled the field guide from my pack and confirmed the plant's identity. The profuse white blossoms grew in huge clusters. Twisting the stems, I broke a dozen of the flower clusters and dropped them into a collecting bag.

"Flowers for breakfast, I guess, Daisy." We headed toward camp. When I spotted the orange tent, I was thigh-deep in a dark green patch of a single plant variety. Elongating stems bore slender, deeply grooved leaves that grew opposite each other. My finger tips brushed the tops of the greenery as I walked. A sting shot through my left index finger. I quickly glanced at the injury. No visible stinger. I rubbed it and the sting abated.

"Well what do you know? Nettles."

Grandma Georgia had served early spring nettles when the timber awoke after a long winter. This was nearly summer, though. The plants likely had grown tough. Maybe the leading tips of new growth would still be tender enough to fix as greens. I decided to find out.

"Where are my gloves?" I slipped the pack to the forest floor and rummaged carefully inside until I found my leather gloves. I pulled the knife from its holster on my belt. The honed edge of the Buck knife sliced easily through the nettle stems. I harvested a bag of the top six inches of all the plants within arm's reach.

"Flowers and nettles for breakfast, Daisy. Let's head to camp."

By the time I had water boiling in a pan over my camp stove, my hunger had intensified to sharp pangs and I felt a little light-headed. I threw a scoop of instant mashed potatoes into my bowl, stripped a cluster of elderberry blossoms into the steaming mixture and stirred. The flowers turned brown, but tasted pleasant mixed with the potatoes. I stuffed a handful of the nettles into the pan of boiling water and ate the elderberry mixture while the nettles cooked. The process of cooking destroyed the stinging quality of the plant and left mild-tasting, nutritious spring greens.

With the sharpness of my hunger satisfied, I cleaned the dishes and returned them to the hanging bag of supplies. I whistled for Daisy. She bounded toward me from a small tree east of camp where she had treed a scolding squirrel. "Let's go for a walk, girl. See if we can find some cattails." I shouldered the pack and we headed toward the field of soybean sprouts again.

Following the edge of the timber, we passed the Two Elms at the home site and headed east along the driveway to the county road. An old bridge spanned the river at the end of the driveway. My grandfather had lobbied hard to locate it here in order to shorten the journey to a small patch of the homestead which fell west, across the river. As a result of his insistence, the bridge was named for our family.

Daisy trotted south, across the bridge. I followed to the midpoint and stopped to look over the concrete rail. The muddy Neosho churned below. Twigs and scattered debris floated eastward in the current.

"Find a damp spot above the river and dig a hole for water?" I voiced the advice of my father regarding a safe water supply. I shook my head. "The entire river bank looks wet. I wonder what he meant?"

We proceeded southward along the county road. Twice we met vehicles, a car and a pickup truck. I waved at their human occupants, but they either ignored me or just stared. "Do I look muddy or something? Like I just crawled out of the river?" I brushed my pant legs and ran my fingers over my cheeks and hair braids. "Maybe I should have brought a mirror."

I suddenly felt very conspicuous and quickened my steps along the road. Locating cattails comprised my morning mission, and I had yet to discover any in the roadside ditches. About a mile south, the river curved broadly eastward and the road followed. When it straightened again, a crossroad intersected the tree-lined road. I turned west and followed the road along the river's meanders. The forest gave way to open ground and more farm land.

Then I met the fallen cottonwood tree. *"Look what they did to me,"* it screamed silently as I drew near. A jumble of limbs lay in a huge mound surrounding the severed trunk of a once-stately tree. Bare ground, churned by massive tires, surrounded the debris in a hundred-foot radius.

The tree was doomed. And yet, it wasn't dead. Fresh green shoots erupted from the trunk and a couple of the larger branches. All the branches lay on the ground. From them, new leaves stretched skyward toward the sunlight. These shoots had sprouted after the tree fell.

I walked completely around the fallen tree twice while Daisy snuffled after small creatures. I sat on a large limb and soaked up the sun while a little breeze stirred the stillness of the June morning. The new cottonwood leaves twisted on their arcing stems. They danced in the morning sunlight. Their serrated edges caught each other and created a rustling song, the unmistakable music of a cottonwood tree. I closed my eyes to listen.

Here I was, alien to the world of humanity, commiserating with a dying tree. How strange.

This tree, though, refused to give up. It spoke to me without words. It sent new growth sunward and clung desperately to the life it once knew. Life is a force that does not give up easily.

I fingered the fresh waxy leaves. "Dance. Dance while you still can," I whispered to the fallen giant. As if in answer, a brief gust of wind teased the leaves and they twisted wildly on their stems. For a moment, a vision of Craig and me dancing in the hospital room filled my mind. He and this tree, comrades in futility, honed in on the beauty of life rather than rolling over in despair. Every single moment was precious, something to cherish and celebrate, even when faced with the specter of death.

That was one reason I came to the woods, after all. An idea called to me and I acted in celebration of life. I would never have the same opportunity, never again be thirty years old. The fragility of existence made every moment vital, every choice ripe with consequences.

Short, fragile and precious, life should never be taken lightly nor wasted. I must make every moment amount to something. I would find a way to honor Craig, Gabrielle, and West Carl. How could I fail? After all, even the trees spoke to me with wisdom and encouragement.

"Thank you, tree," I whispered.

As I returned to camp, the image of a ragged garnet stone protruding from a layer of shiny metamorphic schist entered my mind. When I was a high school student, my family toured Alaska one summer. There was a place in that great state where natural garnet crystals were found in an outcrop along a river. For a moment, I became one of those rough garnets, with jagged edges and dull faces. But one of those faces seemed to shine a little more than the rest. My polishing work had begun.

25
RETURN TO THE COTTONWOOD TREE

To learn how to die cut down a tree.

Antler

The second night stretched long and lonely, like the first. I found little rest. Nightmares plagued my dreamscape so that I resisted even closing my eyes. Far from refreshed in the morning light, I crawled slowly from the tent when the sun's warmth chased the mosquitoes away. I pulled on my boots and reached into the bucket for a refreshing splash of water on my face. There wasn't much left.

"Guess we fetch more water today."

Daisy pranced at my feet. "Hungry? Let's get your breakfast." I dipped a cupful of dog food morsels from our hanging supply bag.

While Daisy crunched her breakfast, I returned to the patch of nettles and the elderberry shrub. A dull ache plagued my belly much of the time. Scavenged meals satisfied my hunger, though they lacked the taste and appeal of home cooking. After tidying the campsite, I grabbed the straps and the bucket and headed for the river to replenish our basic operating water supply.

Fifty yards to the north, I stumbled across a fallen limb, six feet long and a hand's span in diameter. I lifted one end and dragged it across from the tent in my clearing, a place to sit later when I relaxed at the campsite. We returned to the river.

With a fresh half-bucket of water stowed at camp, I slung my pack over my shoulders. "Let's go for a walk, Daisy." She jumped and circled me several times, ready to go. I felt drawn again to the fallen cottonwood tree, like it was my magnet. We retraced the previous day's path to the home site. Stepping through the tangled border vegetation, I entered the timber and kept to the trees. Before long, I stumbled across fallen lumber and a pile of old barn siding. "This must have been the barn my dad talks about." Nestled in an alcove of the rotting lumber, a stand of beautiful orange lilies bloomed.

"Daylilies. Hold on." I dropped my pack and retrieved the edible plant guide. True to my recollection, daylilies received a strong nod as highly edible. "I wonder if Grandma planted these." I pulled unopened buds from long slender flower spikes and dropped them into my collecting bag.

We crossed the river at the Harris bridge and headed south. Today we walked through the timber rather than along the road. At the broad eastward curve which created an arc in the county road, I found a patch of another plant noted for supplying edible greens. "Lamb's quarters—my favorite. Better than spinach. Something different for supper tonight, Daisy." She wagged her stubby tail, sniffed my greens, and walked away. I pulled the young plants and stuffed them into another bag.

At last we plowed through a strip of thick brambles. Across the road lay my cottonwood tree. I stood for a moment to collect my thoughts and calm my heart. Awed by the presence of an honored guide and mentor, I approached the tree with reverence. I propped my pack on a severed branch and perched beside it, calm and at peace. Reaching the shiny new leaves at my side, I smiled as they tickled my fingers and palms. In the midst of a new cluster of leaves, a slender stem with ripening seed pods bobbed. In a few days they would split open. Hundreds of seeds, each carried on a breeze by a bit of fluff that gave this tree its name, would sail through the air. The dying tree would live again through its progeny. What about Craig? Would his life be mirrored through me? Through Phoebe? Did I have the fortitude to raise her in a way that would ultimately honor his contributions to life? His absence seared a hole in my heart.

With eyes shut, I listened to the soft music of the leaves dancing in the morning breeze. The song spoke to me again. My heart filled with gratitude for the miracle of life. Every living thing experienced life through a vast cooperative network of interrelated processes. Plant or animal, rooted or mobile, cottonwood tree or human—we all breathed, but breath alone would not sustain life.

This tree had drawn moisture and sustenance through a complex root system. An intricate network within its trunk and limbs drew water upwards to every trembling leaf as it quaked in the slightest breeze. Energy streamed through those leaves from the sun, nutrients trickled upwards from the soil, air molecules exchanged oxygen for carbon dioxide and vice versa. Complex, continuous processes defined life for the tree. Alone they remained simple processes. Together, they marked its very existence. Tiny seeds born on the wind would carry a spark of life from the once magnificent cottonwood tree. The possibility defined a miracle.

As did my own life. For Daisy and me, similar processes worked together effortlessly and silently to define life as we knew it. Our lungs expanded and we took in oxygen. When they contracted, we expelled carbon dioxide. Through the process of digestion, nutrients and energy entered our bodies. Every needed molecule floated to each vibrant cell, circulating in a flow moved by an unfaltering pulse. And we found our lives, in miracles as big as the tree.

All the systems, all the processes, worked seamlessly and silently together. We never had to give them more than an occasional passing thought. I tried to imagine what it would be like to say to your arm, "Arm, move." And have it refuse. We took so much for granted. Should the balance become upset, as it did for Craig and for this tree, life didn't simply cease. It spiraled in a different direction but it persisted onward until... until what? All the processes, the cooperative systems, once set in motion with a spark of life, carried on the best they could until they stopped. They just stopped. But it took a major catastrophe to stop all the life processes at once.

Death is violent in and of itself. It marks the destruction of a world, a cessation of its rotation. Water no longer flows. Rivers run dry. Rain no longer falls. Tides and currents stand still. Wind ceases to blow. The moon and stars wink off and the sun takes its final curtain. Only a galaxy-sized calamity could put a halt to a planet, birthed from the flames of an infant star, spinning like a top in the Milky Way. Yet we experience such a calamity through death. To watch a loved one die is to watch your world stop turning.

Thinking about Craig and his last moments, I felt shaken. The morning lost its bright appeal. I grabbed my pack and sprinted away. At first, there was no destination in mind. I just had to go somewhere else. Daisy loped easily at my side. After about a hundred yards of fighting the undergrowth, I slowed to a walk. Fluffs of cotton danced through the air, seeds released by another tree. Each tiny puff held great potential, the possibility that it could grow into a majestic tree someday. Phoebe, also, held such promise. If I could provide a nurturing environment for her. If her roots anchored her deeply, and her limbs absorbed life's warmth. If, if, if! How could I serve her potential without a partner? I felt unequal to the task.

I turned toward camp and resumed my jog. I fumbled at the tent door when I arrived, unzipped the flap and dove onto my bedroll. I buried my face in the pillow and fell into a deep sleep.

Dreams took me to the house Craig and I had built.

I tiptoed down the hallway from our bedroom toward the living room. The urgency for silence puzzled me. Was I loathe to wake a napping toddler? No... no. I was loathe to disturb the black bear which sat in the corner of my living room. I peeked around the corner at the end of the hall. The bear noticed me, turned slightly in my direction, and growled.

I retreated to Phoebe's room, closed the door and sank to the floor. A few moments later, she stirred from her nap and cooed happily. I stood up and lifted her from the crib. Then, hugging her to me, I tiptoed back along the hallway and peeked around the corner again. The bear licked its paws and rubbed them over its massive muzzle in a cat-like grooming process. It glanced at Phoebe and me, snorted and shot out of the corner. It loped past the spot where I stood rooted to the carpet, and knocked us against the wall. I clutched Phoebe desperately so that she wouldn't fall. At the end of the hall, the bear leaped into my mirror and disappeared. I saw a bright patchwork quilt draped over its shoulder blades when it jumped.

I woke in the late afternoon, but remained groggy the rest of the day. My arms and legs seemed to weigh about a ton each and I dragged through the preparation of my evening meal. As day waned into evening, I crawled back into the tent. Despair returned to my heart in force. I wrestled internally to prepare my mind for another long night.

Finally, my exhausted brain turned off the questions and I fell into a dreamless sleep.

26
COMPANION

"The breezes at dawn have secrets to tell you."
RUMI

The stillness of pre-dawn reverberated through every cell in my body as I woke. Silence roared. The vacuum of noises played on my mind. Even my internal music remained mute. I couldn't recall a time without a tune playing in my head. From my early days when Mother played classical symphonies on the stereo as I drifted to sleep, or let her fingers fly over the piano keys, somewhere in the recesses of my mind a melody rang. But now, black silence.

My heart quickened. A vague distress, like fingers of panic, clutched my chest. Theme songs had resonated within me for different eras in my past. In desperation, I called them to mind. My life songs included "There's Got to Be a Morning After" from my teen years.

Morning after, where are you now? I ran the chorus through my mind, but it died after the first phrase. "Who Will Buy" hailed from the morning I became engaged to Craig. "You Needed Me" echoed through his ten-month battle with cancer, while "The Impossible Dream" became illustrative of his struggle. Perhaps this wilderness venture was my impossible dream.

My whole life had been marked by music. But in the dark that morning, there was nothing. I shivered. Silence pressed against me from every direction.

As the sky brightened, the timber stirred to life. Gradually the chorus of a wild morning filled the void. A tree branch snapped. Flickers called eerily in a repetitive prehistoric pattern. Squirrels scolded neighbors about the day's breakfast. Red-headed woodpeckers tapped decaying oak trunks. The air buzzed with insect tones. Daylight waxed. I closed my eyes, but didn't sleep. A swollen feeling at the base of my skull signaled an oncoming headache. I rubbed my neck gently in hopes of relieving the ache before it began.

Through the rustling in the timber, I began to hear human voices. Distant. Words undistinguishable. They became a little clearer.

"Hawea! Hawea!" A woman called. "Hawea!"

I sat up. Why would another woman be wandering our timber at dawn? She continued to call as she approached my camp. I peered out the tent's screen door and watched her follow the edge of the river bank from the south.

"Hawea!" She turned straight toward my tent.

I watched in apprehension. Her hardy tan skin appeared darkened by the sun. Shiny black hair parted into two locks that hung to her waist. Each was wrapped in long strips of blue cloth. The part in her hair was painted vermillion, a more brilliant red than I had ever seen. She wore a long tan skirt accented with colorful embroidery. Beaded leather shoes covered her slim feet. A colorful woven cloth hung over her left shoulder.

"Hawea." The maiden shook my tent. I peeked at her and smiled. Her intense gaze didn't seem threatening, even though she didn't return my smile. Her eyes sought mine and narrowed to slits, searching my face. "Hawea?"

I crawled out of the tent. "Hello," I whispered.

She held my gaze. We studied each other for a long moment before she looked around my campsite. She again probed the tent as if she'd never seen such a thing before.

A torrent of strange words flew at me. "Bey yayishe? Dada shka xe hninkhe? Bey yayishe?"

She paused. Then, "Wey Niwako. Zhashe ahni?"

I shrugged and shook my head. "Sorry. I don't understand."

She placed her hands on her chest and nodded as she again said, "Wey Niwako. Niwako." She nodded and tapped her chest as she spoke.

She pointed to my chest. "Zhashe ahni? Bey yayishe?" Hesitantly she said, "Your name?"

I smiled and nodded. "Ann. I'm Ann. You are Niwako?" I gestured to her.

At last she smiled. She began to speak in hesitant English. "I... am... Niwako... Water Woman. Hello."

"Hello," I answered.

"Have you seen my lodge?" Niwako painstakingly asked.

"Your lodge? No. No, I haven't seen a lodge. I don't think there are any around here any more."

The first rays of the sun broke through the trees. A sliver of sunlight flamed across my orange tent. I opened my eyes. Niwako was gone. I crawled out of my tent and stretched in the sun. Again. *It was all a dream.*

My head pounded. After serving breakfast to Daisy I nibbled on a granola bar from my emergency rations. Sitting on the camp log, I leaned against a tree and closed my eyes. I took several deep breaths, willing the tension to leave my head and shoulders. After a few minutes, I felt a little better.

"Let's see, Daisy," I said. "What shall we do today? Looks like we need more water."

I grabbed a couple straps, tied them together and attached one end to the bucket handle. We set off toward the trusty sycamore tree which stretched over the river.

Niwako appeared beside me. With a nod, she moved to the tree, hiked her skirt up around her thighs and jumped onto the trunk. She wrapped her arms and legs around the tree and shimmied down the trunk to the water's edge. I followed her down the tree.

At its base, I cast out the bucket, let it sink and pulled it to the shore. Then I shimmied back up the tree like an inch-worm. My thighs gripped the trunk and my feet pushed upward. I reached out with my arms and pulled forward and then hugged the tree while my feet scrambled up a little further. Exhilarated, I laughed when I reached the top.

Back at camp, I soaked a wash cloth in the water and sponged the sleepiness from my face.

"Let's do some gathering, Daisy."

We set off in search of the day's edible gifts. Niwako tagged along to keep me company. She eased the emptiness in my heart. Time passed quickly with my imaginary friend, as if I had returned to the simplicity of childhood.

Since daylily buds bloom only one day, we headed back to the demolished barn for a new crop of buds. I lingered at the rubbish pile and pawed through the siding planks.

"You know, I might be able to do something with a couple of these," I said.

"What would that be?" Niwako asked.

"They're flat enough that I could use one like this as a small desk top for writing in my journal." From the pile I pulled an eight-inch wide piece that was nearly two feet long.

"Desk? Writing?"

"That may seem strange to you. I brought paper and pens to write things that might come to my mind. Haven't had a lot to say as of yet."

"Why would you need more than one?"

"I was thinking I might be able to rig up a kind of hanging desk with braided vines and leave one or two hanging at different places in the timber. Then no matter where I was, or when I received an idea, I could sit down and write about it."

"I do not understand the value in that."

"I don't suppose you would. It's just one way of sharing thoughts and stories with other people."

"Like our story keepers tell children about hunts and battles from our father's times."

"Yes, like that, I suppose. But when you write them down it won't matter if a story teller suddenly disappears because anyone can read the stories."

"Sometimes our hunting parties wrote important stories
on a big rock. When we follow the game, we see it again every year. But only the story keepers can read all the events from the rock."

"I think that today, I'll search for places to hang some writing planks. I once helped my grandmother pick wild grapes on the west side. Maybe we can locate them again and use the vines."

I pulled another eight-inch plank from the pile of barn siding, stuck the two into my pack and called the dog. "Let's head across the field, Daisy."

We turned away from the rubbish pile, and walked into the wheat field. Rows stretched compass straight along the northern boundary of the Farm. We followed a row that stretched westward from the old home site. Halfway to the tree-line on the west side of the field, the land dipped into a small valley. "Maybe this is where Grandpa used to find arrowheads," I mused. I paused to scour the ground around me for any sign of chipped rocks. Nothing was visible. I stepped from row to row and circled the lower area for nearly half an hour with no success.

"What are you doing?" Niwako appeared at my elbow again.

"I could be wrong, but I think this might be where your lodge once stood."

She glanced around the entire tree-lined field and shrugged. "Hard to say. Might be."

"Sometimes in the past, my family found chipped flint in this area, and even arrowheads."

"Ah." Niwako nodded.

"I never have. It would be kind of fun to find one though."

The arrowhead search produced nothing. At length, I gave up and walked toward the row of trees. Wild grape vines grew profusely along the edge of the timber about a thousand yards south of the boundary line. I dug in my pack for my native food field guide. The entry for riverbank grapes indicated that young leaves were quite edible. I untangled a long vine and stripped a few leaves from its leading tip. After untangling a second vine, I wound each one around an end of a barn plank. I returned the growing tip to the greater mass of vines and threaded the tip in and around some bigger stems until the plank hung as a table top above the forest floor.

"Ta-da. A desk."

I scouted the edge of the timber to look for a peach tree I recalled. The search proved unsuccessful. Perhaps the tree had died. I circled along the field's boundary. By the time the sun dipped low in the sky I could see the orange roof of my tent.

"Home, sweet, home, Daisy," I muttered. My stomach growled. I felt ravenous.

"Let's try those grape leaves. I'll grab a few more elderberry clusters and we can fix supper."

I boiled the grape leaves first. Unfortunately, they were nearly unpalatable. I must have missed their prime. After two tentative bites, I decided I better rely on the elderberry and potato mixture and I tossed the rest of the grape leaves behind the tent. I turned to our hanging supply bag and dug into it for the last of the potato flakes. The bag had spilled. There were only about two tablespoons left that could be fixed. "It's going to be a hungry night, Daisy. Guess tomorrow is the day we head out for more supplies."

I dashed to the nettles and snipped a dozen tops to add to the daylily buds and elderberry blossoms. After the meager supper, I pulled my harmonica from my backpack. I situated myself on the tree branch, stretched out my legs, and leaned against the young tree behind me. Remembering the eerie stillness from the previous night, I played my harmonica until daylight waned.

Maybe a fresh tune at dusk would eliminate the suffocating silence when I woke. After a long drink of water I crawled into the bedroll.

27
CAMP TWO

The most comforting speech in the world,
the talk that rain makes by itself all over the ridges.
Thomas Merton

I woke as the earliest hint of light filtered into the blackness. My bones ached from hours on the ground. I crawled out of the tent and stretched. Daisy joined me. Instead of following the river bank, we planned to hike the gravel roads to the car.

I tied a strap to Daisy's collar.

Niwako appeared beside me. "Are you certain the tether is necessary?"

"I want to reign her in quickly if we meet a car."

"Car? What is car?"

"Right. If you come along, you'll probably find out."

We headed around the edge of the soybean field and down the farm lane to the county road. The sky grew lighter. Our footsteps on the gravel roared in the stillness of dawn. We covered two miles before a distant rumble signaled the approach of a farm truck. I pulled Daisy to me. "Sit. Stay." We waited motionless until the truck passed.

"A car?" Niwako asked.

"Well, a truck anyway. Same idea. Different design."

As the dawn progressed, traffic picked up. We met seven more vehicles in the remaining three miles. Each time I pulled Daisy to my side and we waited for them to pass.

In the growing light, I noted several edible plants and collected a few to compare later with my Peterson field guide. Though I watched for a stand of cattails in the roadside ditches, I saw none. The sun peeked above the eastern horizon as we rounded the last corner. The road straightened and we continued due south for the last leg of our journey.

The day grew warm and sticky in the sunlight. A swarm of gnats appeared in the air. They buzzed around my ears and hair with a thousand tiny whines. I swung my free arm madly to disburse them.

The walk along the road proved smoother than our previous trek along the river's edge. However we lost our sense of wilderness isolation as the vehicles rolled by. I knew why wildlife moved at first light. That slice of time between the dead of night and daybreak is the best time to conduct business and avoid human contact as well.

My car looked like home to me. I pulled a granola bar, dried fruit, and a handful of dog food from the supplies. "Ah—breakfast." I fed Daisy from my hands. Then I leaned against the car and nibbled my morning meal.

Niwako reappeared. "A car?"

"Yes. My car."

"And you store food in your car?" she asked.

"Extra food. Extra water. Other supplies."

"Your car has wheels like those others."

I nodded.

"So it will move?"

"Of course it moves. If the engine is running."
"Why do you store food so far from your lodge?"
"I want to use natural foods as much as possible.

The car is a good hike from camp in order to discourage cheating with packaged food."

"And water."

"Yes. The water is essential."

"You have to come this far for water?"

"Yes. But I filled these canteens with fresh drinking water. They should last a few days."

Niwako shrugged and shook her head.

"You think I'm crazy."

"I cannot see the harm in moving supplies closer to your lodge."

"You might be right. Spending half a day to get water three times a week is a bit ridiculous. Or a whole day. However, I really don't have anything else to do. I'll think on it. Maybe next time."

I reached down to scratch Daisy's ears. When I looked up again Niwako had disappeared. I filled another bag with mulberries before we wound our way back toward camp. This time we headed westward from the car. After about a mile, we came to a bridge that crossed the Neosho River. Under the bridge, a cluster of cattail heads bobbed in the day's breeze.

With the hunting knife, I sliced a bundle of leaves and stalks. I strapped them together and tied them to the top of my pack. Laden with the cluster of cattail leaves, their tips bobbing an arm's length away from my shoulders with every step, I hiked toward the Farm. By the time we reached the Harris bridge, the late morning sun hid behind a low cloud front. Cooler air refreshed us.

Daisy detoured to the railroad boxcar when we passed the old home site. I followed her to the dilapidated relic. She sniffed out a rabbit hiding underneath the structure and yipped in excitement as she darted into a chase.

"This is not my lodge, though it appears like a lodge," Niwako whispered in my imagination.

Three divisions of concrete foundation emerged from the ground north of the boxcar, the only indication another barn once stood there. Walls of trees outlined each room. I stepped through the decades-old growth and entered a space that beckoned to me.

"I wonder why I didn't think to camp here?" I said.

"You could move," Niwako suggested. "Kaw villages are easily moved."

"I'm not Kaw."

"You are on Kaw land. Is this box special to you?"

I glanced over my shoulder to the Two Elms at the home site. "We dreamed of a wedding in the shade of those trees," I whispered.

"Then you should camp here."

I nodded. "What do you think, Daisy? Want to move?"

She wagged her stubby tail.

"Guess it's settled then." I dropped the cattails and extra water canteens before we headed to the tent. We moved everything to the new campsite. I chose a dirt-floored room with dense tree walls for my bedroom and pitched the tent there. An adjacent room with old concrete flooring became the kitchen and living area. I stepped through the tree wall and walked to the shade of the Two Elms. Except for a glimmer of orange, the second camp remained invisible, insuring my privacy. Though the sun shone brightly into my new headquarters, a slight northerly breeze kept the June heat at bay.

Daisy and I scouted the timber along the edge of the cultivated field. We dragged another fallen limb to this camp for a chair in my new kitchen. I spread the cattails across the concrete floor of my open living room and sorted the leaves from the stalks. With the knife, I slit the outer sheaths and cut the tender white inner stalks into chunks. I piled them on a cloth in anticipation of my evening meal. After I tied the leaves into small bundles, I hung them to dry in the trees. Someday I'd weave them into baskets.

A few hackberry branches littered the corners of my new rooms. I selected one about sixteen inches long and three inches thick and ran my knife along the length of the wood. Chip by chip, the stick grew narrower as I whittled the rest of the afternoon away.

By evening, clouds again covered the sun. They grew heavy and dark, an angry slate blue color. "You think it will rain, girl?" I asked Daisy.

We walked a short circuit around Camp Two, scouting the fields for more edible plants. The air felt dense with moisture. Clouds became so dark it was impossible to guess the time of day. Low rumbles of thunder signaled the approach of rain. When the first sprinkles arrived, we returned to the tent. I tossed my pack and the camp supplies inside and we dove in to wait out the rain.

Within a few minutes, the patter of rain drops beat steadily on the nylon roof. I pulled the fleece comforter over us. I thought of little Phoebe. Pangs of longing for her washed over me like ocean waves. Memories flooded my consciousness. Our wedding plans under the Two Elms. Daisy chasing a cat up a tree. Gathering eggs in our chicken house. Grasshopper rodeos. Those happy times of the past were gone forever. Despair born of frustration and loneliness darkened my heart to match the clouds.

28
DELUGE

Nobody started it, nobody is going to stop it.
It will last as long as it wants, this rain.

Thomas Merton

A drop of water stabbed my forehead. The gray afternoon light illuminated hundreds of droplets on the inside of the tent roof. The threat of a cold shower hovered inches away. My heart sank into the depths of despair darker than any I'd ever known. When Daisy and I made the boxcar our refuge, we discovered we shared it with dozens of rats. Their eye-dots disappeared when I screamed but before long they were back.

"Go away!" I shouted.

Scratching noises erupted from every direction. The eye-dots once again were extinguished.

When they returned, I began to sing a tune. Softly, to keep the rats at bay, I hummed the melodies of songs which spoke to my heart, the songs which identified my life. My songs. When I could sing words, I did. When I forgot the lyrics, I just hummed the melodies. The rats stayed away.

I closed my eyes and listened to rain battering the roof and north side of the boxcar. *"If the river starts to rise, you high-tail it out of there,"* my grandmother had said. I whispered her words aloud. The rats disappeared again.

"How much rain does it take before the river overflows?" I said.

Niwako appeared beside me. "Oh, a bit more yet," she said. "It depends more on rainfall in the hills to the north and west."

"And you know this because?"

"There was a flood when I was a child. It is how I got my name."

"Niwako?" I asked.

"Yes—Water Woman."

"Tell me more."

"I was young, a girl of about twelve summers. We had long rains that year also. The people moved from our site here in the river's bend to the hills. Our seer foretold the flood. So we moved. That was the People's way."

"Is that how you were named?"

"No. There is more. The rain stopped. My mother sent me to find wild raspberries. I came back to the river bank. I was intent to fill my skin bag with berries. Then I heard a rippling sound—a rush of water. I looked up and the river was running fast toward the berries where I stood. It was a day—maybe two—following the big rains here."

"What did you do?"

"The only thing I could do. I climbed the nearest oak tree. I climbed high and fast as the water flowed over the ground."

"How long did you stay in the tree?"

"It was days before the water went down. I grew hungry. I ate all the berries I had picked. There was nothing more to eat up the oak tree. I also got very little rest, for fear I would tumble out of the tree in my sleep.

"On the dawn of the fourth day, I could see that the waters were down. The berry bushes had reappeared at the base of my tree. However, the berries that had not washed away were covered in muck.

"As I came down from the tree, I could hear my father and brother calling for me. 'Ho! Ho!' When they found where I had been, my father named me Niwako."

"What was your name before that?"

"As a child, I was called Misata—Little One of the Fifth Moon."

"I've never been quite that close to a flood," I said. "But I did see what high water can do in a canyon."

"Canyon?"

"A narrow gorge between tall mountains. A few years back there was a flash flood in Colorado's Big Thompson canyon. It happened after about a foot of rain fell in an hour. The normally calm, burbling stream was transformed into raging rapids. A twenty-foot wall of water raced down the canyon faster than people could drive out of there. The only way to escape the flood was to scale the canyon walls. Thousands of people were camped there that night. About a hundred and fifty of them were killed in the flood."

"But you escaped any harm?"

"I wasn't among the campers. My husband and I visited friends about a month after the flood. We saw cars sitting in the middle of a calm river. They were full of silt and gravel. Sections of the road were gone, torn free by the flash flood. People escaped with their lives by climbing up, just like you."

"Listen." Niwako cocked her head slightly.

"What? What do you hear?"
"Nothing." "Nothing?"
"Nothing. The rain has stopped."
"Come, Daisy."

I wriggled out of the hole in the boxcar to survey my camp in evening's light. The tent sagged, thoroughly soaked. Water pooled on its floor. I dragged the sleeping bag and my extra clothes from the tent, wrung water from them and hung them over branches to drip. Clouds thinned. For a few moments, sun rays pierced the grayness of the sky.

"Let the sun shine in," I sang. My spirits lifted with the song. I unstaked the tent and draped it over tree branches as well.

Soggy tent hanging on tree limbs

Thunder rumbled in the distance. My belly echoed its rumbling as a dull hunger grew. "Dang, I'm hungry, Daisy. Ever tried eating a cattail?" I found the Peterson guide and reviewed the cattail section. Stalks are edible raw, which was good since the waning light hardly left enough time to cook anything. I nibbled one of the green pieces. It was tough and fibrous.

"How about the other end?" I tried a white chunk and discovered it to be crunchy and tender. Apparently, where the stalks appeared green and began to flatten into the long leaves, they lost their palatability. "White. It must be white. Well, what about the white flower stalks?" I bit a chunk off a cylindrical stalk. "Umm, not bad. Delicate. Kind of nutty."

The last rays of the sun disappeared behind clouds as I brushed my teeth. Rain sprinkled my shoulders again. Daisy and I sprinted to the boxcar. We crawled inside to escape a new downpour. When twilight deepened into night, rain continued to batter the north side of the boxcar. I stretched across the pile of shingles and wrestled a blanket around my shoulders and legs. I could see nothing. Shivering, Daisy crept under the damp comforter. She sighed as she cuddled against my chest. I squirmed. The lumpy pile of shingles dented my skin. My skin prickled with a thousand itches and I shivered under the damp cover. This was going to be a long night.

The scampering of tiny feet returned. Though I could no longer see eye-dots in the night's darkness, I sensed the rats were there. Dozens. Maybe hundreds.

"Oh, God. What am I going to do?" Tired of singing and talking to thin air, I stomped a foot against the floor boards and listened as scores of tiny feet scrambled for shelter. Silence returned but for the rain pattering against the walls. Moments later, the rats were back. I stomped again. They scurried away. This continued long into the night. Daisy dozed fitfully, but I slept very little. I couldn't locate a position that offered comfort to my bones. Every few minutes I stomped to silence the scampering rats.

I want to go home.

But first I needed to get through this night in hell.

Drying the camp after a shower

29
SWELLING OF THE WATERS

Talk to the rivers, to the lakes, to the winds...
John Lame Deer

I awoke with a jerk. For a moment I didn't recall where I lay. Absolute darkness surrounded me. No pinpoint of light, no distant glow, nothing illuminated the surrounding space. I might as well have been blind.

Cold. I felt chilled to my core. Daisy shivered under my right arm. Something poked my ribs. In fact, the entire area felt lumpy. Lumpy and damp. The blanket strewn across us felt heavy with moisture. I stirred. The area around me exploded with a thousand scratching noises. Then there was silence.

Oh, yes. The rats. It was all coming back to me. This was not a dream from which I could awaken. This was my reality. I lay in the boxcar at the Farm, and I slept on a pile of old roofing shingles.

Really? I can sleep like this? Not for long, evidently.

Darkness ruled the heart of night. Darkness and silence, at least when the rats were still.

Silence. I fell asleep to the roar of rain drumming against the roof. Now there was no rain. Was that what woke me? The cessation of a downpour?

I pushed myself to a sitting position. Every bone inside me ached. I ached with the discomfort of the night's sleeping arrangements. I ached with fatigue. I shivered, cold and miserable. That was it. I'd had enough. As soon as daylight appeared, we were packing out. I felt defeated by the wilderness.

Rat scratching noises returned. I slapped my foot against the floorboards. Silence. Now we were back to that routine. My noises disturbed them to silence. Their noises prompted my response.

I stood and stretched my shoulders upward to work out a few kinks. I wrapped the damp comforter tightly around me. Daisy yawned loudly and jumped off the pile of shingles. She sniffed for a few minutes and stopped with a sigh at the base of the shingle pile.

Silence again. I swayed slightly on my feet, exhausted. But my rest for the night was over. Scritch, scritch. The rats. I stomped twice, transferring weight from one foot to another. Scratchy scritch. Stomp, stomp.

For some reason, the words to a song popped into my mind and I sang weakly in the stillness of the night. "Let the sun shine in. Let it shine, shine, shine..." Though my voice sounded plaintively off key, the rats remained silent. I began stepping back and forth in rhythm to the lyrics. A hint of warmth returned to my fingers and toes.

I sang a different song. I sang all the songs I could recall, from children's nursery songs, to folk songs and campfire songs, to themes from various musicals I'd enjoyed over the years. Music from *"The Sound of Music,"* *"Mary Poppins,"* *"The One and Only Genuine Original Family Band,"* *"Oklahoma,"* *"Oliver!,"* and *"Mississippi Melody"* filled the forlorn boxcar. I turned to Christmas carols. I concluded with "Jesus Wants Me for a Sunbeam." My heart pounded as I danced through each song, but I kept the rats quiet. By the time daylight showed through holes and cracks in the boxcar walls, I flushed with welcome warmth.

It's strange how vision adapts. Wiggling into the boxcar's interior in yesterday's waning daylight, I saw nothing at all inside besides the pinpoints of light reflected in the eyes of my reclusive neighbors. I relied on my fingers and ears to explore the enclosure. After hours of total darkness, the tiniest rays of light revealed objects that had previously been hidden. I saw the shape of the mound of shingles where I'd spent half the night. I sat down on it and studied the boxcar in the dingy light.

To my right, in front of the south door, half a dozen automobile engines and transmissions leaned against each other. Or did they come from tractors? I didn't know. Beyond them, ancient farm equipment was scattered helter-skelter across the width of the boxcar. Curved tines of a cultivator, a horse-drawn plow, a corn sheller, scythes and sickles from a time long since gone emerged in the gloom.

To my left, old household equipment stood against the wall. I identified old furniture, an antique treadle sewing machine, wash tubs, and a cabinet of empty canning jars mingled with a few old tin and enameled stove pans. A pile of milled lumber filled the center of the room. The growing light revealed a square box four-feet high standing in the northwest corner. I carefully picked my way to its side and discovered that a dusty turntable hid under its hinged lid. The family's Victrola stood watch over the chaotic boxcar interior. I ran my fingers around the edge of the lid and tried to imagine the Victrola spewing forth music for my father and his childhood family. Where would it have stood in my grandmother's house? The Victrola must have been relegated to obscurity in the boxcar when my grandmother moved the house to town.

And why had she moved the house to town? Because the Farm was prone to floods. Enough of this musing. I had work to do if I was to escape before another miserable night descended.

I peeked through a nail hole of daylight above the Victrola. What I saw took my breath away. Water stood everywhere. How much rain had fallen anyway?

Returning to the pile of shingles, I found the supplies I'd shoved into the boxcar the previous day. I folded the comforter and slid everything adjacent to the ragged access gap in the north door. After rolling my damp jeans above my knees, I wiggled backwards on my stomach through the aperture and splashed into ankle-deep water. A jolt shocked my body. *Geez, it's cold.*

"Daisy?" She leaned out of the boxcar, wagging her tail. She looked at me with puzzled eyes. I lifted her to the sodden landscape, pulled the supply bag to the opening and probed it for our breakfast. Dog food for her. Emergency granola bar for me. I slipped the bar into my shirt pocket and offered dogfood kernels to Daisy in my cupped hands. She crunched eagerly until the last kernel disappeared.

I surveyed our situation while we ate. High, thin clouds raced across the sky. Patches of blue showed through here and there. Surely the rain was over and the sun would shine before long. It could just as easily start raining again though.

The orange tent remained draped across the branches of the tree-lined wall. It swung lightly in a brisk morning breeze. The lowest corner appeared heavy and thick. I splashed to the tent and reached inside to find an overlooked water canteen. I withdrew the container and shook it. A swallow or two of water sloshed in the bottom. I probed the tent again.

What is that in the very tip?

My matches, soggy with rain water. Every last one of them ruined. There would be no fire today.

But that was not all. Something else.

What's this? No – my extra film.

All the spare rolls of Ektachrome were stored in a little film caddy, which was now at the bottom of my soggy tent. Ruined. There would be no more pictures either.

That's okay, I told myself. *We're getting out of here today.*

"Let's check it out, Daisy."

I splashed toward the Two Elms, slipping and sliding most of the way. A hundred feet beyond the trees, a low mound of earth marked the excavated foundation of my grandmother's house. It rose above the water's surface, a roughly circular hill twenty-feet in diameter. We scaled the three-foot high mound. Mud oozed through my bare toes and caked my feet up to my ankle bones as I circled the mound to survey the surrounding farm land.

Water, water, everywhere.

The tenacious tops of the wheat crop waved feebly above the surface of the water. My heart sank. I thought of my grandmother and the despair she must have felt as the water crept into her house decades ago.

"We've got to get out of here," I said to Daisy. I slid down the mound and splashed toward the location I thought marked the farm lane. Everything was under water.

Wish we had a boat.
But I would have to rely on my legs.

Flood water cut off our escape route.

A draw marked the low spot between the house site and the county road. As we approached it, the water deepened. Daisy splashed ahead of me and reached a point where she began to swim. I followed until water lapped at the rolled denim above my knees.

I'm going to have to swim out.

Daisy reached the low spot on the submerged driveway. She drifted south, gaining speed. Her paddling became intense as she strained against a hidden current in the waterway.

"Come, girl," I called. "You can do it. Come here."

She half-turned, glancing at me, eyes wide. The whites of her eyes showed her apprehension.

"Hold on, girl. I'll get you."

I splashed toward her. Frigid water soaked my jeans to my thighs. She continued to float downstream. Lumbering through the water, my progress was a snail's pace compared to the current flow. I was losing her.

"Hang on, Daisy. I'm coming." I shouted to reassure the frightened dog.

I retreated to shallower water and lunged along, keeping pace with the sodden brown head of my little friend. As she neared the river's normal course, the current picked up. Floating debris coursed alongside Daisy. I looked ahead and noticed one area where the floating twigs slowed and danced in little eddies. With renewed determination, I lunged toward that spot. As I splashed toward it, I disturbed some driftwood which began to float alongside me. I swept up the largest chunk, a branch about two inches across and eight inches long. Reaching for my straps, I corded the end around the chunk of wood as I ran.

Daisy approached the stiller water. When she was as close to me as she was likely to be, I hurled the driftwood into the current with every ounce of strength I could muster. "Fetch, Daisy! God, let her get close enough to grab it."

The dog strained toward my tethered branch. She snapped her jaws. Missed. "Try again, girl." The second time her incisors caught the crumbling bark on the sodden wood.

"Good girl. Now hang on." I tugged on the strap. Daisy held fast. She turned in the current and aimed toward me. I reeled her in, looping the strap around my elbow and hand as she drew nearer. At last, Daisy paddled under her own strength. She headed for my legs. I lifted her out of the water and carried her toward Camp Two. She shivered in my arms, whining.

Standing within the tree-lined room outside the door, it dawned on me that now the water level marked an inch above my ankle bones. The river was still rising. The chill of the water permeated my flesh. I convulsed into violent shivering. I boosted Daisy into the boxcar and crawled in behind her. Desperate to find some warmth, I stripped the wet clothes from my body and wrapped both of us in the damp comforter. There was no way we would be able to swim out of here. Not with a current like that. We'd have to stick it out until the flood water receded.

How long would the river rise? How high would it get? Visions of water seeping into the boxcar flooded my mind. I had to find higher ground. My grandmother had climbed into her house attic. It was now seven miles away. Niwako climbed a tree. Or so I supposed. Where was my native companion when I needed her?

The closest trees large enough to offer shelter were the Two Elms. But the lowest branch seemed twenty feet high—far out of my reach. And though Daisy had been known to climb trees, she couldn't jump that high.

I turned to the boxcar. Maybe I could find a way to climb to its roof. Perhaps I could find a trap door of some kind to open from the inside. I studied the ceiling in the dim light. At the west end was a square doorway, like my grandmother's attic entrance. How could we get to it though? Perhaps the old Victrola would serve as a ladder. Donning my spare set of clothing, I scooted some of the old farm tools from below the spot I had identified as a possible doorway. The path between the Victrola and the roof access had to be cleared as well. By the time I had moved the stored items out of the pathway and stacked them in new piles, I had warmed myself again.

I dragged the heavy music machine along the newly cleared path. When it stood in the corner below the roof access, I opened its front doors and stepped onto the shelves. Balancing with care at each level, at last I crawled onto the square lid, compressed into a crouch. I slowly stood. My hands barely reached the square access area. I pushed. It didn't budge. I banged against the square. It echoed back, firm and unmoved. Unable to dislodge the doorway, I crouched until I could reach a pipe that lay on an adjacent pile of castoffs. I prodded the doorway with the pipe, clanging harder, and more desperately against the square, to no avail. The doorway remained firm and fast.

"Suppose there's some kind of ladder outside?" I asked Daisy. She perked up. I jumped to the floor and we left the boxcar again. The water was even higher on my legs. I parted a wall of trees and struggled through the limbs at the east end of the rail car. Hidden partly by brush and small trees, a rusty ladder to the roof was bolted to the planks of the boxcar wall.

"Thank you, God."

With an energy born of desperation, I began packing items for an ascent. I could make thirty trips hauling things in my small pack. Or I might be able to wrap the supplies in the flattened tent and draw up the bundle from above. I opted for the latter idea. I moved the nylon tent to the boxcar floor and spread it flat. Carefully, I stacked my blankets, three canteens of drinking water, my field guide and our emergency food supplies. I brought the corners together, wrapped two straps around the bundle at right angles and knotted them together. I pushed myself out the door and stood in water—now two more inches above my ankles. I slid the tent to the center of the opening, straps hanging to the water below. With my camera around my neck, I put my backpack on backwards so that it draped loosely in front of my chest.

"Daisy, you want a ride?"

She splashed to me. I lifted her and wrung water from her feet and legs the best I could, then guided her hind feet into my pack. After zipping the main compartment mostly shut, she wiggled in the front pack, licking my face trustingly.

"I know. This is strange, isn't it? But I won't let you fall."

With a hand on the boxcar to steady my path through the rising water, I plunged around the end and pulled through the thicket until I stood at the ladder. After testing its anchor bolts, I reached above my head and pulled us upwards until my toes found a grip on the lowest crossbar. One by one, we climbed the ladder's rungs. When the roof was level with my chest, I unzipped the pack. Daisy squirmed onto the boxcar. I set the pack and my camera as far onto the roof as I could reach and descended to the flood water again.

The tent bundle stuck in the boxcar opening so that I had to work it through a little at a time. When finally I held the lumpy parcel in my arms, I wrapped the long strap around my hand and dangled the package, testing its viability. The extraction from the boxcar had rearranged the objects wrapped inside. The balance seemed off-center, but the straps held.

I wrapped my arms around our supply bundle and stepped carefully to the ladder. With my chest, I pinched the collection to the wall of the rail car while I wrapped the short strap around the second rung up. I began to climb. Looping the other strap around the rung second from the top, I watched as the free end dangled back to brush the top of the bundle. I backed down to the rising water – another inch higher on my ankles, wrapped the dangling strap securely around my right hand and lifted the nylon bundle slightly to release pressure on the other strap, which I detached from the ladder.

With a tug downward on the looped strap and a boost from below with my upper chest and shoulders, I inched upwards with the supplies. At the halfway mark, the rusted upper rung split and bent outward. The tent bundle dropped fully onto my shoulders. The strap flew over my head to dangle in the water below. The load shifted. Through a gap in the tent over my left wrist, one plastic bag of Daisy's food, a canteen of fresh water, and my edible plant field guide tumbled from the load and splashed into the muddy water.

I shrieked. Swaying on the lower rung, I struggled to regain my balance. With a coarse scraping sound, the rung under my right foot gave and I dipped backwards.

30
JOYFUL LIKE A BIRD

When I rise up
Let me rise up joyful
Like a bird.

Wendell Berry

For a few mad seconds, I worked feverishly to shift the tent bundle back into balance. I pressed the bottom of my bare foot against the wooden planks of the boxcar. Lacing both my hands around the aged welds that held the rungs to the upright bars of the ladder, I curtailed the sway of the load.

I closed my eyes and took several deep breaths. I pulled myself toward the ladder and sandwiched the bundle between my chest and the remaining rungs. I shot my right hand upward for a higher hold. Swinging my left knee sideways, I found the next welded rung with my toes. I hopped my right leg upward along the planks and repeated the process. Hardly daring to breathe, I ascended one rung at a time until I balanced at eye level with the roof.

I extracted several more items through the gap in the tied bundle and set them on the edge of the roof before I boosted the remaining bundle to the top and scrambled over the edge to join Daisy.

Crawling to the center of the roof, I opened the bundle to inventory our supplies.

"I'm sorry, Daisy." I grabbed the dog and pulled her into my arms. We'd lost half her food, a third of my fresh water and the field guide. Even if we managed to ration the supplies we had until the water receded, my resource for checking the edible qualities of wild plants was destroyed. Why, oh why, hadn't I left some of that on top of the Victrola?

I sobbed into the damp fur over Daisy's shoulder. She twisted in my arms and licked my cheeks. "You have no idea what just happened, do you? Guess we'll have to eat sparingly. Hope the river goes down before we're totally out of food. Niwako said she was in the tree three days. Three days. You think we'll be up here three days? Oh, God."

I closed my eyes and lay on the roof, curled around Daisy. In only a few minutes, I drifted into an uneasy sleep.

The warm rays of the afternoon sun woke me hours later. I opened my eyes to a sparkling blue sky. The clouds were gone. My face burned with the sun's heat. "Geez. How long have I been out?" I struggled to sit up. Shards of pain whipped through my spine, hips, and shoulders after hours on the hard roof. I rubbed my eyes, crawled to the edge of the boxcar and looked down. The water level now reached the boxcar floor.

"At least the rain is gone. How long will the water rise?"

I spread my spare clothing, bedding, and the tent across the roof to finish drying. I mentally divided our remaining food into three days, two meals each day. It would be a lean three days.

I counted the kernels of the remaining bag of dog food. For a moment, I held one kernel in my palm, wondering how it would taste.

No, really? I'm thinking about depleting the food supply of my faithful and only companion? I shook my head and returned the kernel to the bag. I counted out twenty of them.

"Here, Daisy. You want supper?" She crunched each bite. Then she looked up and wagged her tail.

"I know. It's not much, is it? I don't suppose you'd eat mulberries or a bit of cattail?"

I prepared a portion for myself, a raw cattail stalk cut into inch-long bites and a handful of mulberries, soggy with their own juice. I offered a bite of the cattail to the dog. She sniffed and licked tentatively, but wouldn't eat the morsel.

"I know it's not what you want, girl. We've got to stretch our food, though. It has to last until the water goes down and we can walk out of here."

Visions filled my mind. I saw us lying unconscious, shriveled from malnutrition and dehydration, covered with welts from insect bites, and sunburned to a crisp. Our future loomed bleak and precarious. I thought of Jesus, alone in the wilderness for forty days. Did he feel similar moments of despair? I prayed silently for the strength and resilience necessary to survive the flood.

A bird fluttered to a limb in a tree below me, its wings flashing sun yellow as it flew. I crawled to the edge to get a closer look. Startled, the bird launched into flight toward the closer of the Two Elms. A white rump patch and another flash of yellow helped me identify the flicker.

Moments later I heard its call. "Flicker. Flicker. Flicker. Flicker."

Niwako appeared at my side.

"You've been deafeningly quiet lately," I chided her.

She shrugged. "You have climbed to safety. You did not need me."

"I lost some supplies. We have very little food."

"You will survive."

"I'm not so sure. The future looks bleak."

"How will you lift your spirits?"

"Not a clue."

"How did you survive the night?"

"What—last night?"

"Yes, when you heard the—"

"Rats?"

She nodded.

"Well, I sang and stomped my feet to keep them quiet."

"My people had a dance for courage when they feared the future. Dancing gives strength."

"Strength. Courage. Fortitude." The memory of Craig's dance in the hospital brought tears to my eyes. My chest heaved with a gulp of air.

The flicker repeated its two-note call.

"The bird calls you to dance," Niwako said. Then she was gone.

"Flicker. Flicker. Flicker. Flicker." The calls floated across the flood water. I stood. Stepping with the rhythm of the woodpecker's invitation, I turned around, drumming my feet on the boxcar. Other forest voices replaced the flicker's call. As I continued to tap, the air filled with the peaceful cooing of doves, a cardinal, the caw of a crow. High in the blue sky, a red-tailed hawk circled and dove. It screeched distantly above the watery scene. Tree frogs chirped, squirrels scolded, insects buzzed and a Harris sparrow sang its heart out. Had there been music all along and I just didn't hear it? Or was the entire timber waking up, refreshed after the long rain?

Earth's symphony swelled. I spun and danced. When I slowed to a peaceful sway, I stretched my arms straight out to my sides. The sun settled onto the tops of the trees to my right. A full moon rose to my left. I lifted my palms so that in my line of sight the sun rested in my right hand and the moon in my left. With the creatures around me, I rejoiced. From horizon to horizon, my reach encompassed all that I could see. My heart soared and I embraced the entire earth within it.

When the sun dipped behind the western tree line, the spell broke. The mystical, joyous connection with God's natural world ebbed in the waning light. I lowered my hands and found Daisy standing at my side. I scratched her head. My heart felt at peace. I breathed a silent prayer of gratitude for the light of the moon. This night would be a far cry from the absolute darkness of the last one.

Another facet of my ragged garnet gleamed in my mind as the last rays of the sun disappeared.

I pitched the now-dry tent by tying its cords to seams and bolts on the roof. I spread the bedroll, spare clothing, and comforter inside the tent, folding a few layers as a simple cushioning mattress. My spare clothing became a pillow. As the last red glow of the sun faded, Daisy and I crawled under the comforter. I slept almost immediately.

A few hours later, I woke, groaning. My head spun and my bloated belly burned. Waves of nausea shook my core. I thrashed the covers off and shot from the tent. I took one step toward the south edge of the roof and reeled with dizziness. Dropping to my knees, I crawled to the edge and heaved over the side. When the nausea passed, I wilted with exhaustion. I spent the rest of the night prone at the edge of the roof, alternately trembling with uncontrollable shivers and writhing with a clawing fever. The nausea returned several times. I shivered in the moonlight, too weak to move, the taste of bile lingering on my tongue.

As dawn colored the eastern horizon, the fire in my belly eased. Weak, I crawled back to the tent and collapsed on the bedroll. I spent a miserable day drifting in and out of a surreal consciousness. The sun warmed the tent. Daisy moved outside to sit in the short shadow it cast on the roof. Chills swept through my body and I drew the comforter around me.

Once I woke to hear Daisy lap at a pool of rainwater. Other than that she sat within my reach. If a dog could be worried, she certainly was. I managed to dig out a handful of food for her. She ate each kernel with dainty delicacy. Another time, I twisted the cap off a water canteen and sipped a couple of cool swallows, only to have the nausea return almost as soon as the water entered my stomach. Mostly I spent the day asleep, or wishing for sleep, sicker than I could recall I had ever been in my life.

In late afternoon, the sickness had passed. I crawled slowly from the tent and sat next to Daisy. Weakness made each of my limbs feel like it dragged a ton of bricks. "I guess maybe the mulberries were spoiled. What do you think?"

She batted her tail against the roof.

I sipped more water. This time it felt easy on my stomach. The worst was over. I had nothing to eat, though. Chances seemed slim that I would find anything edible below before the flood waters returned to the river channel. I crawled into the tent before sundown and fell into a deep and restful sleep.

31
THE VOICE OF THE TURTLEDOVE

*There is fine music everywhere in nature between
moss-covered stones and foliage... music beyond the
eardrums. We have had to create flutes and violins to
leave impressions deeper in than the eardrums, where
nature used to play.*

Thor Heyerdahl

When I woke the moon shone in a clear night sky.
The inside of the tent glowed with an eerie deep orange
light. My stomach contracted with sharp pains of hunger
and I felt desperate to find something to eat. I sat up and
reached for my water canteen. A couple sips of water
assuaged the sharpness I felt in my middle for a moment
before the discomfort returned in force.

"Oh, God." I winced in pain. A heavy shroud of
despair settled on my shoulders. I had really botched
things. My recent life seemed plagued with inadequacies
and poor decisions. Daisy and I suffered because of my
ineptitude.

"Hawea," Niwako greeted me. She appeared across
the tent from where I sat, luminous in the moonlight.

"Hello to you too," I said hoarsely. "You show up at
the strangest times."

"Maybe you need someone to talk to."

"Maybe I do," I admitted. "I sure do miss my husband. It would be nice to talk to him. He could've helped me get through this mess."

"Why can you not talk to him?" Niwako asked.

"He has died. I guess you wouldn't know that."

She shook her head and waited expectantly.

"He got sick—seriously sick with cancer. We did everything we could think of, but in the end, he died anyway. I failed him."

"Why do you say that?"

"I was unable to find a cure."

"Why was it up to you to find a cure? Are you a medicine woman?"

"No. But I was his wife and closest friend. He depended on me and I let him down."

"Sometimes it is the right day to die."

"But it wasn't—things were just starting to look up for us. We lived through two heartbreaking losses together, and then God sent a child to us. We had everything to look forward to. And he got sick."

She had no answer.

"He died by inches. Little by little, he slipped away from me and became a child, frightened in the dark. I couldn't calm those fears." I rocked, arms crossed in front of me as if I could comfort myself with a hug. "I feel like I failed him."

"You are very hard on yourself."

"I have to be."

"Why would you have to be?"

"Because it's true. I thought I could do anything I wanted, if I put my mind to it. But I failed. Our two babies died before they were born. Then Craig got sick and died. I feel as if everything was my fault. I should have saved them but I didn't. When it gets right down to it, I can't do anything right."

"Do others shun you for these failures? Is that why you are here?"

"No. I think they understand. I believe they've forgiven me, but I can't. I just can't let it go. Night time is so hard, so filled with memories and guilt. I miss my family. I miss the life we had. How do I get beyond this? How can I live with myself? How can I make it through each long and lonely night?"

"Sometimes," Niwako said, "Things are beyond our control and outside of our understanding. You should accept your limitations. Be kind to yourself."

"Be kind to myself," I mused. "How do I do that?"

The call of a meadowlark pierced the morning stillness from behind my tent. "Tow-hee-and-lickety-split. Tow-hee-and-lickety-split." I woke from the dream, startled.

"Be kind to myself. I wish I knew how to do that."

"Tow-hee-and-lickety-split," the lark sang again.

Really, a meadowlark? Here? Above the flood? Either it was lost or—dare I hope?—the flood waters had disappeared. Quietly I twisted around to where I could peek out the tent for a glimpse of the morning songster.

Not quietly enough. The feathered herald dove from the roof with a flash of yellow and black. It fluttered to a precarious perch on a nearby tree. The thin branch danced under its weight. Again the meadowlark burst into a short, labored flight to a limb on the nearest of the Two Elms.

I sighed. Hunger stabbed at my middle. I reached for my drinking water. The canteen sloshed, half-empty.

Slowly I savored a few sips as the cool draught tumbled to my stomach.

I crawled to the corner of the boxcar nearest the Two Elms, swung my legs over the side and gazed absently toward the meadowlark's now-hidden perch. As I peered down from the roof, I was relieved to see that the water level indeed was lower than it had been at sunset. Bits of debris and mud caked the emerging bushes a good six inches below the highest water mark. My hope and determination sprouted anew. The water was going down. As if to acknowledge the sunny turn in my spirits, the lark called again.

"Tow-hee-and-lickety-split."

"Really? Who—who—who?" a dove responded with peaceful coos.

For a couple of minutes the two sang a duet, as if in a zest for life after the uncertainty of a long storm. I felt kinship with the birds. Together the lark, the dove, and I had survived the storm. The worst was over. We could sing again.

"Be kind to yourself," I echoed Niwako's parting remark. The storm was over and a new day dawned. Surely things could only get better now.

I pulled myself tall and moved to the center of the roof. Extending my arms straight out from my shoulders, again I cradled the image of the sun in one hand and that of the moon in the other. I inhaled deeply, held my breath, and closed my eyes. As before, a mysterious energy coursed into my fingertips and latticed throughout my body.

The meadowlark heralded the dawn. The dove repeatedly cooed.

United with the songsters, I felt comforted. Together we had huddled in our shelters as the life blood of the planet drenched us all, and dampened our hope and optimism. We could do nothing but simply wait while time stood still. Now that the rain was over, the sun dawned in a cloudless sky. The flood waters receded. Our lives could continue as if they had never halted. We survived.

I curled my fingers into fists, as if I could tangibly cling to the energy which seemed to flow between the sun and the moon. A beautiful symphony swelled triumphant inside my head and I was one with all of God's creation.

After the moon sank below the tree line, I returned to sit on the edge of the boxcar roof, legs dangling below. Another face of my rough garnet had received a vigorous buffing to make it shine.Daisy nudged my arm and whined. I draped a hand over her shoulders and scratched her fondly.

"Hungry, girl? Me too. But the food is gone. We'll get out of here as soon as the water is low enough we can wade across that draw."

I gazed at the ebbing flood waters. A tree along the river line beyond the Two Elms shuddered and drew my attention. Its limbs shook again. Surrounded by fresh green boughs of neighboring trees that stood tall and strong in the morning stillness, this tree stood out among all of them because it was moving. Not only were many of its limbs shaking and shuddering, a darker green colored its leaves. Deep pinpoint shadows shook with the low hanging branches. It was almost as if—

"Squirrels! I bet squirrels are jumping around in that

tree. But why? I wonder why they are only in that one tree?"

The answer struck my mind and I jumped as if I had received an electrical shock. "It's a mulberry tree. Why didn't I see it before? Come on, Daisy. We're going to have fresh mulberries for breakfast."

I stuffed two collecting bags into my pockets and threaded my arms through the straps of the backpack so it hung in front of my chest. Daisy jumped a little as I lifted her, and kicked clumsily when I lowered her into the pack. I zipped it half way and backed carefully onto the rusty ladder. Grasping the upright supports and kicking around the broken rungs, we descended with no problems. I stood in cool water half way to my knees.

I unzipped the backpack and leaned forward. Daisy splashed eagerly into the water. After shifting the pack onto my back, we sloshed eastward toward the tree that danced. When we were twenty feet away, the squirrels scolded us fiercely. They shot from the shaking limbs, exiting in all directions to the safety of other trees. The mulberry tree was mine. With branches that sagged under the weight of thousands of berries in all stages from green to overripe, I knew the tree could provide sustenance for weeks. It was a mystery how I had overlooked it previously.

Eagerly I grabbed a handful of the dark berries. Their sweetness was absolutely the most delicious thing I had ever tasted. I offered some to Daisy. She ate them, but with little enthusiasm. Her eyes drooped and I almost heard her say, "Is this the best you can do?"

I ate several dozen mulberries and then made myself stop when I sensed that my stomach would reject them if I ate more. After filling a bag for later, we sloshed along the trees toward the draw. Fifty yards to the north, I noticed a low bush that was covered with small, green berries.

"Gooseberries!" I squealed. Never had I imagined that I would be so happy to see a gooseberry bush. Though my father and grandmother shared a fondness for tart pies made from this wild fruit, I had never learned to appreciate them. However, food was food. I spent a few minutes stripping small green berries from the bush into another bag. As I closed the bag, I popped one into my mouth.

Sour. My lips puckered like a prune as my tongue pulled away from the tart seed-filled berry. This would be a challenge. Maybe if they were mixed with some mulberries, a sweet-tart mixture would be palatable.

"Come, Daisy. Let's check out the draw."

She splashed ahead of me in water up to her shoulders and soon started swimming.

"Still too deep. But maybe tomorrow we can hike out, if the water keeps going down."

We turned back toward the Two Elms and the boxcar. Daisy splashed ahead and crawled onto the low mound at the house site. She shook water from her back. With a yip, she darted through weeds toward the center of the mound.

I sloshed out of the water and stood in the mud of the mound. Across the raised area, Daisy wagged her tail in excitement, her teeth closed around a small rabbit that lay on her front feet. The rabbit struggled weakly for a moment and then became limp. Daisy trotted proudly toward me and laid the rabbit at my feet.

"You caught it, girl. It's yours. Go ahead and eat it. I wish I could cook it for you."

She nosed the rabbit and pushed it toward me. "It's okay. Go ahead." I stepped over the rabbit and through the weeds. Daisy grabbed her prize and tore into its sodden pelt. She ate quickly before we splashed toward the boxcar again. As we scaled the broken ladder, she panted happily in the pack at my chest.

32
TALKING WITH BUTTERFLIES

We are here to witness the creation and to abet it.
Annie Dillard

The dog scrambled to the roof. I pulled myself over the edge and crawled to the center. I ate a couple fistfuls of mulberries and threw in a few gooseberries for good measure. Mixed with the sweet mulberries, the gooseberries tasted pretty good. I rolled the day pack into a makeshift pillow and lay back against the roof. With a sigh, Daisy flopped down beside me. Eyes closed, I basked in the morning sunshine.

After a moment, something tickled my right forearm. I opened my eyes to find a butterfly sitting on my arm. The hackberry emperor flexed its wings slowly in the sunshine. It probed my skin with its curled proboscis. Soon another spotted tan butterfly fluttered to my left arm.

I sat up slowly. I drew my knees in and propped my hands on top of them. Within a few seconds, a swarm of the small brown and ivory butterflies arrived. More than a dozen lit upon me. In slow rhythm they fanned their delicate wings. I held my breath until I couldn't hold it any longer. Then I breathed shallow inhalations and held tree-still. Each emperor butterfly tickled my skin and tasted my dried perspiration. I felt blessed in an affirmation of acceptance by these creatures of the natural world. It was enough to give me hope and renew my determination to complete the forty day plan. I could do this. With this kind of affirmation from the natural world, how could I give up now?

Minutes later, the butterflies fluttered upward. The first one flapped and rose into the slight breeze and the rest followed as if they were part of one being. They twittered in the morning air, scissoring randomly until they disappeared into the leaves of a young hackberry tree at the edge of my kitchen patio below.

"You are connected," Niwako said behind me.

"They are connected anyway."

"Don't you feel kinship with the butterflies?"

"Yes. I suppose you could say that."

"Every living thing draws strength through common breath."

"We're connected on the winds?"

"On the wind of the Great Spirit."

In my imagination, I looked at her. "Do you suppose then that my dad would receive a message I send on the wind?"

"Your dad?"

"Yes. My dad. Today is Father's Day and I'd wish him a wonderful day."

"What is Father's Day?"

"In my world, it's a day we designate once a year to honor our fathers."

"And you don't honor them the other days?"

"Of course we do. But Father's Day is special. It's a day to celebrate and tell your father how much you appreciate him."

"Is there such a day for honoring mothers?"

I nodded. "Mother's Day is earlier in the spring."

"You have already honored your mother then."

"And celebrated my motherhood. That is a bittersweet celebration for me."

"I don't understand bitter-sweet."

"Happiness mixed with sadness. Because of my lost children."

We became silent. I closed my eyes and let the breeze play against my cheeks and ruffle my hair.

"You seem very quiet. What thoughts are in your mind?" Niwako said.

"I'm thinking about families. Actually, I've been thinking about one mother and one son in particular."

"Who?"

"Mary and Jesus. They are important to the development of my culture's values."

"Why do you think of them?"

"I just figured something out. I feel kinship with Mary."

"Did you know her?"

"No. She lived centuries ago on another continent. Her story is written in our holy book, the Bible."

"How do you feel kinship with someone long gone?"

"She was the mother of Jesus, the leader of my faith."

"Is he an important man?"

"Many people think so."

"He is your leader."

"Yes. I'm here today because of him."

"I did not see him."

"No. You can't exactly see him. But when he was my age, he spent forty days alone with God in the wilderness. He seemed to draw strength from God's creation. That's my hope for myself."

"If you follow him, how is it that you feel kinship with his mother?"

"It's like this, Niwako. The record tells us that Mary was his mother, but God was his father."

"The Great Spirit."

"Yes. Jesus was connected to the Great Spirit from the very beginning. He affected people even before he was born. As a child, he met wise folks who sensed his connection to God. People recognized him as a great teacher."

She listened patiently.

"I've been trying to imagine how that made Mary feel. The ordinary cycle of life was upset for her. Topsy-turvy."

"Topsy. Turvy," Niwako echoed.

"If she was anything like me, she must have felt overwhelmed by the way her child affected others. Mysterious things must have happened almost every day. I bet she remembered every one of them. Jesus was trained, disciplined, and educated by God himself so that his wisdom quickly surpassed that of his own mother."

"I still don't understand your kinship with this woman."

"I think it's because the rest of us have to wait until we die to find the wisdom that Jesus possessed all along. When we pass into the spirit world and enter God's presence, I think we will find that moment to be the greatest adventure of our lives. At least I hope that it will be so. To enter God's presence would have to be an exuberating experience. Perhaps we'll instantly learn the most fulfilling wisdom we will ever learn."

Niwako nodded.

I continued, "I think I understand a little of what Mary felt, of the awe that filled her heart with expectations as her oldest son grew up. Jesus knew that wisdom before his death. My two babies were also with the omniscient God of love from before their births. Their limp little bodies yielded up spirits which I never had a chance to nurture or to teach or to watch unfold. They were nurtured by God alone from the very beginning, as Jesus was."

"You feel kinship with the mother of Jesus because your babies are connected to the Great Spirit."

"Yes. Someday, Niwako, when my days on earth are done, those two precious babes will take my hands and show me around in Paradise. But until then, I'm still here, still struggling to get through each day... still growing... still learning."

With a sigh, I turned toward the morning sun.

"Where is your father this day?" Niwako redirected my thoughts.

"I'm not sure. He may be in Hays. Or he might be closer, at his cabin in town a few miles away."

"How would you honor him if you were together?"

"Our family celebrations usually involve a special dinner. Maybe I'd help fix a cake or a pie for dessert. I'd give him a card filled with meaningful words. Perhaps a little gift."

"You could do that at any time."

"Yes. I could. But today when I think of him, I feel devotion and gratitude tug at my heart."

"Is this day different than other days you honored your father?"

"I think it is. He helped me so much over the last year while my husband became weaker. And he had confidence in me. More than I have myself. I can relate to the child's love for the parent. You see, Jesus spent three decades living quietly in a domestic situation. He and his mother must have been close. He worked in a village as a skilled carpenter. She knew that someday this would all come to an end, but she didn't know when that would be."

"When did it end?"

"He was thirty, like I am now. Imagine the meeting between mother and son which launched the three-year ministry that would forever shake the world. Jesus returned home from a day of work and hung his carpenter tools in their usual place. His mother greeted him with her usual smile. Then she probably studied his face for further signs, wondering, 'Is the moment coming near?'

"This time, rather than his usual loving embrace, Jesus held her at arm's length and gazed a long moment into her eyes. He said softly, 'It is time.'

"A chill shot through her body. 'Must you go, my Son?'

"'You know it is ordained.'

"'But wait a little longer—I beg you. I fear for you.'

"He held her tightly in his embrace before he answered, 'I cannot delay any longer. It is time.'

"Tears welled in her eyes. She gasped for breath. She desperately clung to him as if he could pass her the strength to face the uncertain future. At last she nodded to him and whispered, 'Go then, my son, and do what you must do.'

"The next morning he left Nazareth to journey to the Jordan River where he was baptized by John. He began his public life with a forty-day sojourn in the wilderness."

"And here you are, in the wilderness today," Niwako said.

"Exactly. I know—I can feel—what a comfort it was to Jesus to have his mother's approval and confidence."

"Do you think he would have stayed home if she insisted?"

"No. I think he would have gone just the same without her blessing. But it was so much better to have it. I understand because my dad sent me off with the same unwavering confidence."

"He sent you here?"

"He gave me his blessing. You see, after Craig died, I sat in his university office, struggling with the decision to embark on this journey. 'I had this idea,' I told him. 'The thing is, if I do this, I would be away from Phoebe for several weeks. And it has to happen soon. This summer is the only time in my life when I could do it.'

"'Then do it,' he said. 'I have great faith in your ideas.'

"His endorsement was enough to give me courage to proceed. Without even knowing what it was I intended to do, he said, 'Do it.' Just as I imagine Jesus' mother said to him.

"What better definition of parenthood is there, Niwako? To watch your child grow, to see him mature, and to turn this child loose in the world with your confidence—that is what being a parent is all about. Knowing I have the support of a parent behind my task put a song in my heart and filled me with love. My dad believes in me. I must find the strength to believe in myself."

There was silence for a few moments.

"He is a man worthy of great honor," Niwako said.

The hackberry emperor butterflies chose that moment to rise from the leaves where they hid below us. The small swarm fluttered upward in the morning breeze and headed west, dancing across the tops of ripening wheat.

"The butterflies might carry your wishes to your father," Niwako said.

I nodded. "Thank you, Daddy. Happy Father's Day." My wish rose on the morning breeze and followed the butterflies toward the horizon. I watched them disappear in the distance.

33
DRYING OUT

*When you walk across the fields with your mind pure
and holy, then from all the stones, and all growing
things, and all animals, the sparks of their soul come
out and cling to you, and then they are purified and
become a holy fire in you.*

Hasidic saying

The following morning at daybreak, Daisy and I
descended the ladder. I returned to the top and stuffed
my grimy extra clothing and as much of the bedding as I
could into the pack. I tied my boots to a strap on the top,
clipped on my empty water canteens, and backed down
the ladder to stand in mud.

I shook the shrubs surrounding the base of the
ladder and parted the branches to scrutinize the ground
below. Sure enough, there was the canteen which
splashed into the flood water during my initial ascent to
the roof. I picked it up and tapped it against the boxcar
to dislodge some of the muck. I looked back below the
bushes. After a minute, I discerned a rectangular shape
covered in black ooze. My Peterson *Field Guide to Edible
Wild Plants*. I picked it up, my heart sinking. The book
looked like a total loss.

"What are you holding?" Niwako asked behind me.

"This is the book I dropped into the flood water. My field guide."

"A book?"

"Yes. Full of important information regarding what plants are safe to eat and giving warnings about those that are not."

"I can't see how you would pull that kind of information from the box."

"It's more than a box. It has about three hundred pages of illustrations and written descriptions. I don't know how I'll be able to get along without it."

"What are pages?"

"I'd show you if I could."

"Can it be washed?"

"Washed... Maybe. It might be possible to rinse the mud away, but the paper pages would be so soggy they'd stick tight together when they dried. They'd be unreadable."

"You should not give up without trying."

I glanced toward my native friend. "You're right."

I submerged the field guide in our utility bucket and sloshed it slowly back and forth until the cover was free of mud. Holding the book at arm's length, I tested the pages. Their saturated condition made them stick together. When I tried to separate the pages, they tore. I submerged the book in the bucket again and opened the cover. I fanned the pages apart until they floated freely, anchored by the binding. Taking care to keep the pages separate, I lifted the book. With the cover spread into a full circle and the pages fanned apart, I set it upright on the boxcar floor.

"Maybe it will dry like that and at least part of it will be useable. Hope it's the part I need."

Daisy trotted toward my beckoning whistle. We slipped eastward through the mud. When we passed the mulberry tree, I filled a small bag with fresh berries. I popped a handful into my mouth as we turned toward the draw. Water remained across the farm lane but now it was only ankle-deep. Daisy splashed across and I followed.

When we arrived at the gravel county road, I dried my feet with a camp towel and put on socks and boots. We stepped briskly along the road. An hour and a half later, I stood beside my Plymouth. Relief and joy washed over me as I walked the last few paces. Standing at the front bumper I ran my hands tenderly along the edges of the hood. I wanted to hug the car.

Chuckling, I shook my head. I spread the comforter across the front seats and fished the car key out of a pocket on the pack.

"Come, Daisy. Let's go to town."

She jumped eagerly to the passenger seat. I drove to my parents' cabin on the south edge of town. Nobody was there. After locating the hidden key I unlocked the door. For the rest of the morning, I laundered my camp clothes and bedding. In a long hot shower, I lathered my entire body twice and relished the clean water as it washed over my head and shoulders and ran in rivulets to my toes.

When the stream of hot water became tepid, I finally turned it off and dried myself with a folded towel from the bathroom shelf. Wrapped in the towel while my clothing washed, I sampled a few of the items left in the refrigerator and headed to the soft, inviting bed for a nap. I felt like Goldilocks enjoying the absent hospitality of the three bears, but I knew my parents would have welcomed me had they been home.

The bed—oh what luxury to recline on a mattress! I pulled the clean sheets around me and with a contented sigh drifted off to sleep. The raucous buzz of the clothes dryer at the end of its cycle woke me. I dressed in clean, warm clothes and turned to Daisy.

"Would you like a bath?"

She wagged her tail enthusiastically and gave me a doggy smile. Her tongue extruded over her front teeth. Her brown eyes sparkled. I dug an old wash tub from a corner of my dad's garage, ran water from a hose and added a couple gallon jugs filled with fresh hot water from the kitchen tap. I patted the edge of the tub. Daisy, my water-loving dog, eagerly jumped in. Energized after her bath, she raced in circles around a young catalpa tree in the yard. Every few seconds she stopped to shake. Bath water sprayed from her nose to the tip of her stubby tail. I laughed at her frenzied delight.

After folding my laundry, I filled all the canteens with cool, fresh well water and replenished the supply in my car reserve. As I headed toward the door for the last time, I paused at the wall telephone. A sudden longing to hear Phoebe's voice tugged at my heartstrings. I picked up the phone and dialed my sister's number. It rang and rang until I finally gave up, dejected.

"Guess they went to town," I mumbled. "Or they're outside."

I secured my folks' cabin. Daisy and I got in the car and headed to my grandmother's house in town. She was almost always home, and today was no exception. She laughed heartily when she opened the door. Her arms flew wide and she embraced me with a loving hug.

"I've been a-wondering how you did in the rain. Did the river come up?"

I nodded that it had.

"That's what Mrs. Campbell was a-saying. Thought it was out of its banks."

"Yes, it got pretty high," I said.

"What did you do?"

Not wanting to alarm her, I glossed over the details, but I briefly described the last few days.

"The boxcar, huh? Isn't it locked?"

"Yes, it is."

"You got a key?"

I shook my head.

"How'd you get in?"

"There was a kind of rotten spot in the corner of the door."

"Big enough to get through?

"Barely."

"You going back?"

"Yes."

She shook her head. "I don't know. I worry about you so."

I smiled. "I'll be fine. After all, you lived out there for years."

She laughed. "I did. Yes, I did. I've got chicken and dumplings on for dinner. Can you have a bite with me?"

"I'd love to."

The warm chicken broth over biscuit dough was heaven to my neglected stomach. With the dumplings, Grandma served fresh green beans from her garden. It was an exquisite combination. She brought out ice cream and my favorite homemade brown sugar raisin cookies for dessert.

"Take some with you," she urged as we cleared the dining table.

"Okay. You talked me into it. Hey, do you mind if I try to call Kay? I'd like to find out how Phoebe's doing."

"No. Go ahead."

While she ran the dishwater, I dialed my sister's number on Grandma's rotary phone. It rang and rang. Still no answer. With a sigh, I replaced the receiver in its cradle.

After we washed dishes, Grandma Georgia handed me a small container of cookies. She ushered me out the door with a warm hug. She grabbed my wrist as I turned to go and pressed a small key into my palm.

"For the boxcar," she said. "Now you can open the door."

"Thank you, Grandma." I hugged her again, clutching the precious key.

"You be careful now," she called as I backed the car out of her driveway. I waved through my open window and drove away.

I parked the car again, carefully sorted food supplies and added a three-day ration to my pack. Shouldering it, I clipped the heavy canteens to my belt, locked the car and whistled for Daisy. As we tramped back to the Farm along the road, the optimism in my heart was tempered slightly with the disappointment of missing Phoebe. I hesitated. I thought about turning back, running to the car, and driving straight to my sister's home where I could sweep my girl into my aching arms. The warmth of the sun brought me back to the gravel road. The rain was over. Flood waters had receded. I had survived the worst. I couldn't quit now. I would be abandoning my best shot at discovering the purpose for my new life. I had to persevere to the end of the forty day sojourn. I must.

With renewed determination, I turned west and stepped briskly along the road.

Back at the boxcar, I unlocked the padlock on the door. Heaving against it with all my might, I managed to roll its rusty wheels along their tracks until a four-foot opening gaped from roof to floor in the side of the boxcar. There was the field guide, pages drooping together. Gingerly, I lifted the tome, testing the pages. They remained slightly damp. Not soggy, as I left them, but damp enough to be pliable. I pulled out my knife and slid its long blade between the pages where they drooped together before setting the book back on the boxcar floor to finish drying. Encouraged, I boosted myself up to sit in the doorway. I surveyed the tree-lined rooms of Camp Two. Mud and muck caked the surfaces and corners. Recalling the rats, I decided to leave the tent on the roof and just use the boxcar and the old foundation for day activities.

I scaled the ladder with the pack, unloaded my laundry and our food rations, stacked them carefully in the tent and zipped the door shut. Then I returned to ground level and whistled for Daisy.

"Let's go for a walk."

We circled eastward again to the tree-lined river bank. Although running high, all the flood water was contained within the banks. A brisk current carried flotsam and debris along its course. We went to the mulberry tree for supper's fresh supply before turning south, following the edge of the trees along the river. At the end of the farm road, where the cultivated field broadened as the river meandered eastward, we turned west and tramped along a row of sodden soybeans until we met the tree line again on the west side of the field. The plants had matted to the ground, but new growth already turned upward toward the afternoon sun.

I turned north, following the trees. A hundred yards later, I located the grape vines where previously I had tied the plank of barn siding for a wilderness writing desk. The plank was gone, washed away in the flood water.

When the crop rows stretched straight eastward to the boxcar, I turned and traipsed through the bowing crops again. The wheat didn't look well at all. I doubted it would be able to stand again after submersion in the floodwaters. About halfway across the field, a low rise in the land led me up a small hill. Fifty yards beyond the crest, a small white rock caught my eye between the rows. When I stood above it, I reached down and picked it up.

"An arrowhead." Smiling, I turned it over. I fingered its rough edges reverently. "Well, would you look at that."

Niwako appeared at my left shoulder. "Ummm," she mused. She reached forward to touch the chipped flint with her index finger. "It has my brother's mark."

"Your brother? You can tell by looking who made an arrowhead?"

She nodded. "His flint-napping skills were very refined. He took great pride in his work, so he made a special notch as a signature mark. This one, here. See?"

The artifact in my hand—the first arrowhead I had found in my entire life—took on new meaning. I rubbed it against my shirt tail to clean a bit of mud from the stone. Then I pocketed it carefully and headed to the boxcar, alone with Daisy again. I felt certain that my discovery was a sign that my luck had changed. Everything would be fine.

34
POLISHING FACETS OF GRIEF

Go forth, under the open sky, and list
To Nature's teachings, while from all around—
Earth and her waters, and the depths of air—
Comes a still voice.

William Cullen Bryant

Fresh matches, fresh batter, and fresh berries helped me create a gourmet meal the following morning on my camp stove. Pancakes sizzled on the griddle. I drowned them in a steaming sweet-tart sauce of mixed mulberries and gooseberries. After breakfast I cleaned up and packed for a morning walk. The fallen cottonwood tree called me again. Whistling for Daisy I headed out the driveway toward the Harris bridge.

The draw on the farm lane was water-free, but remained sticky with mud. It was the only soft spot we encountered. From the bridge, I noted that the river had dropped a few feet, though it still ran higher than normal. We traipsed along the road. Daisy bounded into the trees but her progress paralleled my own. Twice I heard her scuttle through the underbrush in hot pursuit of some small creature. Once I saw a rabbit leading her on a frenzied chase. She came up empty every time this morning. The timber had returned to normal, its creatures wild and free.

As I rounded the last turn in the road, I listened intently for the rippling music of the cottonwood leaves. Not a breath of air stirred. The rustling I anticipated eluded me. My heart fell when I saw the tree. It no longer sprouted fresh green leaves. They had been replaced by brittle brown tufts.

"Hey there," I whispered. "Was that flood too much for you?"

A few leaves fluttered to the ground. I sat on a limb to listen but there was nothing to hear. The tree's voice had been silenced. Sighing, I collected my pack and trudged north, back to camp.

The following days blended together, growing into weeks. They were filled with regular routines that involved collecting fresh produce from the river bank, daily forays across the fields or into the trees, and time spent thinking, dreaming, or writing. I fell into the rhythms and my heart knew seeds of contentment. Now and then when I needed conversation Niwako showed up. The tedious buffing of more faces of my rough gemstone continued through each day and each week.

I woke at first light to complete morning activities before the blazing summer sun wrung rivulets from my face and torso. First chore was to secure breakfast from the natural garden along the river bank. Fortunately for me, the field guide had been salvaged to where I could use it. Each day I became more confident in my own ability to identify the edible plants provided in the timbered riverbank area without the guide. I was living my dream. As an adolescent, I had been fascinated by a newspaper article entitled "Ever Tried Eating a Cattail?" The article and accompanying photos had launched me into a fascination with native plant identification and use.

"Early man," wrote Roger Tory Peterson in the field guide's editorial note, "was probably a vegetarian." His son Lee identified over a thousand plant species offering edible and nutritious parts at various times of the year in eastern North America. Other people might call them weeds. To me they represented God's garden, scattered randomly along my path, mixed with a wide variety of non-edible—even poisonous—plants. But for those who cared to learn, dinner was free for the taking.

The staples of my wilderness diet consisted of eighteen different wild plant species. Some provided berries or seeds. Some offered edible flowers. Quite a few were classified as greens. Cattails, daylilies, mulberries, elderberry blossoms, and gooseberries continued to provide sustenance as the days and weeks passed. After the flood, I found a stand of cattails along the southern edge of the river's bend. When the flower spikes appeared they produced a coat of yellow pollen. To collect this flour-like substance, I shook the spikes inside a collecting bag. It made a good addition to pancakes.

I tried redbud pods. The young pods of early summer resembled peas, but those I boiled in June were too mature and tough to be edible.

A wide variety of wild plants, including some woody vines and trees, yielded fresh top leaves or young shoots to cook as greens like spinach. If I could have, I would have added bacon, hard-boiled eggs, and vinegar to the greens prior to serving, but I had none of these ingredients.

Curly dock leaves, just as they unfurled, were edible. They became bitter with age, and needed to be cooked in two or three changes of boiling water to be palatable. I collected only tender young leaves and found the flavor to be better than that of grape leaves. But they were the same sickly green color as grape leaves when cooked.

I tried milkweed once, harvesting the young tender top leaves and buds, only about five or six inches of the top part of the plants. After washing the tips, I covered them with boiling water, boiled them a minute, drained, and covered them with more boiling water. After changing water five times, I boiled the plant fifteen minutes. My trusted field guide explained that using cold water in the water changes would seal in the bitter flavor. Boiling water removed it. Cooked carefully I found the milkweed to be very palatable.

Dandelion crowns, just below the surface of the soil, were tasty. I clipped away the dark green portions of the leaves, leaving just the blanched whitish area above the root and the developing flower buds. Boiled five minutes, they were quite acceptable.

I found lamb's quarters to be mild and pleasant, tasting better than spinach. This plant was plentiful and easy to identify. Boiled five minutes and seasoned with peppergrass seeds, it became one of my favorite wild foods.

Woodland nettles thrived in the timber. Through June, I was able to collect the tips of the growing plants and they were still edible when boiled. The first person who sampled stinging nettles must have been really hungry. It would never have occurred to me to eat plants which fought back had I not already known my family headed to the timber for nettles every spring.

The top leaves and stems of redroot pigweed were a tasty source of greens, also readily available and easily identified. Boiled ten to twenty minutes without changing water, I found pigweed greens to be tasty. They were a bright green when cooked. Greens which retained their color after cooking seemed to taste better than those which became dull green.

Young leaves of the yellow sweet clover plant collected before flowers appeared could be boiled for five minutes and served as greens. However, I found their flavor rank and unpleasant.

A number of plants found in disturbed areas produced seeds with a peppery flavor. I collected the dried seeds of peppergrass and shepherd's purse to season the greens and elderberry potato mixture. The peppery flavor was very faint. Another plant that yielded a tart intense flavor was the violet wood sorrel. The clover-like leaves with heart-shaped leaflets needed no cooking. I enjoyed nibbling them as a snack while hiking, as well as adding them to other dishes to spice them up.

After the early morning walk to gather breakfast, I relaxed in the shade of my tree-lined rooms from mid-morning until late afternoon. When the sun dangled low above the western tree line, we left for another foray. On days when the breeze hid and not even a leaf stirred, the oppressive heat became an oven. I couldn't muster energy for much of anything.

The bundled cattail leaves finally dried. Recalling a lesson in basketry from my youth, I soaked a few of them until they were pliable. Then I wove them crudely around a framework of green twigs to form a primitive basket. I pulled a few of the long leaves into fibers and braided them into twine. After winding the twine's midpoint around the neck of my arrowhead, I fashioned the twine into a loop. The chipped relic became a pendant.

Each morning, noon, and night I scribbled the day's events in my journal and wrote letters to be delivered at a later date. More and more, I found myself writing to Phoebe, telling her about my wilderness adventures. Thoughts of her occupied nearly every moment.

Though less frequent, nightmares still occasionally woke me screaming from an uneasy sleep. When this happened my heart could be comforted if I left the tent and lay outside under the stars. Their twinkling beauty across the dome of heaven calmed my anxieties and gave me fresh perspective.

Time passed. One day blended seamlessly into the next one. The routines became a comfort and stilled the unrest in my heart. My gemstone of life was slowly taking shape. Each day's activities served to polish another facet a tiny bit more. Soon, I thought, my gemstone would be complete and I would be able to begin the next chapter of my life.

35
METEORITE CRATER

*I know a painting so evanescent that it is seldom
viewed at all, except by some wandering deer.
It is a river who wields the brush.*

Aldo Leopold

Every three or four days, Daisy and I made supply
trips to the car. On each third supply run, I drove to
Grandma's house for a brief visit. Late in June I again
dialed my sister's number. This time, she answered. She
chattered of Phoebe's days, the outings, the play times,
the cute things she had said and done. Then she gave
the phone to Phoebe. When I heard my toddler's bright
voice, I choked up and could hardly talk.

I didn't want to return to the boxcar. An invisible
chain of memories locked around my heart. It pulled me
in the opposite direction, toward my baby girl. But in
only a few more days, my sojourn would be over. I
decided to persevere.

The following morning, Daisy and I wandered
through the timber toward the location of our first camp
site. I stopped at the elder bushes and clipped a couple
of the flower clusters. Though the plant had recovered
from the flood, its blooming season now waned. The
remaining blossoms lost their brilliant sheen, and
thousands more littered the ground at my feet. Tiny

green berries replaced the petals. I clipped half of the remaining flower clusters to garnish the pancakes of my next meal.

Daisy bounded through the underbrush toward the river. Circling through the trees, I skirted the edge of the nettle patch, now waist high. A few yips toward the south told me Daisy had found something to chase.

I wondered if I would recognize the small clearing where I first pitched the tent. The undergrowth filled the spaces with flourishing plants. They grew so fast in the summer heat I imagined I could actually see the leaves unfurl. I struggled through the jungle and stumbled into an area encircled by young trees. This was it. This had to be it. I discovered the limb I had dragged into my first camp. It remained wedged between two tree trunks. Lowering my pack to the ground, I sat on the branch. I remembered the view from the first days of my quest and marveled how quickly things changed in the timber.

The tops of grasses a few yards south waved slightly. Without a sound, a doe stepped into view. The deer trail. I had forgotten. I ducked a little lower to watch unseen. A spotted fawn trailed its mother along the narrow path. Transfixed, I watched their silent progress.

As the deer neared my hiding place, a distant anguished bark pierced the usual morning chatters and buzzes. *Daisy.* I whipped my head toward the yelp. Startled, the deer pair bounded away.

When a second distressed yelp echoed through the trees I stood up and grabbed my pack. "Daisy? Where are you, girl?" I thrashed through the undergrowth.

A hundred yards into the woods, I realized I would not be able to find her unless she continued to bark. "Daisy? Daisy!"

I heard a frightened yip. She sounded further away than before. I turned and walked a few feet in the other direction, stopped and called again. Slowly and painstakingly, I trailed the desperate yelps, calling to her in reassurance every few feet.

After what seemed an eternity, the yelps petered to miserable whimpers. They seemed close. If only I could catch a glimpse of her familiar liver brown and white markings through the summer weeds. A dread for what I would find crept into my heart. What could have happened? Was she injured? Had she tried to chase a squirrel up that century-old oak tree over there, only to fall on her back? Had she broken a leg? Did she find some kind of snare that a stranger set and forgot?

Heart pounding, I parted the last barrier of brush between us. A circular depression, fifteen feet across, filled a small clearing at the base of the ancient oak. Mud filled the shallow sink area. Daisy stood mired in the mud. She wiggled feebly and whined.

"Are you stuck, Daisy?"

She wagged her stubby tail.

"Do you suppose this is the meteorite crater Grandma talks about? Looks like a mud puddle to me. Let me think a minute."

Slowly and carefully, I walked around the edge of the mud crater. With each step, I bent the border grasses and sedges to the ground and placed my boots squarely on top of the plants. Daisy whined as I moved away from her.

"Hold on girl, I'll get you out. Somehow." After completing the circle with no problem, I came back to the spot where Daisy was closest to the edge. She faced the opposite direction.

I stepped left two paces so she could see me, leaned over the deceptive mud and stretched my arms toward her as far as I could reach. My fingertips bridged the gap between us and I scratched her head. She craned her neck around, licked my hand, and wagged her tail. I sensed her distress melt away. She trusted me to get her out of the quick mud.

I could barely reach her from where I stood. There was no way I would be able to find leverage to release her legs. I gave her head another pat and pulled back.

I set my pack on the ground, well away from the edge of the muck, and dug out my straps. With them in hand, I retreated to the base of the oak tree. I looked across at two other trees spaced irregularly around the area. Which was closest to Daisy? Counting paces, I returned to the mud's edge. Nine paces. I made my way to the other trees and counted paces to Daisy from them, adding a couple as the distance across the mud increased. Nine paces beat fourteen and seventeen. The oak tree would be our anchor.

I wrapped a strap around the oak, knotted the loop firmly, and gave it a test tug. It held. At the free end, I attached a second strap, and the third to the end of that one. Standing at the edge of the muck, the extra length of the strap looped around my right forearm, I swung the end over the mud and tossed it toward Daisy. It fell ten inches wide of her reach. I pulled it back, and tossed again but it landed off the target.

"Third time's charm," I muttered and tried yet again. The tip fell across Daisy's shoulders. "Can you get it, girl? Grab the strap. Fetch."

She craned her head around, snapping at the air, unable to reach the strap which dangled across her back.

I retreated to the base of the tree again. After a quick search, I located a stout twig. Wrapping the free end of the strap around its center I secured the stick. At the shore of Daisy's mud pot, I tossed it toward her. It landed beyond her a couple feet.

"Get the stick, Daisy."

I tugged it slowly toward her head.

"Fetch, girl. You can do it."

She snapped up the stick when it was within reach.

"Good girl. Now hang on."

I gave a tentative tug. She tightened her jaws.

"That's right. Hang on."

Her shoulder muscles rippled as she attempted to move her feet. I tugged harder, and she clamped down on the rope and stick. I leaned against her bite and wrenched backwards with all my might.

The stick broke. Daisy loosed her hold on the strap and I crashed to the ground.

36
TRAPPED

Two are better than one,
...For if they fall, one will lift up the other.

Eccl 4:9,10

"There's got to be a way to get you out, Daisy. Give me a minute."

I pushed myself to my feet and began a methodical sweep of the vegetation, looking for something— anything—that might provide an idea for a way out of this mess. Fifty feet to the south I found a three-foot limb with a girth wider than my boot by half. Maybe, if this limb would float on the mud, I could use it to get close enough for a firm hold on Daisy. I dragged the branch to the edge of the mud and extended it toward her. I wrapped the strap a couple times around my waist and stepped gingerly onto the branch. Balancing carefully, I bent forward to pet her again before I reached below her rib cage, my knuckles brushing the surface of the mud. I tugged upward. Daisy didn't budge.

"That's not going to happen. Okay. What about your feet?"

I grabbed the leg closest to me and worked it upwards. A gripping suction fought every small gain we made, but finally her foot came free from the mud. I stretched upward to unkink the cramps in my thighs, but I didn't let go of her foot.

"Now for another." With a deep breath, I leaned close to her again and worked to extricate her other foreleg. I placed her feet on the limb and stretched my legs again.

Her third leg required greater concentration to extract from its prison of goop. Slowly, I worked her foot upwards, each fraction of an inch a harrowing ordeal. Daisy, growing impatient, began to jerk a little. I feared she would slip off the branch and land back in the mud. With my left hand, I assisted her balance on our log raft. My leg muscles strained to keep my own equilibrium. I leaned into the straps looped around my waist and worked Daisy's right hind leg free with my dominant hand. Slowly her foot moved upwards until the mud released it with a long slurping sound. She clawed desperately against the limb.

Noting that our branch had settled lower in the mud, I turned immediately to work on her fourth leg. It loosened quickly. In the fraction of a second when she broke free from the quick mud, I boosted her to safety. Daisy flew through the air. Simultaneously, the shift in our equilibrium threw me off balance. I slipped. My whole weight fell against the straps around my waist.

The knot at the tree broke loose. I tottered, flailing my arms. The floating branch tipped sideways in the mud. In a desperate effort to regain my balance, I stepped left. Into the mud. My right foot slammed down beside the left one. I swayed for a moment before I caught myself and stood upright.

I inhaled sharply and lifted my right knee. It didn't budge. I tried the left knee. Heavy as my Kimball piano, it remained frozen in place. I could move neither foot. In seconds the mud surrounded the tops of my boots and the cool ooze closed around my ankles. I was trapped.

I tugged at the strap encircling my middle. It was slack. I removed it from my waist and tossed the end toward Daisy. It would be no help to me now. Straining against the mud, I worked one foot at a time. Instead of releasing me from the muck, the suction intensified. As if starving fingers from the depths of the earth clawed hungrily at my boots, I sank lower.

Heart beating madly, I bent forward and reached into the mud with my fingertips. I withdrew them quickly. No problem. Why couldn't I just lift my feet? I grabbed my right ankle with both hands and tugged upwards. Nothing. It was my weight. My own body mass locked me firmly in the mud.

The bright sun marched across the blue sky, oblivious to my plight. Shadows crept across the imprisoning crater. I was helpless to follow them. I squirmed in the heat whenever the fickle shadows left me exposed. Except for the cool mud around my feet, I became drenched in sweat and a monstrous thirst left my tongue feeling like a wad of cotton in my mouth.

I sipped a swallow of water from the canteen strapped to my belt. How long would the water last? How was I going to free myself?

Every time I jogged one foot or the other, it sank deeper into the mud. By the time evening shadows stretched around me, the surface of the mud surrounded my legs halfway to my knees.

Daisy remained nearby. She occasionally circled the bog sniffing, but most of the time she lay at the shore watching me. Now and then she whimpered as if puzzled why we weren't moving out of here, back to our camp and to supper. To control my growing panic, I spoke to her.

"I know. I've really done it this time, haven't I? There has to be a way out of this. I just can't think what it is." Daisy, of course, had nothing to say. Niwako remained hidden. I was on my own.

As the sun sank out of sight, a black despair rose from the cool mud and wrapped my heart in a hopeless fog. A chill crept up my legs. I shivered uncontrollably. My teeth chattered. I wailed into the thickening gloom. Daisy whined. She twirled tightly in the nearby grasses and traced a bed for herself. She settled down for the night. Every few minutes I rubbed my arms to pull warmth into my body. Fatigue overwhelmed me. My hands fell limply to my sides. I swayed in the darkness, disoriented, struggling to remain conscious.

The minutes of that long night dragged into hours. My head drooped. Just as I nodded to sleep, I jerked awake, desperate to remain on my feet through the darkest hours. The third time I nodded off, I woke with a start, my heart pounding. The scream that echoed in my ears was my own. I felt defeated. I didn't have the strength nor the will to keep myself upright any longer.

37
A GLIMMER OF HOPE

Those who are dead are never gone.
They are there in the thickening shadow.
The dead are not under the earth:
They are in the tree that rustles,
They are in the wood that groans,
They are in the water that sleeps.

Birago Diop

This would be the end. Who would find me? How long would it take? Silently, I bade farewell to Daisy. I bent my knees and sank to a squat. As the moist coolness of the bog soaked into the seat of my pants, I looked at the stars sparkling overhead. I bowed my head and tried to relax, shivering sporadically.

"Ann! Annsy!" a voice in the distance called my name.

"Craig?" I answered softly.

He appeared, illuminated by the starlight so that his blond hair carried a soft glow as he walked into view.

"Craig?" I said again. This was not the shell of a man who slipped away from me during the previous winter months. This was Craig, the man who knew birds, who had been my closest companion and friend for ten years. Dressed in jeans and a t-shirt, he swished through the forest undergrowth in his worn hunting boots, his favorite denim jacket hanging loosely from his shoulders.

He marched confidently right up to Daisy and crouched beside her. She didn't stir.

"Craig—you okay?" I said hoarsely.

"I'm fine," he answered. "You?"

"Well...," I shrugged and gestured to the smooth surface of the mud. "I kind of got myself into a pickle."

He smiled wryly. "I see that. What're you going to do about it?"

"I don't think there's anything I can do. I've been stuck for hours. I can't get out." My voice broke into a frightened whimper.

"Hey—hey. Don't give up. There's got to be some way out of this."

I shook my head and drooped. "I wish you'd tell me what it is."

"This is something you have to figure out."

"I can't, Craig. I've done everything I can think of and nothing works. I just get sucked in deeper."

"Well, don't give up. Never give up."

"Why not?"

"You've got to keep going for Phoebe. For our daughter."

I sobbed.

"Ann, get hold of yourself. You have to find a way out of here. Phoebe needs you."

"She needs you too."

"Yes. Well, we both know that can't be. You, however, are still here."

"Yeah. Here. Stuck in the mud. Just like I'm stuck in a joyless world. Look at me. Look at this mess I've made. I just can't do this any longer."

"Of course you can. You've got to."

"But I can't. I miss you so much, Craig. I can't stand it. I'm so lonely—it's like—I'm that tree in the forest—that tree falling in the forest. And there's absolutely nobody around to hear me fall."

"Unlike a tree, though, you can walk out of the forest and find someone to share your future."

"Are you saying you think my wilderness idea was a mistake? That if I could leave, I should?"

He shook his head. "All I'm saying is that you're not too likely to meet any new people while you're hiding from everybody. No wonder you're lonely."

"And it's okay with you if I find a new companion?"

"Life is for the living, Ann. You need to do what's right for you and Phoebe and that would not include giving up and letting go."

"I've made such a mess of things. Who'd want me anyway?"

"Why do you say that?"

"Well, just look. Here I am. Stuck. Phoebe might need me. But I can't get out of here. I failed you when you needed me most. Everything that was important over the last few years—I failed all of it. I'm such a misfit. Poor excuse for a human being."

"You're too hard on yourself. Why do you think you should be able to control life and death? You're only human."

"But I let you down. We had everything going for us—and I didn't find the treatment that could cure you. Everyone I love, I let them down when they need me most."

Craig was silent for a moment before he responded. "I don't think you let me down. I think you kept your promise. You stayed with me to the end. Did you ever stop to think that if there had been any way—any treatment available—any cure—the doctors would have found it? That wasn't your job. None of us can live forever. That's a fact. It was my time."

"But—"

"Wait. Let me finish. You are only human. You can't control who lives and who dies. You just have to do the best you can to love the people you're with as long as you can. And I'm tellin' you, the cycle doesn't end when your heart stops beating. Just because you can't see beyond doesn't mean there's nothing there."

"I know."

"I don't think you do. I think you're feeling so sorry for yourself right now, you can't think straight."

"But I miss you."

"And you always will. But here's the thing. I'm always going to be here. So are the babes. We will live through you as long as you hold us in your heart."

"It's so hard. You knew it would be hard on all of us when you were gone."

"Hard. But not impossible, Annsy. Draw strength from our love. Then through your actions and the passions of your heart, we will make our mark on the world. Live your life. Make it as full as possible. That's the best honor you can give the babies and me. We want you to live."

These words branded my heart. I whispered, "But what if I can't get out of here?"

"You need to believe in yourself. You have everything you need to get out of the mud."

I shook my head. "I'm not strong enough. Just like I wasn't smart enough to find your cure, or healthy enough for the babies."

"It was enough. Try to understand. You did all that you could do and it was enough. We knew we were loved. And death is not the end. So go easy on yourself. Try to forgive yourself for your human limitations. Nobody is blaming you for anything. When you face what seems like impossible odds, give it all you've got. That will be enough. That's what faith is all about."

"Faith?"

"Yes, faith. You do what you can with what you've got."

"So what do I have that will get me out of this mess?"

"Think."

"You're not going to tell me are you?"

"You have what you need. Trust that it will be enough."

"I have my knife. An empty canteen. This arrowhead around my neck. My belt. A shirt."

Craig listened patiently. "Keep going."

"Then there are the straps, but I can't reach the end I untied. My pack is sitting over there out of reach. This stupid branch that I fell off to begin with."

"And?"

"And... well... Daisy, I guess."

"You have Daisy. Good old girl. She has not left your side all night."

"Daisy?" I repeated her name. She yawned and stretched. As I watched her, I realized that a dim light had filled the night's void, signaling the approach of dawn. This night was almost over. I glanced back toward my vision of Craig. He slowly receded up the slope and into the darkness of the trees.

"Wait! Don't go!"

He paused. "Believe in yourself," he reminded me distantly. Then he was gone.

38
WILDERNESS OF THE HEART

Do not fear, only believe.

Mark 5:36

"Believe," I muttered softly. "What I have will be enough. Daisy has not left my side." My attention turned back to the spaniel. "Daisy, how are you going to help me get out of this mess?"

She wagged a little to let me know she heard me. Then she began to pace back and forth along the smashed grasses, sniffing the ground as she walked.

I stood. As I pushed upward from my crouch, the surface of the mud under the seat of my pants clawed at me. It released me with a slurping noise. I straightened my knees. Needles of pain shot through my legs as life returned to my calves and feet. I flexed my knees and worked through the pain.

I inhaled deeply and looked around. How could I get out of this dilemma? If only the knot in my straps had held.

Maybe—maybe—Daisy could assist with the straps. Where was the end I had released?

In the gathering light, I searched around my ankles. The free end of my strap draped across that limb and dangled in the mud. I stretched toward it. The strap tantalized me four inches beyond my reach. I let my shoulders drop. As my hands fell to my sides, my left fingertips brushed the hilt of the knife sheathed on my belt. *The knife.*

With renewed energy, I released the blade from its carrier. Reaching once again toward the near end of the strap, I stabbed the woven nylon on the point of the blade and drew it toward me. My heart lifted as I wrapped it around my palm.

I tugged against the length and dragged it down the hill. I looped the strap around my left forearm as I collected its length. Maybe I could toss it over the closest branch above my head. I clasped the free end and swung the loops forward and back in preparation for an upward pitch. I heaved the strap with every ounce of strength I had. It fell to the muck below my knees, far short of the target branch. I tried again with the same result. After two more unsuccessful tries I paused to think.

"Well if not up, maybe out?" I recalled the distance to the ancient oak tree. Nine paces, but it was behind me. A smaller tree with a four-inch trunk grew in front of me almost straight in line with my orientation. I swung the loops and pitched. The strap fell short. I needed more weight on the end I tossed. What about the canteen?

I pulled the nearly-empty water jug from its holster on my belt, shook it, and savored the last sip of water. I unbuckled my belt and slipped the canteen's harness off. I snapped the container back into its cradle and ran the strap through the loops. After knotting the strap, I tested the missile with a few gentle swings. I heaved it toward the tree. It landed on the ground, short of my mark. I pulled it back and tried again. This time it fell beyond the trunk.

"Fetch, Daisy." She headed toward me, tracing the strap's course to the edge of the crater.

"No, no—go around the tree, girl. Around!" I pleaded with her, to no avail.

We tried again with the same result. How could I convince her to loop the strap around the tree before she returned it to me?

Once again, I tossed the canteen, strap trailing behind it, to a spot just beyond the young tree. Daisy waited for my command. With a sudden inspiration, I pulled the arrowhead pendant off my neck. I heaved it toward the little tree, just to the other side and called, "Fetch!"

As Daisy shot toward the arrowhead, I tugged on the strap so that the canteen wiggled a tiny bit in the grass. Daisy saw the canteen and pounced on it, then turned around and retraced her steps, threading the strap around the tree's trunk.

"Yes! Good girl, Daisy."

She dropped it at the edge of the mud. With the tip of my Buck knife, I skewered the canteen's holder and pulled it to my grasp. Now I had straps to tug. Releasing the canteen, I tossed it into the grass. I wrapped the straps tightly around my hands and pulled. I lifted one foot and pulled on the straps with all my strength but I remained stuck.

I took a deep breath and closed my eyes. *Believe in yourself. Faith is trusting that what you have to offer will be enough.*

Enough. Really? It sure didn't seem that way. I opened my eyes and found my gaze drawn to the tree branch which had tipped under my weight the previous afternoon. *Stupid branch.*

It dawned on me that the branch rested higher in the mud than it had with me standing on it. It floated.

I could float. If I could float in water, surely I could float in this elusive puddle of mud. *That has to be it.* If I spread my weight over a print the length and width of my body instead of just my feet, then I should float. Shouldn't I? I would be a human raft and pull myself to firm ground.

I imagined my whole body dripping with mud. Shuddering, I stared at the little tree, so close and yet out of my reach. I had to get out of this mess. Floating on the muck appeared to be my one remaining option. I took a deep breath and resolved to try. Bending my knees, I lowered myself to the surface and swung both arms over my head. The chill from the wet mud shocked my entire backside. I caught my breath. Forcing myself to relax, I lay prone on the mud. Slowly, ever so slowly, my feet inched upwards.

Yes. That's right. I'm floating.

I heaved against the cords wrapped around each hand. Like a massive ship, I turned slowly until my entire body was aligned with the little tree. When I tugged on the straps now, I slithered toward the shore. Kicking did absolutely no good. I shortened the straps as I moved, winding more loops around my hands. Inch by agonizing inch, I pulled myself to firm ground. At last I dragged my hips ashore. I sat up and continued the backward progress, walking on my hands. When only my boots remained in the mud, I lifted one leg at a time and planted my feet on the smashed grass. I walked to the top of the rim. Elation filled my heart like none I had ever experienced. Daisy pranced at my feet.

I knelt beside her and hugged her long and hard. "We did it, girl," I said. "Now let's go home."

Late that afternoon I parked my loaded car in front of my sister's country home. Phoebe and her cousins played outside on a swing set. When I opened the car door, Daisy bounded toward the children, tail wagging furiously. I headed toward the swing set. Phoebe slipped from her cousin's grasp and toddled toward me at a run. I picked up my pace and in three steps we collided. Swinging the child into the air, I turned a full circle and brought her to my chest in a bear hug.

"Ma-ma!" she said.

Tears in my eyes, I looked at my daughter. Here was my future. This was my passion.

"Mama's back, Phoebe," I whispered. "Mama's back."

I've got you babe

39
DAY FORTY

*You are a child of the universe. No less than the trees
and the stars: You have a right to be here.*

Desiderata

Raindrops splattered against the roof of the tent. The drumming sound jogged my mind into consciousness. I opened my eyes to total darkness. For a moment I couldn't remember where I was. I rolled over in my sleeping bag and threw an arm across Daisy. She sighed and crept a little closer, quite willing to cuddle in the humid chill of the night.

Oh yes. This was it—the last official night of my forty days. Spread over the better part of a year since I left the Farm, I had scheduled a few weekends alone, returning to the tent in various locations to complete my sojourn in Plan B. The days of solitude provided time for quiet meditation.

Though never again at the Farm, I tried to be creative in my camping locations. On one occasion or another, the orange tent sprouted like a bright flower in every corner of my home acreage. Once, we camped in the chicken house. Once in the woodshed. Yet another time, we spent a night in my dormant vegetable garden.

Right now, I was under the hedge trees at the north edge of my twenty acres. And it was raining. I pulled Daisy a little closer and hugged her.

After few minutes, the pattering of the rain ceased. Deep silence reigned. Then, miraculously, a mockingbird called from its roost in a tree above my bed. As it ran through its repertoire of stolen calls, I marveled that it sang in total darkness. "Only a mockingbird," I muttered to Daisy. She smacked her tongue and lips, content in my arms.

Gradually the air inside the tent took on a dim glow. Morning approached. I crawled from the sleeping bag.

"Ready girl? We better get going."

Winding the car through the spring green hills, I drove toward Butler County Lake along a route I had never before driven. We found the headwaters first. I circled the entire lake before parking near a picnic shelter on the north shore. I stuffed a rain jacket in the top of my pack, and we set out eastward, trekking across the inlets of the headwaters with the intent to hike completely around the small lake.

A great blue heron waded in the shallows. At my continued approach, it beat its great wings to lift into flight, its long legs dripping water as they trailed behind. A bullfrog moaned its low croak. The frog plopped into the water and slid beneath the calm surface between cattail stalks. Aside from myself, there were no other people at the little lake this morning. I was totally alone. Again.

"Woman lonely. Woman alone," I whispered into the morning breeze. A feeling of restlessness tugged at my heart. There was not a soul on earth who knew where I was at this moment.

About mid-morning, the clouds broke. Sunshine winked from dewdrops that hung heavily on the roadside plants. I paused in a picnic shelter across the lake from my car, sat on top of the table, and dangled my feet on the seat plank. A cliff swallow's nest, lumpy with bits of dried mud, hung under the eaves of the shelter roof. The swallow darted to its nest and disappeared over the edge. When it reappeared, it glanced pointedly down at me and I peered back.

The water of the lake sparkled in sunshine. I breathed deeply and felt at peace. Nature could be an effective tonic for the soul. Too bad the effects were so fleeting. Now that the forty days were officially over, I knew I would continue to need periodic retreats into the beauty of the countryside. Days such as this one served as times of centering and healing. Considering the frequency with which Jesus was reported to spend time apart on a mountain or in a garden, surely he felt the same need for rejuvenation through God's natural world. I wondered how he felt at the conclusion of his forty days. Was he refreshed and strengthened? Ready to attack the monumental tasks set before him? When he returned to the world of humanity after his long separation, was it a symbolic beginning of his life's work, filled with excitement, apprehension and conviction?

For me this day seemed just another day. I knew I would continue to fight depression and loneliness. I would periodically need to refresh myself in the beauty of God's wilderness. I would continue to polish my gemstone every day of my life. This day represented a new beginning for me but it was just another day.

Life would go on. There was no golden moment at the end of my quest, no story-book ending, no happily-ever-after. Events, even milestones of life, were more like beginnings than endings and I expected to encounter numerous unforeseen challenges in the future.

When I held Craig's hand for the last time on the night of his death, I felt crushed under the weight of a heavy future, alone and lonely. What I didn't know at that time, but had since learned, was that I didn't have to bear my whole future all at once. I could face it moment by moment. In fragments, the empty future became bearable. Each moment held its own challenge, but when I filled them with little things and little joys, life was bearable. Moment by moment I would find the strength to laugh and to love again.

The tornadic gale of life events had calmed to a gentle breeze. When taken one moment at a time, the torrent of uncertainty that represented my future was tamed to a manageable breath of air that stirred the tall grasses as it whispered through them. I no longer had to cower in hiding from the winds of life. I felt confident that I could launch myself into the breeze. I knew I could fly.

40
Rise Up and Ride

We live in all we seek.
                                    Annie Dillard

Getting cuter every day

Three years later

Quietly, I slid from my sleeping bag to stand barefoot on the frigid cabin floor. Five other women, science teachers in various Kansas schools, slept soundly in the other bunks of our assigned cabin. Not wanting to miss the early morning bird walk, I had slept very lightly the previous night. I shivered in the pre-dawn air and dressed quickly. I drew my jacket onto my arms, grabbed my small backpack and stepped outside. I turned to the door, pulling with one hand and restraining with the other, until a barely audible click signaled that the door had securely closed.

Facing the growing light on this Saturday morning, I stepped briskly toward the publicized meeting location. "Shoo-wee. Shoo-wee." A mockingbird called to the right of the path. I hustled toward the trailhead, eagerly anticipating the planned activity at my first science teacher convention. The Kansas Association of Teachers of Science held a spring gathering annually at the state-owned Rock Springs 4-H camp.

After arriving at Rock Springs with other teachers from my high school the previous day, I immersed myself in the evening activities. KATS Camp bustled on Friday with hundreds of us finding our lodging, sharing dinner in the immense dining hall, and attending evening presentations.

But at dawn on Saturday, few stirred for the bird watch. About fifteen hardy souls waited at the trailhead, coffee mugs warming most of their hands. A quick glance around revealed no familiar faces. No, wait. There was one. He caught my eye and offered a smile. Mike Fell shivered, his jet-black hair stuffed into the hood of his sweatshirt. His brown eyes twinkled in my direction.

Another teacher in Winfield, Mike chaired the district's science curriculum committee. He taught at the middle school, while I was assigned to the high school. Our paths rarely crossed. This morning, however, we gravitated toward each other.

"Morning! Did you sleep okay last night?" he said.

"Not really. I was afraid I'd oversleep. You?"

"Me neither. Had a snorer in my room. I don't think I slept at all."

The facilitator for our bird watch called us to attention. The group listened quietly for a few minutes. We heard the mockingbird again. And a cardinal. Then "Fi-bi. Fi-bi."

"Listen," Mike whispered. "A phoebe."

I grinned with delight to hear the songbird for which my daughter was named. I dropped my pack to remove binoculars while others scanned the tree branches in search of our feathered soloists. Mike pulled binoculars from his pack.

We weaved across the terrain toward a wetland area. The two of us brought up the rear. In soft voices, we chatted. We dropped further and further behind the rest. I learned that Mike was a single father. He was raising twin sons who were ten weeks older than my Phoebe. He lived a few miles outside of Winfield, in a house he designed and built mostly by himself.

I spent most of the rest of KATS Camp with Mike. When he offered a ride home, I eagerly accepted. At my house, he asked about a couple of framed arrangements of butterflies on my wall.

"Those are Craig's Mexican butterflies," I said. "He collected them about ten years ago when he was in Chiapas doing research with a professor."

"From Hays?"

"Yes. How'd you know that?"

"I think I may have met Craig down there."

"Really?"

"In my senior year at Southwestern College, I went with a group to Mexico. Since my biology professor knew the Hays professor really well, we spent a couple days in Chiapas with the team from Hays."

"You met Craig before I did."

KATS camp became the threshold of my new life. I was lonely no more. Mike and I married that summer. Phoebe and I moved into his earth-sheltered home twenty miles south of our own on the same highway. Thirteen months later, seven and a half years after Craig and I buried our sweet baby girl, I gave birth to a healthy, beautiful daughter. Phoebe gained a new daddy, and she grew up with twin brothers and a baby sister. When she was twenty-one, Phoebe married the love of her life. Five years later, she became the mother of our first grandchild.

I married Mike when I was thirty-three. My entire new life began when I surpassed the age that Craig achieved. I marvel at that. These have been precious years, every one of them a gift, more treasured because he was not granted that gift. I will never forget him, or our children Gabrielle and West Carl. They will be part of me all of my days. But life is for the living. So I cherish them quietly in my heart. Freed from the wind's shadow, standing on my own, I plunge headlong into the winds of my life.

Feel the wind blowing, rustling our souls,
moving and moving and making us whole.
Our spirits can soar and dip and glide,
and we want to rise up and ride.

And the wind blows...
Rise up and ride.

Ann Zimmerman

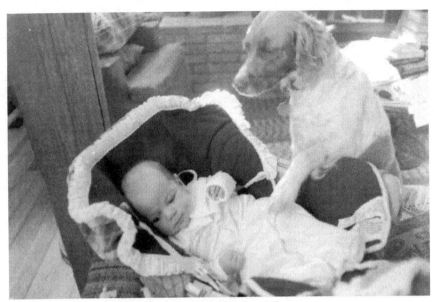

Daisy meets baby Elynne

Sisters

Proud Gransy with Phoebe's son, Donte

Donte kissing his aunt Elynne on her wedding day.
Photo courtesy Vijay Sherring.

ACKNOWLEDGEMENTS

Life is a journey that at times seems like a wild ride. To those who have touched my life in this latest adventure, I am forever grateful. The process of writing and rewriting brought many new friends into my life, and renewed many old friendships.

I extend thanks to my community of writers and fellow word weavers: The Fighting Hamsters critique group of Kansas Writer's Association, with special appreciation to April Pameticky and Ray Grizzly Racobs; to writers closer to home including Carol Martin, Dr. Steve Swaim, Roxy Callison and Amanda Porter; to the excellent writing instruction of William Bernhardt and my friends from his workshops, especially Grace Wagner, Renee Roberts and Doris Degner-Foster; to my team of readers and reviewers including (but not limited to) Dora Gross, John Scott Holman, Millie Horlacher, Lynne Hunter, Sharon Martin, Barry McGuire, and Joyce Teubner; to Jan Hathaway for my photograph; and to Rik Tanos for guiding me through the publication process. My deepest appreciation goes to Debra Ferris and Nancy Sturm who have shared much of this adventure with me.

With humility, I acknowledge the artistic contributions of poets represented in *Earth Prayers from Around the World*, edited by Elizabeth Roberts and Elias Amidon. Additionally Aldo Leopold, Albert Schweitzer,

Ann Zimmerman, Annie Dillard, John Muir, William Cullen Bryant, and Thor Heyerdahl provided thoughts which open or close various chapters.

With a note of tenderness, I recall posthumously the support and encouragement of several significant people. My parents, Helen Peterson Harris and Wally Harris were my biggest fans. I wish they were here now. Tom Junkins displayed unbounded enthusiasm for writing his memoirs and was generous with his encouragement. Vic McClung requested a chance to read my story after receiving a terminal diagnosis of his own. His request launched me into this writing journey. Marvin Swanson, my writing mentor and dear friend from earlier years, could always ask a question to help me grow. And of course, Craig, who lived this story with me and remains part of me to this day.

With greatest thanks, I acknowledge my family. Mary, Kay, and Sheryl gave their support and encouragement. Brandon provided a psychological sounding board for the story's emotions. Ryan helped create the cover design. Elynne provided me with a writing retreat. Phoebe lived this story with me then— and now. But especially I am grateful to Mike, my new partner and best friend, who provided artistic suggestions. His unconditional faith in the validity of my journey bolstered my confidence. And—most of all—he proved to me it is indeed possible to love again.

I feel fortunate to have shared part of my journey with all of you, as well as others who preferred to remain anonymous. Without any one of you, my journey would have been quite different.

Made in the USA
Charleston, SC
24 April 2015